A H 00117912 T
W9-AGX-601

EP 3/5 3450

CORPORATE GOVERNANCE

Corporate Governance

What can be Learned from Japan?

SIMON LEARMOUNT

OXFORD
UNIVERSITY PRESS

Great Clarendon Street, Oxford OX2 6DP

Oxford University Press is a department of the University of Oxford.
It furthers the University's objective of excellence in research, scholarship,
and education by publishing worldwide in

Oxford New York

Auckland Bangkok Buenos Aires Cape Town Chennai
Dar es Salaam Delhi Hong Kong Istanbul Karachi Kolkata
Kuala Lumpur Madrid Melbourne Mexico City Mumbai Nairobi
São Paulo Shanghai Taipei Tokyo Toronto

Oxford is a registered trade mark of Oxford University Press
in the UK and in certain other countries

Published in the United States
by Oxford University Press Inc., New York

© Simon Learmount, 2002

The moral rights of the authors have been asserted
Database right Oxford University Press (maker)

First published 2002
First published in paperback 2004

All rights reserved. No part of this publication may be reproduced,
stored in a retrieval system, or transmitted, in any form or by any means,
without the prior permission in writing of Oxford University Press,
or as expressly permitted by law, or under terms agreed with the appropriate
reprographics rights organization. Enquiries concerning reproduction
outside the scope of the above should be sent to the Rights Department,
Oxford University Press, at the address above

You must not circulate this book in any other binding or cover
and you must impose this same condition on any acquirer

British Library Cataloguing in Publication Data

Data available

Library of Congress Cataloging in Publication Data

Learmount, Simon.
Corporate governance: what can be learned from Japan? / Simon Learmount.
p. cm.
Includes bibliographical references and index.
1. Corporate governance—Japan.   2. Industrial management—Japan. I. Title.
HD2741 .L37 2002   658.4–dc21   2002067185

ISBN 0-19-925291-2
ISBN 0-19-926908-4 (pbk.)

1 3 5 7 9 10 8 6 4 2

Typeset by Newgen Imaging Systems (P) Ltd, Chennai, India
Printed in Great Britain
on acid-free paper by
Biddles Ltd, King's Lynn, Norfolk

Acknowledgements

This book would not have been possible without the cooperation of those people who gave their valuable time to be interviewed. I am extremely grateful to them. I am indebted also to the Development Bank of Japan (DBJ) who awarded me a Shimomura Fellowship, which not only funded the fieldwork but also greatly facilitated my access to companies. Colleagues at the DBJ's Research Institute of Capital Formation, especially Mr Hanazaki, Mr Mogi, and Mr Sakurai, have helped me more than perhaps they realize. The research was also funded in part by an R. A. G. Monks Award at the Judge Institute of Management Studies, University of Cambridge, for which I am very appreciative. I am also extremely grateful for a Daiwa Foundation Fellowship (jointly held at the Judge Institute of Management Studies, the ESRC Centre for Business Research and Oriental Studies, all at University of Cambridge) that enabled me to write this book. I would also like to thank Sir Adrian Cadbury, Ronald Dore, John Hendry, John Roberts, Takaya Seki and Hugh Whittaker as well as David Musson and three anonymous reviewers at Oxford University Press for their encouragement and very helpful criticism along the way. I have also benefited from constructive discussion with participants at various seminars where initial results from this study were presented, especially those at the Royal Institute for International Affairs, the Tokyo Stock Exchange, the University of Oxford, and the Japanese Ministry of Economy, Trade and Industry. For her enduring support, perseverance, and inspiration, special thanks are due to Akiko Saito.

Contents

List of Figures

List of Tables

Introduction

Over the past decade, interest in the way that companies are governed has mushroomed across the world. Numerous countries have implemented corporate governance codes, business schools have appointed new corporate governance professors and introduced core courses on the governance of the corporation, and all manner of corporate governance consulting and advisory firms have sprung up. Many international bodies are taking a keen interest in the subject, as effective corporate governance is now widely seen as essential for the creation of a coherent and efficient global financial architecture. For example, the IMF, the World Bank, and the OECD have all recently established working groups to study and make recommendations about corporate governance, and in 1999 the G7 committed itself to encouraging the implementation of global corporate governance standards:

We attach high priority to [...] the OECD's recently-approved core principles on corporate governance, and the World Bank's continuing work with the OECD and other international institutions to encourage their broadest possible adoption and implementation in emerging market and industrial countries. (G7, 1999)

The explosion of interest in corporate governance, and the drive towards global standards in particular, are largely bound up with the recent spectacular increase in the concentration of shareholdings in the hands of large institutional investors. Over the past three decades, holdings of shares by insurance companies and pension funds have grown considerably at the expense of holdings by individuals in many developed economies. For example, institutional investors accounted for 47.1 per cent by value of UK ordinary shares at the end of 2000, while individuals held just 16 per cent of the total. In 1969 the figures were almost the reverse, with institutions accounting for 21.2 per cent of shares and individuals for 47.4 per cent (Hill and Duffield 2001). It is widely argued that this new concentration of shareholdings means that institutional investors now have both the ability and the incentive to monitor and discipline company managers (Black 1992; Maug 1998); formerly, individual shareholders were thought to be too numerous and too widely dispersed to exert adequate corporate control, giving managers the potential to become entrenched and able to act in ways that maximized their own utility.

This particular view of the compass of corporate governance is strongly informed by (Anglo-American) economic theories of the firm, especially 'agency theory', which explicitly casts managers as 'agents' for the shareholder–owners of companies. In its popular form, the stronger participation and influence of institutional investors in the affairs of companies is seen as the rightful reassertion of company control by its owners (*The Economist* 1994; Monks and Minow 1995; Monks 2001). The argument that shareholders can 'own' a company has though been long disputed (Dodd 1932; Fama 1980; Donaldson and Preston 1995; Kay and Silberston 1995; Blair 1995), and some have suggested that the embracing of these economic theories simply reflects the project of owners of capital (namely the increasingly powerful institutional investors) to protect their own interests (Davis and Thompson 1994; Jackson and Carter 1995). Others have pointed out some of the disincentives and impracticalities of institutional investors playing a more significant role in corporate governance (Davies 1997; Learmount 2001), and some have questioned the economic value of institutional investor monitoring to either companies or the investors themselves (OECD 1998*b*; Romano 2001).

Nevertheless, Anglo-American economic theories of the firm are now coming to dominate academic and institutional approaches to corporate governance across the world, largely as a corollary of the growing influence of (mainly American) institutional investors. The biggest twenty-five American pension funds increased the proportion of foreign equities they held from 4.8 per cent of total assets in 1991 to 11.2 per cent in 1996, and gross US activity (both purchases and sales) in foreign securities has grown from just $53 billion in 1980 to nearly $5.8 trillion in 2001 (source: US Treasury). Accordingly, 'the implication is that global companies seeking global equity financing will more and more have to come to terms with the expectations of these US investors' (*Financial Times* 1998). And the largest American institutional investors have not been slow or timid to express their expectations, producing numerous corporate governance codes for the different countries in which they invest, and creating influential associations such as the International Corporate Governance Network (ICGN) which actively co-ordinate and promote their interests across the globe.

I am strongly in favour of greater shareholder involvement in the governance of companies. However, the current dominance of the Anglo-American approach to corporate governance does seem to risk prematurely curtailing broader, potentially valuable research on the governance of companies, as well as possibly proscribing good corporate governance practices that do not exactly fit its propositions. In particular, it glosses over many of the issues which should be at the heart of the debate about the governance of modern corporations, such as what a company is, what its goals are, whose interests it serves, and at a more practical level the interaction and prioritization of the interests of parties involved in a company, and the constraints and obligations incumbent on those who run companies. As a result, debate on corporate governance is poorer, and policy decisions are arguably not as well informed as they could be.

My main aim in this book is to broaden the debate on corporate governance a little, by drawing on an empirical examination of the governance practices of fourteen Japanese companies. I expand upon the reasons why I have chosen to study Japanese companies in Chapter 1, but in short Japanese corporate governance has for a long time been thought to function differently from the Anglo-American shareholder-focused system (Albert 1991; Charkham 1994), and therefore these companies seem to offer especially productive subject matter through which different approaches to corporate governance might be explored. Furthermore, a secondary aim I have is to contribute to the understanding of how Japanese companies are actually governed in practice. Japanese business practices have for a long time been the subject of intense interest and speculation among the media, policy-makers, business professionals, investors, academics, as well as the general public, and yet there have been few in-depth, empirical studies of these practices in context. This is especially true as far as corporate governance practices and processes are concerned; for example, how do Japanese boards of directors really operate, how do shareholders interact with companies, how are the relationships between companies and their main banks effected on a day-to-day basis? My experience working with Japanese companies in the past told me that most existing interpretations fall short of presenting an accurate picture; they tend to be based on inferences from broad statistics, or anecdotes relating to a limited number of high-profile corporations. Without some proximity to business practices and processes themselves, it is difficult to gain an accurate understanding of exactly how Japanese companies really are governed.

The companies that are examined in the book were selected to provide a cross-section of Japanese industry, and include some of the largest Japanese multinationals, as well as some small, entrepreneurial companies which at the time of the research were in the process of being listed on the Japanese Stock Exchanges (all the companies were guaranteed anonymity as much of the data provided was commercially sensitive). The bulk of the fieldwork was carried out while I was based at the Japanese government's policy bank, the Development Bank of Japan, which was extremely supportive in helping me gain extensive first-hand access to these companies. The findings I present are based on close analysis of internal company documents and financial information, as well as interviews with company presidents, directors, auditors, managers, union representatives, and employees. I was also able to interview a range of 'external' parties, including suppliers, customers, main banks, foreign and domestic shareholders, as well as analysts, rating agencies, and other relevant parties. By extensively recounting the views of these interviewees, this book enables readers to gain some closeness to the meanings that participants *themselves* attribute to their experiences inside the Japanese corporate governance system.

I find that Japanese managers do not feel, and are not in any practical sense accountable to shareholders. But at the same time, in none of the companies studied are management or employees entirely unaccountable or immune from outside influence. Instead, it seems that a complex system of responsibilities, reciprocal obligations, and trust inherent in the particular socio-economic relationships within and between companies, is important for guaranteeing the accountability of company directors and employees. The resultant 'socially endogenous' system of corporate governance depends on an exacting system of close interpersonal scrutiny and sanctioning on the one hand, and processes that encourage and reward prosocial behaviour on the other. Given the appropriate socio-economic context, such a system appears to be a particularly effective means of directing and controlling a company, as it not only sanctions unwanted behaviour, it also rewards behaviour that conforms to the collective goals and values of all company participants (including shareholders, creditors, suppliers, customers, and employees).

In expounding upon the way that this system of corporate governance works in practice, it is possible to understand better the difficulties that Japan is facing as it adapts to the rapidly changing global product and financial markets. For example, the mainstream view discussed earlier suggests that 'good corporate governance' essentially requires strong and clear lines of accountability to shareholders and transparency to the financial markets. The Japanese system is widely perceived to be lacking in these respects; as such it is often characterized as being deliberately secretive and subject to cronyism. In this book I suggest that while the foundation of such criticisms may well be correct (the system is opaque, shareholders have not played a major role in the way companies are governed, directors do not feel themselves to be accountable to any specific 'other'), to then surmise that there is no corporate governance in Japan, or that the existing system is in some way blameworthy, is erroneous. Most of the companies I studied are governed well, albeit very differently from their Anglo-American counterparts. This is not to say that there are no shortcomings, or that there is no change taking place. But, by attempting to understand how Japanese corporate governance works in practice, it becomes easier to understand the changes that are taking place and address the weaknesses of the system in its own terms, rather than simply dismissing it as an anachronistic and inappropriate form of corporate governance.

To return to the primary focus though, by unpacking the system by which Japanese companies are governed, this book urges reflection on current understandings of corporate governance, especially in a global context. It does not refute the idea that the governance of companies can in many cases be improved by, for example, company directors being more strongly held to account by shareholders, or greater transparency to capital markets, but it does challenge the *pre-eminence* of 'solutions' such as these to the 'corporate governance problem'. What is advocated in this book is a re-consideration and broadening of the current conceptual scope of corporate governance, so as to facilitate and encourage other potentially valuable ways of exploring and understanding how companies are governed, which will ultimately benefit practice. The ideas that I delineate point to the possibility of a form of socially endogenous corporate governance, which draws on the voluntary reciprocal obligations and responsibilities enacted in everyday individual-level and organizational-level socio-economic interactions, rather than governance based solely on the exercise of power and control of one party over another.

Book Structure

This book comprises a detailed empirical study of corporate governance practices and processes in 14 Japanese companies, which is used to cast light on issues of corporate governance more generally. Although the arguments of the book are essentially aimed at an academic audience, the book has been written so that it is equally accessible and relevant to those involved with corporate governance issues on a day-to-day basis, including financial services providers, lawyers, policy-makers, and of course company directors.

In Chapter 1 I review some of the different ideas which inform current ideas about what corporate governance is, in order to provide the context for the arguments which follow later in the book. In this chapter I draw a distinction between ideas based on economic theories of the firm on the one hand, and what I call 'organizational' theories on the other. I discuss how economic approaches tend to see the firm principally in contractual terms, are guided by assumptions of utility-maximizing self-interested human behaviour, and tend to posit the protection of investors' capital as the 'corporate governance problem'. Organizational theories by contrast tend to begin with a more complex concept of the firm, allow for other-oriented behaviour, and can conceive the governance of companies as routinely involving multiple relationships. While economic approaches currently predominate in the burgeoning field of corporate governance research, there are many criticisms of their fundamental assumptions. Organizational approaches, by contrast, tend to be poorly developed theoretically.

In Chapter 2, I narrow the spotlight onto the Japanese corporate governance system, identifying four key issues on which discussions have traditionally concentrated, namely the weakness of shareholders, the importance of the company–main bank relationship, the role of employees, and the role of senior management. I survey the numerous studies which have contributed to the current understanding of Japanese corporate governance, but find them disparate, engendering the variety of often competing emphases and interpretations which will be familiar to anyone trying to come to terms with 'the Japanese corporate governance system'.

In Chapter 3 I argue that the reason for the confusion about how Japanese corporate governance works in practice, is that up until now there has been a lack of inquiry and analysis which is 'close to the action', in other words research that draws directly on the actual, everyday socio-economic actions and interactions of businesspeople and other company participants. In this chapter I present information about how the research I carried out attempts to address this problem, by conducting detailed case study research in fourteen different Japanese companies. I go on to discuss which companies I chose to study, how the research was carried out, and the strengths and weaknesses of the approach that I adopted. Often such methodological justification is excluded from books such as this, but it is dealt with in detail here, as I argue that it is central to what this book is trying to achieve, namely an analysis of how corporate governance practitioners themselves experience and understand the system to operate.

In Chapters 4–7, I present my analysis of the data gathered from the case studies I carried out. Each chapter addresses one of the principal themes I identified earlier, namely the role of shareholders, the role of the main bank, the role of employees, and the role of senior management in the governance of each of the fourteen companies. The limited number of companies surveyed clearly prevents me from trying to generalize from these findings to Japanese industry as a whole, but where appropriate, relevant industry-level or economy-level data are presented to allow me to expand or elaborate upon the case study specific findings.

In the final chapter, I draw together the findings, and discuss their implications for future research and understanding of corporate governance, both in Japan and in general. In particular I propose that a system which draws on the reciprocal obligations, responsibilities and trust generated in everyday socio-economic interactions at the individual and organizational level, appears to be a realistic means of governing a company. To Anglo-American eyes, at first glance this may appear woolly, opaque, and impenetrable: certainly not a foundation upon which a reliable system of corporate governance can be constructed. However, I argue that a 'socially endogenous' system of corporate governance is anything but unreliable; indeed, a system which can make use of social controls that are part of everyday socio-economic interaction is likely to be more exacting and effective than the more familiar Anglo-American system that aims to 'discipline' managers only through exogenous hierarchical controls.

The Japanese system I delineate is, though, principally a closed system, which in the context of globalization (of capital markets in particular, where large institutional investors increasingly expect their demands to be heard by companies in which they invest) may not be sustainable in its current form. Nonetheless, the commonly advocated 'solution', that Japanese companies must adapt to the demands of the international markets and move towards the more 'open' Anglo-American system of corporate governance, is not the only possibility for change. Another plausible scenario, which my analysis suggests may be possible, would involve the international investor community, over a period of time, being progressively incorporated into the existing Japanese system. In practice, what we observe actually taking place in the companies I studied is adaptation of the two systems, rather than the substitution of one system for the other: companies are providing better information, concentrating more on returns on equity, engaging more openly with their shareholders, but at the same time international institutional shareholders are also beginning to communicate more extensively with Japanese company managers, understanding the particular way that Japanese firms are organized and operate, and learning how they can play an effective role given the way the system operates.

In conclusion, by unpacking the system by which a number of Japanese companies are governed in practice, this book urges reflection on the currently pervasive, narrow definition of the 'corporate governance problem': it is much more than ensuring clear accountability of corporate managers to shareholders. The book ends by commending a more extensive consideration of how companies are and might be governed in the future. Given the limitations of the empirical study, it is beyond the scope of this book to suggest definitive alternatives, but I hope at least to go some way towards pointing out possible future directions that might be considered by practitioners, researchers, and policy-makers alike.

1

A Review of Corporate Governance Ideas

1.1. INTRODUCTION

Corporate governance is 'the system by which business corporations are directed and controlled' (Cadbury 1992; OECD 1999). However, this simple definition belies the range of theories and ideas which inform contemporary analyses of corporate governance and corporate governance systems. In this chapter I want to explore briefly some of these theories and ideas, and in particular consider why the shareholder–director relationship has arguably become the locus of thinking about the governance of the corporation. I suggest that the pre-eminence of economic conceptualizations of 'the corporate governance problem' may risk prematurely curtailing broader, potentially valuable research on the governance of companies. I conclude by setting out the case for empirical research of the Japanese system of corporate governance that neither accepts nor rejects *a priori* any definition of 'the governance problem'.

1.2. CORPORATE GOVERNANCE AND THE ECONOMIC THEORY OF THE FIRM

Berle and Means (1932) are widely acknowledged as the forefathers of contemporary thinking about corporate governance. They argued that in the earliest days of American industrialization when companies were organized to deal with major projects, such as the construction of railways and canals, company owners were able to monitor the managers they employed to look after their projects. At this time companies tended to be private institutions, and were administered on the basis that they were private property. However, during the second half of the nineteenth century in the US, professional managers established strong control within what were becoming large multi-divisional corporations, and shareholders, who were granted the benefits of limited liability, became increasingly numerous and dispersed. Berle and Means termed this process 'the separation of ownership and control'. They suggested that because of the resultant changes in the nature of shareholder–manager relations, the traditional conception of the corporation, as an entity actively owned by shareholders, broke down. The effective disintegration of the private corporation signalled the arrival of the corporation as a social institution:

Neither the claims of ownership nor those of control can stand against the paramount interests of the community. . . . It remains only for the claims of the community to be put forward with clarity and force. Rigid enforcement of property rights as a temporary protection against plundering by control would not stand in the way of modification of these rights in the interest of other groups. When a convincing system of community obligations is worked out and is generally accepted, in that moment the passive property right of today must yield before the larger interests of society.   (Berle and Means 1932: 312)

Berle and Means proposed that:

the 'control' of the great corporations should develop into a purely neutral technocracy, balancing a variety of claims by various groups in the community, and assigning to each a portion of the income stream on the basis of public policy rather than private cupidity.   (ibid. p. 313)

However, in lieu of a well-defined system of responsibilities to society, Berle in a slightly later paper conceded that a system of accountability to shareholders was the most likely interim alternative:

You cannot abandon emphasis on the view that business corporations exist for the sole purpose of making profits for their shareholders until such time as you are prepared to offer a clear and reasonably enforceable scheme of responsibilities to someone else.   (Berle 1932: 1365)

The legitimate exercise of power within this owner/control dichotomy became a central element of the managerialist conception of the firm, which dominated research on the firm until the 1970s (Chandler 1962; Bratton 1989).

In the 1970s, however, new economic theories of the firm emerged to challenge the pre-eminence of managerialism. The publication of Alchian and Demsetz's (1972) seminal paper *Production, Information Costs and Economic Organisation,* followed by Jensen and Meckling's (1976) paper *Theory of the Firm: Managerial Behavior, Agency Costs and Ownership Structure* introduced the idea of the firm as a nexus of contracts among individual factors of production. Previously, classical economics had conceived the firm as a single-product entity with a commitment to the maximization of profits, and what went on within the firm was considered to be of subordinate interest to what went on in markets. But for the first time this new theory allowed economics to analyse the firm itself; the neoclassical view was able to incorporate the workings of the firm into economic theory by explaining it as a constantly renegotiated contract, contrived by an aggregation of individuals each with the aim of maximizing their own profit:

It is common to see the firm characterized by the power to settle issues by fiat, by authority, or by disciplinary action superior to that available in the conventional market. This is delusion. The firm does not own all its inputs. It has no power of fiat, no authority, no disciplinary action any different in the slightest degree from ordinary market contracting between any two people. (Alchian and Demsetz 1972: 777)

For economists used to treating the firm as a 'black box' it was claimed that 'the foundation for a powerful theory of organizations is being put into place' (Jensen 1983: 324).

In this view, the pre-eminent position of shareholders in a company is not based on an idea that they 'own' the company. Instead, the primacy of shareholders is legitimized by the idea that they are the residual risk takers of the company (Alchian and

Demsetz 1972). The argument in its basic form is that when production is undertaken by a team, which can be more efficient than individual production, it is difficult to determine exactly who is responsible for what part of the joint effort. As such, individuals have an opportunity to 'shirk'. In order to prevent shirking, a 'monitor' is required: the monitor is able to make contracts with all the other parties and pay them according to their opportunity cost, and in return for monitoring the team is entitled to claim the residual value created, which incentivizes the monitor not to shirk herself. In the public company, it is generally assumed that it is the shareholders who have the most at risk, with all other parties benefiting from (reasonably) complete contracts. As a consequence it is the shareholders who have most to lose if the company fails, and most to gain from effective monitoring of the other company participants. Fama (1980) makes the point about the irrelevance of 'ownership' explicitly:

... ownership of capital should not be confused with ownership of the firm. Each factor in a firm is owned by somebody. The firm is just the set of contracts covering the way inputs are joined to create outputs and the way receipts from outputs are shared among inputs. In this 'nexus of contracts' perspective, ownership of the firm is an irrelevant concept. (1980: 290)

The principal assumptions underpinning agency theory, as this neoclassical economic theory is now best known, are that parties to a contract will act to maximize their own self-interest, and that all actors have the freedom to enter into a contract or to contract elsewhere. 'Agency theory' explicitly casts management as 'agents' for shareholders (usually termed 'principals'), and their relationship is conceived to be a contractual one based on market exchange. However, given the assumption of self-interested motivation of actors, it is assumed that this relationship creates an 'agency problem': how is the 'principal' able to prevent the 'agent' from maximizing his own self-interest (Jensen 1994)? For agency theorists, this constitutes the corporate governance problem.

Further to this neoclassical conceptualization, the idea of firm as contract has at the same time been developed in a different form by new institutional economists. Whereas neoclassical economics sees the market as the only way to organize efficient contracting, and the firm is seen simply as an artefact of constantly renegotiated contracts, new institutional economics conceives the firm to be a discrete, relatively permanent hierarchy which exists as an alternative to contracting in markets. Like neoclassical economics, new institutional economics is concerned with ensuring the efficiency of private contracting, but rather than concentrating on the maximization of profit, the focus of study is generally perceived to be the minimization of transaction costs. This notion was originally put forward by Coase (1937), but has been developed in particular by Williamson (1979, 1985).

For Williamson, 'Since any issue that can be posed as a contracting problem is usefully addressed in transaction cost economizing terms, and since corporate governance falls within this description, the subject of corporate governance becomes grist for the transaction cost economics mill' (1984: 1201). For transaction costs economists, the governance problems of firms are perceived to proceed from a number of contractual hazards, including self-interested opportunism, informational asymmetries, asset specificity and small numbers bargaining, and the problem of bounded rationality (Williamson 1984, 1985). 'Corporate governance' is concerned with discovering internal measures and mechanisms which reduce the costs associated with these contractual hazards to an efficient level: the external discipline of the market cannot be relied on to mitigate these problems, as it has 'limited constitutional powers to conduct audits and has limited access to the firm's incentive and resource allocation machinery' (Williamson 1975: 143).

Notwithstanding the slightly different conceptualizations of the 'governance problem', it is the ideas of economists that currently dominate the way corporate governance is generally understood. These theories have reified the idea of the firm as a production mechanism, with the primary purpose of maximizing returns on the capital invested by shareholders. As a consequence 'corporate governance' is now commonly conceived to centre on a single problem, namely how the owners of capital are able to protect their investments:

> ... corporate governance deals with the ways in which suppliers of finance to corporations assure themselves of getting a return on their investment. How do the suppliers of finance get managers to return some of the profits to them? How do they make sure that managers do not steal the capital they supply or invest it in bad projects? How do suppliers of finance control managers? (Shleifer and Vishny 1997: 737)

1.3. CRITIQUES OF ECONOMIC APPROACHES

The ideas of economists have provided numerous insights into the workings of the firm, and have enriched our understanding of some of the dynamics of organizational behaviour; for example they remind us that there is lots of self-interested behaviour in organizational life (Perrow 1986), and they have helped researchers think about risk, outcome uncertainty, incentives, and information systems (Eisenhardt 1989). However, there are many critiques of the simplifying assumptions that these economic theories make, especially among organizational researchers whose work shows that organizations are characterized by imperfect information, inefficiencies, multiplex incentives, and contextual influences (Perrow 1986).

Consequently, there are calls for analyses which acknowledge these organizational realities, rather than which rely on the tenuous suppositions that underpin economic conceptualizations of the firm (Martin 1993). Eisenhardt, for example, a staunch defender of agency theory concedes that

> Agency theory presents a partial view of the world that, although it is valid, also ignores a good bit of the complexity of organizations. Additional perspectives can help capture the greater complexity. (Eisenhardt 1989: 71)

As for transaction costs economics, there has also been an acknowledgement of the limitations of the original simple dichotomization of markets and hierarchies. For example 'intermediate' modes of governance have been put forward (Williamson 1991), and the theory has been refined by Hart and Moore (1990) who develop their view of the firm as a collection of jointly owned physical assets, and more recently by Rajan and Zingales (1998) who propose the firm as a nexus of specific investments which cannot be replicated by the market. There has also been a slow but gradual acceptance among transaction costs economists that socially embedded personal relationships play an important role in economic exchange (Zaheer and Venkatraman 1995).

There are, however, those who suggest that the refinement of these contractual theories of the firm is inadequate, and that many of their fundamental assumptions are so inaccurate that they discredit the entire approach. For example Moran and Ghoshal (1996) strongly criticize Williamson's (1975, 1985) pessimistic assumptions about organizations as well as human behaviour and motivation:

[Economic] theories of today are dominated by a profoundly pessimistic view of organizations, concerned far more about the unintended consequences of organizing than about organizing for their intended purpose, and by an even more skeptical view of individual–organization interactions, grounded in the assumption that the human role in organizations is largely passive and frequently pathological . . . the all-pervasive concern for shirking, opportunism, and inertia in organizational economics.   (Moran and Ghoshal 1996: 70)

Moreover the normative implications of economic theories are perceived to be dangerous: Ghoshal and Moran (1996) criticize the fact that these theories create the conditions which encourage the type of behaviour they assume:

Social sciences carry a special responsibility because of the process of the double hermeneutic: its theories affect the agents who are its subject matter. By assuming the worst, this theory can bring out the worst in economic behavior. By assuming opportunism and establishing it as his base case, Williamson is blind to forces that work to confirm or discredit the validity of his assumptions . . . In the process, his theory is likely to encourage the very behavior that it takes for granted and seeks so hard to control.   (Ghoshal and Moran 1996: 39)

In terms of their specific relevance for analyses of corporate governance, a number of other criticisms have been levelled against mainstream economic approaches. For example, O'Sullivan (2000) has argued that an important shortcoming of these approaches is that they fail to incorporate a systematic analysis of innovation or production in their conceptual frameworks. Failing to include the production side is critical as it risks promoting different claims (especially the claims of shareholders) on corporate revenues 'whether or not their contributions to the generation of these revenues make those returns possible on a sustainable basis' (O'Sullivan 2000: 42). At a more general level, it has also been suggested that the predominant economics-derived theories are ethnocentric in their conceptualization and development, and that the bulk of empirical evidence used to support them have been drawn principally from Anglo-Saxon sources, in particular the US and UK (Boyd *et al.* 1996). Gilson (1994) suggests one reason for this:

. . . the American system seemed to represent the evolutionary pinnacle of corporate governance, so other systems were either less far along the Darwinist path, or evolutionary deadends; neither laggards nor neanderthals made interesting objects of study. (Gilson 1994: 132)

In sum, there are a growing number of criticisms of the usefulness and validity of economic theories of the firm as explanatory frameworks upon which to base analyses of corporate governance. This has led to wider reflection on the assumptions which underpin current mainstream academic conceptualizations of corporate governance, and calls for broader analyses which embrace the social, cultural, political, institutional, and interpersonal as well as economic aspects of corporations (Starkey 1995; Turnbull 1997).

1.4. ORGANIZATIONAL APPROACHES

The 'stakeholder approach' to the firm is one framework that has been proposed by organizational researchers as an alternative to economic theories for thinking about the governance of corporations. Although the intellectual lineage of these ideas can be traced back to the work of Clark (1916), Dodd (1932), and Berle and Means (1932), the stakeholder approach is usually attributed to Freeman (1984) who argued that economic theories were based on outdated images of the firm, so a new way of thinking about business organization was required:

... the emergence of numerous stakeholder groups and new strategic issues require a rethinking of our traditional picture of the firm . . . We must redraw the picture in a way that accounts for the changes. (Freeman 1984: 24)

At its core, the 'stakeholder approach' is concerned with challenging the amorality/ immorality of mainstream economic conceptualizations of the firm, and refuting Friedman's (1970) famous proclamation that 'the only business of business is business'. However in spite of some fifteen years having passed since the publication of Freeman's 'call to arms', the development of a rigorous and useful 'Stakeholder Theory' of the firm still seems a long way off. Most work in this field continues to be preoccupied with justifying a stakeholder approach to the firm, rather than the construction of systematic theory to describe more adequately contemporary organizational practices.

Those researchers who have attempted to develop a stakeholder theory have frequently relied on adapting economic theories, rather than constructing afresh an alternative conceptual framework for the firm. For example Jones (1995), explicitly recognizing that the principal shortcoming of the stakeholder approach is its lack of testable theory, proposes an instrumental theory of stakeholder management. He argues that the economic literature focuses on devices to align interests of principals and agents, through incentives, monitoring mechanisms and governing structures that reduce the potential for opportunism to an 'efficient' level at which the cost of further reductions outweigh the benefits. By promoting stakeholder thinking in such contractual situations, he argues that it is possible to reduce transaction costs. He draws on the example of Japan, where he suggests that the voluntary adoption of standards of behaviour limit or eliminate the potential for opportunistic behaviour.

This is, he argues, a more efficient way of contracting: moral sentiments may solve the problems of opportunism in markets and hierarchies better than the incentives of economic theory. Although Jones offers some useful insights into the behavioural assumptions of economic theories of the firm as well as characteristics of the market, ultimately his argument is simply a variation of economic theory, based on the premise that ethics in business transactions are economically efficient.

The problems associated with such attempts to reconcile stakeholder ideas with economics are addressed by Wood and Jones (1995). They argue that such works frequently rely on 'a serious mismatch of variables which are mixed and correlated almost indiscriminately with a set of stakeholder-related performance variables that are not theoretically linked' (p. 231). More importantly, stakeholder ideas are 'sanitized' in the attempt to engage business practitioners, compromising the potential of the approach to allow more complex analyses and understandings of the business–society relationship.

Building on this sense that the stakeholder approach has 'no real theoretical status' which sends out 'a maddening variety of signals' (p. 853), Mitchell *et al.* (1997) have attempted to provide a basis for a stakeholder theory by offering a means to separate stakeholders reliably from non-stakeholders. They propose a dynamic model of stakeholder salience that explicitly recognizes situational uniqueness and managerial perception to explain how managers can prioritize stakeholder relationships. This model is argued to be descriptively accurate, placing managers at the centre of the theory, as it is they who determine which stakeholders are salient. It also allows for observed variability/contingency of managerial values, rather than assuming only self-interested behaviour. Their approach still requires some development, especially in unravelling some of the difficult issues associated with legitimacy and power which are at the heart of the model, but it does support the normative core of stakeholder thinking and is moreover amenable to empirical operationalization and the generation of testable hypotheses.

Another theoretical development, which was initially established to challenge the agency model, is stewardship theory (Donaldson and Davis 1991; Davis *et al.* 1997). Stewardship theory proposes that a manager is the steward of a company's assets, not an agent of the shareholders. In this view the 'separation of ownership and control' described by Berle and Means is not a problem to be overcome, but was a positive and inevitable development enabling the effective management of complex organizations. The theory suggests that depth of knowledge, commitment, access to current operating information and technical expertise are important requirements enabling a company to be run effectively. Consequently, it is argued that the economic performance of a firm increases when power and authority are concentrated in a single executive (i.e. a dual CEO/Chairman), who is not distracted by external non-executive directors. In this respect stewardship theory directly challenges agency theory, where the monitoring role of an independent board and a powerful Chairman, who can represent the interests of shareholders against the self-interest of executive managers, is conceived always to have positive effect on performance.

There has been some limited empirical support for the claims of stewardship theory. For example Muth and Donaldson (1998) carried out an empirical study examining the boards of 145 of the largest companies on the Australian Stock Exchange. The findings were that the more independent the board, and with the split of CEO-Chairman, the lower the returns to shareholders and the lower the levels of sales growth. As such stewardship theory provides an interesting challenge to analyses of corporate governance grounded in agency theory, but its full theoretic contribution is yet to be developed (Davis *et al.* 1997).

Another concept which may be useful for the study of corporate governance, is that of trusteeship (Kay and Silberston 1995), which appears to vary slightly from the concept of stewardship outlined above (although both are yet to be fully developed, so it is difficult to distinguish clearly between them). Trusteeship is borrowed from the concept in English law which governs the behaviour of someone who controls and manages assets which they do not beneficially own themselves. The notion of a board of directors as the trustee of company assets, like the idea of stewardship, is argued by its supporters to capture the roles and responsibilities of the board more accurately than the economic theories discussed earlier. However, trusteeship emphasizes, perhaps more than stewardship, that managers have a wide range of motivations other than simply maximizing their own benefits; when faced with a situation which brings no direct personal advantage a manager may still base his/her action on a sense of duty and identification with the organization (Etzioni 1975). Kay and Silberston discuss some of the implications of the theory as follows:

. . . the duty of the trustee is to preserve and enhance the value of the assets under his control, and to balance fairly the various claims to the returns which these assets generate. The trusteeship model therefore differs from the agency model in two fundamental ways. The responsibility of the trustees is to sustain the corporation's assets. This differs from the value of the corporation's shares. The difference comes not only because the stock market may value these assets incorrectly. It also arises because these assets of the corporation, for these purposes include the skills of the employees, the expectations of customers and suppliers, and the company's reputation in the community.   (Kay and Silberston 1995: 92)

For trusteeship, the non-executive director is a valuable creative force on the board of directors, not the representative of the shareholder interest as put forward by agency theory, nor the interloper described by stewardship theory. The concept of trusteeship appears to offer a potentially interesting source of ideas for thinking about corporate governance, but its operational details are not well developed, and there are no empirical studies that have yet drawn on its ideas.

Finally, some researchers have recently suggested that organizational trust might constitute an alternative to the direct monitoring and control mechanisms which characterize economic approaches to the governance of companies (Powell 1996; Roberts 2001*b*). Theories of organizational trust have mainly emerged in the context of a growing interest in inter-firm collaboration, strategic alliances, partnerships and joint ventures (Powell 1996; Zaheer *et al.* 1998), but as they have developed they have also begun to be used to explore board processes and inter-firm governance processes.

Organizational trust has been recognized as an issue with implications for the way that companies are governed by transaction costs economists, who have attempted to extend and amend their theories to account for the phenomenon (Williamson 1993; Bromiley and Cummings 1995). The underlying assumptions of their approach to trust is that humans are self-interested and opportunistic; therefore, the concern of transaction costs economics is to understand the constraints and sanctioning mechanisms that exist to enforce trustworthiness. In this view, trust is essentially a calculative phenomenon.

However, the organizational literature distinguishes between calculative and non-calculative forms of trust, challenging the dominance of this 'rational choice' economic model of individual motivation. This nascent literature builds on insights from other disciplines including psychology, sociology, political science, and sociobiology. As yet there is little integration of the various disciplinary approaches; for example, personality theorists tend to focus on trust as an individual dispositional trait, sociologists tend to focus on trust as an institutional phenomenon, and social psychologists see it as a social phenomenon (Lewicki and Bunker 1996). Consequently, it is still very much an embryonic body of theory in the organizational literature (Kramer and Tyler 1996), and is claimed by some to be characterized by a lack of definitional and conceptual clarity (Blois 1999).

Yet, it does appear to have some potential as a means of elaborating some important governance issues. For example, Roberts (2001*b*) discusses trust within UK boards of directors as a 'socializing' process of accountability, which is argued to complement the 'individualizing' processes of control. Within a board of directors, trust is possible given 'the collective nature of the group's formal responsibility, the face-to-face structure of meetings, and the relative balance of power between members' (p. 1563). Accountability through surveillance, monitoring, and control in this context is conceived of not as an inferior or deficient alternative, but as a solution to the problem of trust at a distance, where the processes associated with atomized individual interactions circumscribe the development of trust.

Powell (1996) also discusses the potential for a trust-based form of governance between firms. He explores four different forms of inter-firm cooperation, which he suggests operate in different ways depending on the type of cooperation being pursued. The first example he gives is of trust operating in geographically proximate companies, such as those in Silicon Valley or north-central Italy, where small-scale production units seem to operate on a different logic to integrated mass-production firms. In these networks he argues that the risks of the individual business units are attenuated through a trust which develops out of a cooperative infrastructure, depending not just on geographic proximity but close social networks. His second example concerns the importance of trust in rapidly developing technological fields where R&D networks engender a type of trust between individuals based on common membership of a professional community. This is a non-calculative type of trust where cooperation is 'thickened' through the sharing of ideas and knowledge. Third, he identifies the type of trust that builds up in close-knit business groups. As an example he discusses Japanese corporate networks, where he says the type of trust which is built up is calculative and dependent on the maintenance of reputations. Finally he discusses the trust found in strategic alliances, which again he identifies as a form of calculative trust since the 'terms' of the type of trust are usually spelled out in a contract. He concludes that in all of these different forms, trust is shown not to be simply a cultural value or an outcome derived from calculation, but requires sustained interaction as it is learned and reinforced.

In sum, there are a number of different (and competing) organizational approaches which have the potential to contribute to the understanding of corporate governance. All tend to acknowledge the complexities of organizational life, but they also tend to be poorly developed theoretically. This may be a function of their relatively recent development (compared to economic approaches), as well as the lack of empirical research which they have generated to date.

1.5. CASE FOR AN EMPIRICAL STUDY OF JAPANESE CORPORATE GOVERNANCE

In spite of theoretical developments in the organizational research field briefly reviewed above, it is economists' ideas, in particular agency theory, which have come to dominate thinking about corporate governance among practitioners and policy-makers as well as academics. Given the particular way that economists conceptualize the 'corporate governance problem', the pre-eminent focus of corporate governance research and policy is the elaboration of hierarchical mechanisms that can help capital providers to 'control' the behaviour of company managers. For example, the World Bank, which along with many other international financial agencies is actively promoting global standards of corporate governance, claims in a recent report:

What makes corporate governance necessary? Put simply, the interests of those who have effective control over a firm can differ from the interests of those who supply the firm with external finance. The problem, commonly referred to as the principal-agent problem, grows out of the separation of ownership and control and of insiders and outsiders. In the absence of the protections that good governance supplies, asymmetries of information and difficulties of monitoring mean that capital providers who lack control over the corporation will find it risky and costly to protect themselves from the opportunistic behavior of managers or controlling shareholders. (World Bank 1999)

I would argue that focusing attention in this way seems to run the risk of prematurely curtailing broader, potentially valuable thinking about how companies are or should be governed. Given the incipient state of theoretical and empirical research on corporate governance, it seems prudent to address the issue of corporate governance without accepting or rejecting *a priori* any definition of 'the governance problem'.

In order to contribute to our knowledge about corporate governance, in what follows, I present the results of an empirical study which attempts to throw some light on the way that Japanese companies are governed in practice. There are several justifications for having chosen to consider the Japanese system of corporate governance as a topic for this book. First of all, in spite of being the second largest economy in the world, comparatively little empirical research has been conducted on the Japanese system of corporate governance in comparison with Anglo-American systems (Boyd *et al.* 1996). As such, an empirical analysis of the Japanese system provides a useful addition to knowledge about this major world economy's corporate governance practices.

But more importantly, the Japanese system appears to offer good potential to examine closely the different economic and organizational conceptualizations of corporate governance that I have discussed in this chapter. Recently there has been a growing interest in Japanese corporate governance, much of which derives from research into issues around globalization and international economic integration (Berger and Dore 1996; Crouch and Streeck 1997; Hopt 1997). Many of theses studies adopt, explicitly or implicitly, capital-centred economic theories as their principal analytical framework. However, resultant analyses appear to be far from consensual, and more pertinently, some of these studies call into question the adequacies of economic analytical frameworks to explain certain aspects related to corporate governance systems: the Japanese system is often cited as 'evidence' to substantiate the claims of many of the various 'organizational' theories of corporate governance. For example Jones (1995) discusses the case of Japan to support his argument about the reduction of transaction costs through 'stakeholder thinking'; Kay and Silberston (1995) draw on the example of Japanese governance in elaborating their notion of trusteeship; Powell (1996) suggests that governance within Japanese corporate networks operates on the basis of a (calculative) form of trust. Nonetheless, such claims are usually based on secondary source analyses, and have not been subject to empirical scrutiny.

In sum, the Japanese system appears to constitute potentially productive subject matter through which to explore and contrast economic and organizational approaches to corporate governance, as well as being a valuable study in itself. In the following chapter, I review *current* interpretations of Japanese corporate governance, aiming to crystallize for the reader mainstream views of what makes the Japanese system so different from its Anglo-American counterpart.

2

Current Views of Japanese Corporate Governance

2.1. INTRODUCTION

'Corporate governance' is currently an extremely hot topic in Japan, and is keenly discussed by businessmen, investors, government policy-makers and the media. A survey by the Tokyo Stock Exchange in 2001 found that 97.4 per cent of Japanese listed company directors were either interested or very interested in corporate governance. This is remarkably high given that the term was only coined in Japan in the mid-1990s: an archival search of Japanese national newspapers reveals that it has only been used with any frequency since 1997,[1] and not at all before 1991.[2] The term was used initially by the Japanese media mainly in conjunction with cases of corporate impropriety: scandals involving payoffs to *sokaiya* (Japanese corporate racketeers), bribery of politicians and false accounting, involving well-known companies such as Nomura Securities, Ajinomoto, Mitsubishi Oil, Yamaichi Securities, and Sumitomo Corporation, have all been labelled as problems of corporate governance.

Such scandals are not without precedent in Japan (as elsewhere in the world), but as growth in the Japanese economy ground to a halt following the bursting of the 'bubble economy', many have begun to question the viability of (what is perceived to be) the idiosyncratic 'Japanese way' of running companies. Moreover, weak economic performance in Japan coincided with strong growth in the American and European economies during the late 1990s, adding fuel to speculation that Japanese business practices have become outmoded in the rapidly globalizing economy. Issues such as corporate disclosure, accounting practices, board structures, and the role and influence of shareholders have begun to be more carefully scrutinized, in particular as a long-term trend towards Anglo-American style of capital market financing appears to be emerging.

If the domestic and foreign media are to be believed, the 'realities of the global marketplace' have finally caught up with Japan, and are forcing a profound

---

[1] Prior to 1997, all articles which mention 'corporate governance' appear to concern countries or companies outside of Japan.

[2] In 1997 Nihon Keizai Shimbun had 338 articles mentioning the term 'corporate governance', up from twenty-three in 1996, seventeen in 1995, and eleven in 1994. The Yomiuri Shimbun had eight articles in 1997 and none previously, the Asahi Shimbun thirty in 1997, six in 1996, eight in 1995, and three in 1994. The term does not appear to be mentioned in any national Japanese newspaper prior to 1991.

questioning of the soundness of the rules and customs by which Japanese companies are governed. The solution, that one invariably hears from policy-makers and commentators alike, is that Japan must conform to the 'the global standard'. By this, they mean that Japan will among other things have to adopt the Anglo-American style of corporate governance. For example

Many Western critics of the Japanese system have long argued that the country only need become more Anglo-Saxon to escape the malaise. . . . It may sound arrogant, but that doesn't make it any less true. (*Financial Times* 1998)

In this view, traditional components of the Japanese corporate system such as the main bank system, cross-shareholding, lifetime employment, and so on, are condemned as anachronistic, inefficient, and untenable in the interdependent global marketplace.

Since 1997 numerous Japanese organizations, including Nikkeiren (the Employer's Federation), Keidanren (Federation of Economic Organizations), Keizai Doyukai (Association of Corporate Executives), and the Liberal Democratic Party have produced working papers and policy recommendations which advocate radical changes to Japanese corporate governance practices. For example, in its paper entitled 'Urgent Recommendations Concerning Corporate Governance' published in the autumn of 1997, the Keidanren claimed:

The issue of corporate governance in Japan is now the subject of widespread discussion of various sorts. In order to maintain and strengthen their international competitiveness into the twenty-first century in the context of an age of megacompetition, Japanese businesses must realize a form of corporate governance that meets global standards. (Keidanren 1997)

As well as these long-established domestic organizations, many foreign and domestic institutions have also contributed to the profusion of recommendations, proposals, and principles for the reform of Japanese corporate governance. These include international institutional investors like CalPERS (the California Public Employees Retirement System), newly formed interest groups such as the Corporate Governance Forum of Japan, and various research groups including, for example, the Nomura Research Institute, the Mitsubishi Research Institute, and the Ministry of International Trade and Industry sponsored 'Study Group on the Corporate System needed for the Twenty-First Century'.

Almost all documents highlight, to a greater or lesser extent, a perceived need for Japanese corporate governance to become more like the Anglo-American model, where shareholders play a critical role monitoring and disciplining companies. Commonly, it is argued that this will have a significant impact on the revitalization of the Japanese economy, forcing companies to focus their attention on company profits above all other considerations. It is only very occasionally that the inevitability of radical reform and convergence towards this Anglo-American shareholder-focused system of corporate governance is questioned. For example, the Nihon Keizai Shimbun, in a rare diversion from its usual line predicting a greater role for shareholders in the Japanese corporate governance system, acknowledges in one article that:

Tighter shareholder oversight might be cited as the cure for the problem, but the textbook answer rings hollow amid the realities of Japanese corporate culture.   (Nikkei Weekly 1998)

The issue that this statement raises is an important one: in spite of the apparently overwhelming publicly expressed weight of opinion in favour of realigning Japanese corporate governance practices more closely with the Anglo-American shareholder-focused model, there seem to be many privately held reservations about how or whether this might be feasible given existing practices in Japan. One of the key problems here is that, compared with research on, say, British and American corporate governance practices, detailed studies of the way that the Japanese system of corporate governance works *in practice* are few and far between, as it is such a recent topic of concern: for example, there appear to be *no* studies which have attempted to explore the governance of Japanese companies as an integrated system. Most interpretations of the Japanese system of corporate governance actually appear to have evolved from previous research that was originally conceived to explore and explain the relative success of Japanese companies in the 1970s and 1980s.

In this chapter I aim to present a review of the various studies and research that either directly address the governance of Japanese companies, or have strongly informed current interpretations of the 'Japanese corporate governance system'. The review is structured around four main themes which I suggest are central to extant conceptualizations of corporate governance in Japan. These are the role of shareholders, the role of the main bank, the role of employees, and the role of senior management. For each of these themes, there are a variety of interpretations of their relevance and importance for the Japanese corporate governance system, and this review serves to highlight these different, and sometimes contradictory interpretations.

2.2. THE ROLE OF SHAREHOLDERS

Shareholders of Japanese companies are commonly perceived to have been prevented from playing an active role in the governance of Japanese companies; however, pressures associated with changing patterns of corporate finance, especially the demands of international institutional investors, are forcing companies to be increasingly attentive to shareholder rights (Kester 1996; Ide 1998). In this section I explore this characterization in the light of various theoretical standpoints which have been used to explain Japanese shareholding practices, especially those associated with the pervasive cross-shareholding structures and industrial groupings observed in Japan. The implications of these different perspectives for analyses of corporate governance are examined.

The system of stable shareholding is widely seen to be an important feature of the Japanese corporate system, where the majority of shareholders are believed to

Table 2.1. *Proportions of stable shareholders in Japan*

Stable shareholders (%)	With this number (%)
10	0.8
20	0.8
30	2.0
40	4.9
50	17.3
60	32.7
70	30.8
+	10.6

Source: Shoji Homu Kenkyu Kai (1990).

Table 2.2. *International comparison of common stock ownership (%)*

	Japan (1994)	US (1994)	UK (1993)	Germany (1993)
Financial sector	44	45	62	29
Banks	26	3	1	14
Insurance	16	4	17	7
Pension funds	0	26	34	0
Mutual funds	0	12	7	8
Other	2	4	3	0
Non-financial sector	56	55	39	72
Corporate	24	0	2	39
Public authorities	1	0	1	4
Individuals	24	48	18	17
Foreign	7	6	16	12
Other	0	1	2	0

Source: OECD 1996.

have agreed to waive control rights, not to sell to third parties, and to consult with the firm whose shares are held in the event that they are disposed of (Sheard 1987). A study by Shoji Homu Research Centre (see Table 2.1) confirms the prevalence of stable shareholders. Furthermore, shareholding in Japan has been dominated not by the institutional investors who are becoming increasingly powerful in Anglo-Saxon economies, but by financial institutions and other companies (see Table 2.2).

Share turnover rates on the part of insurance companies, banks and other companies, are generally low and show considerable stability (see Table 2.3). These ownership patterns and low share turnover rates tend to support the view that shareholding in Japan is essentially characterized by large, stable, reciprocal exchanges between business partners and a small proportion of actively traded shares.

Table 2.3. *Share turnover by type of investors in Japan*

	1978–81	1982–85	1986–89	1990–92	1991–94
Insurance Companies	1.9	1.8	3.0	4.9	6.0
Companies	12.0	12.6	35.4	8.5	5.9
Banks	6.0	8.7	42.8	12.3	14.6
Investment Trusts	118.7	109.7	115.5	65.3	58.7
Foreigners	71.4	75.8	144.6	61.4	49.1
Individuals	54.8	54.9	78.8	24.9	19.8

Source: Economic Planning Agency 1995 (not strictly comparable, as 1978 figures are only for Tokyo Stock Exchange).

As a result, it is commonly assumed that companies are protected from the 'discipline of the market', which could be exerted by the active trading of underperforming equities by independent shareholders (Monks and Minow 1995).

Some economic historians suggest that it was the nature of corporatization in Japan following the Meiji Restoration that strongly contributed to the emasculation of shareholders and the associated genesis of stable interlocking shareholding (Fruin 1992; Yamamura 1997). It is argued that the existence of household forms of organization, rapid economic change, the need to adopt foreign technology quickly, and the relative scarcity of capital compelled the majority of companies to specialize, and precluded diversification or rapid expansion. However, as some companies began to establish nationwide rather than local or regional businesses, they realized the need to create economies of scale and scope. Rather than developing vertically or horizontally integrated companies, networks of closely or loosely allied groups of companies, which are commonly known as *keiretsu*, were established. Partly to raise capital and partly to cement business relationships, shares were often sold to friendly companies and institutions, rather than on the open market. Masaki (1979) reports the explicit advice of Mitsubishi Bank and Mitsubishi Mining in offering stocks for the first time in 1928 as an example of the type of understandings that commonly accompanied such share exchanges:

Since these stocks are offered for a long-term investment, such action as immediately selling them should be abstained from in the light of moral obligation to the company. If it is necessary, however, to sell them, inform the head office beforehand so that we can buy them back at the selling price. (p. 46)

Okazaki (1994) suggests that the 1940s wartime planned economy also strongly influenced the development of the stable shareholding system. At this time, the government felt that the stabilization of manager–worker relations needed to be prioritized in order to contribute to the war effort, so efforts were made explicitly to attenuate the power and authority of shareholders *vis-à-vis* companies. For example, the Japanese Cabinet on 7 December 1940 passed an Act entitled 'The Outline of the Establishment of a New Economic System' which viewed shareholders, managers, and employees as equal participants in the firm. This had the effect of strengthening the role of managers, and refocused firms away from a simple pursuit of profit (Okazaki 1994).

The main theoretical perspective which has been developed by economists to explain the continuing resilience of stable shareholding is the 'risk-sharing' hypothesis, initially proposed by Nakatani (1984). Nakatani found that rates of profitability and sales growth are lower for companies with extensive cross-shareholdings, but also the variability of these profits is lower. Therefore, cross-shareholding is argued to serve as an implicit mutual insurance scheme, 'in which member firms are insurers and insured at the same time' (p. 243). This approach is argued by Nakatani to improve the welfare of the corporate constituents jointly, rather than prioritizing returns to any one particular group: 'the firm in any of the corporate groups maximizes the joint utility of its corporate constituents—employees, financial institutions, stockholders, and management' (p. 228). Nakatani suggests that although this system may not optimize firm-level profitability, it is not necessarily inefficient as there may be benefits from increased macroeconomic stability.

However, since the late 1980s stable/cross-shareholding and the *keiretsu* system have come under considerable attack. The system was first questioned by the US government, which, during the US–Japan Structural Impediments Initiative Talks that began in 1989, suggested that cross-shareholdings were anti-competitive. Also the system was widely condemned in the US following the well-publicized attempt by greenmailer T. Boone Pickens to purchase a stake in Koito, a Toyota group parts manufacturer, on the grounds that it showed a total disregard for the 'rights' of shareholders in Japan (see Monks and Minow 1995).

Such criticisms sometimes make reference to claims that stable shareholding grew significantly following the progressive liberalization of the capital markets between 1965 and 1975, which is interpreted as a determined effort by companies to place a majority of shares in safe, friendly hands in order to prevent foreign shareholders from gaining controlling interests in Japanese companies (Okumura 1975). According to this conceptualization, stable shareholding structures are deliberately and consciously constructed by companies to protect themselves from the outside influence of shareholders. The fact that Japanese companies have traditionally held their Annual General Meetings (AGMs) almost exclusively on the same day (2345 of the 2387 listed Japanese companies held their AGM on 26 June 1998), and the majority last less than 30 minutes, is also frequently given as supporting 'evidence' that in Japan shareholders' rights are deliberately suppressed by entrenched managers (Monks and Minow 1995).

Furthermore, it has recently been argued that declines in corporate performance during the 1990s are in some part attributable to the inattention company managers pay to shareholders, who have not been able to carry out their monitoring role (Watanabe and Yamamoto 1993; OECD 1996). For example Wakasugi (1997) suggests that 'the poor performance of the Japanese stock market is attributable in large part to Japanese companies' emphasis on growth at all costs and neglect of shareholder returns—both of which can be traced to the overall governance system's lack of adequate representation of shareholders' interests' (p. 146).

It is now frequently claimed that because of the ongoing deregulation of the Japanese financial system, which commenced in the mid-1980s (for a comprehensive review of financial deregulation measures in Japan since 1984 see Japan Securities Research Institute 1998) changes to the cross-shareholding and *keiretsu* system are inevitable (Monks and Minow 1995; *The Economist* 1995; Nikkei Weekly 1998). For example the OECD (1998*a*) asserts that '[i]n countries such as France and Japan, traditional interlocking finance/industrial groupings have begun to lose cohesion as cross-shareholdings are liquidated' (p. 21). Frequently, predictions about the collapse of the cross-shareholding system and the reassertion of shareholder rights are simply assumed to be inevitable given the growing reliance on equity financing in Japan, for example

> One explanation for the growing acceptance of shareholder culture as the ultimate measure of corporate performance is partly because the larger companies in continental Europe and Japan are relying increasingly on bond and equities markets, as opposed to traditional bank credits, as the most cost-effective means of obtaining finance. (OECD 1998*b*: 21)

Although there is evidence to suggest that some cross-shareholdings are reducing, claims that the whole system of cross-shareholding is collapsing have not been empirically substantiated. Indeed, there are some indications that underlying attitudes to shareholding in Japan are not changing at all. For example, an amendment to the Commercial Code in 1993 reduced the cost of shareholder derivative lawsuits (whereby a shareholder can sue directors on behalf of the company), which was widely interpreted as an important step boosting shareholders' ability to influence company management (see e.g. OECD 1996: 180). However, in 1996 there were only 200 such actions, most of which did not involve listed companies, and none of which involved opposition to management decisions or performance issues (all were concerned with illegal actions by management) (Nikkei 8 September 1997).

Some researchers have suggested that focusing attention solely on the equity exchange fails to capture the importance of business relationships themselves. For example, Clark (1979) argues that cross-shareholding is an *expression* of the business relationship between firms, but does not constitute the substance of the relationship itself. In a similar vein, Gerlach (1992) claims that Japanese inter-corporate networks, of which cross-shareholding is one supporting element, are neither rational economic monitoring arrangements, nor are they attempts to prevent shareholders from influencing managers. Instead they represent 'the long-term balancing of a complex set of interests as firms singly and collectively move through broader business networks' (p. 161). Inter-corporate alliances are argued to serve as an important organizing framework for market relationships in Japan, and are more pervasive across the whole of the Japanese economy than cross-shareholding figures themselves reveal.

Gerlach suggests that group-wide activities within *keiretsu* (including joint industrial and public relations activities, social centres, dining rooms, health care centres, holiday resorts, and even inter-group marriage agencies) serve to integrate groups socially, establish a coherent identity between group members, and position the group within the wider business community, rather than just serve narrow economic interests. Gerlach limits his analysis to core members of the main *kigyo shudan* (large industrial groups) and consequently fails to explore relationships between companies in other less formalized alliance structures which he argues are pervasive in Japan. Nonetheless, his research points to the limitations of economic analyses of Japanese shareholding, which tend to focus attention narrowly on the issue of protecting invested capital, to the exclusion of other, possibly important issues, which may be relevant to the role that business partners play in the Japanese corporate governance system.

Gilson and Roe (1993) also argue that the economists' search for a 'corporate monitor' fails to do justice to the complexities of the Japanese industrial system; the exclusive focus on solving the agency problem has concentrated research on the ability of banks to monitor companies, whereas they argue that studying the effect and implications of *keiretsu* type organization is at least as important. They suggest that through this it is possible to discern that the corporate group system that has developed in Japan is not just a solution to the problem of protecting investors' capital; instead it 'functions not only to harmonize the relationships among the corporation, its shareholders, and its senior managers, but also to facilitate productive efficiency' (1993: 872).

Gilson and Roe suggest that by developing this conceptualization of *keiretsu*, one arrives at a different analysis of how governance might operate in Japan. They argue that intense product competition and relation-specific investment interact to generate a strong monitoring structure, which prevents the 'cooperative entrenchment' of *keiretsu* managers: all members of the *keiretsu* suffer if a joint-effort does not succeed in the product market. Moreover, monitoring of individual firms in a *keiretsu* is enabled through the movement of executives between companies, as well as through the options of exit (they can stop transacting) and voice (they own shares and so can intervene in management) that each company possesses. The drawback of their analysis is that it is principally based on the vertical *keiretsu*, set up to facilitate joint production, and is less immediately relevant to the horizontal *keiretsu* and *kigyo shudan*.[3] Nonetheless, their arguments are valuable in suggesting, like those of Gerlach do, that mainstream agency theory explanations of cross-shareholding and the *keiretsu* system might be limited, and may not capture some important elements of the Japanese industrial system.

Although the analyses of Gerlach (1992) and Gilson and Roe (1993) call into question the value of the agency model of the firm for understanding Japanese corporate governance, the analytical frameworks they use are still essentially (transaction cost) economic ones, and as such seek to gauge how opportunism and self-seeking behaviour are mitigated in Japan. The work of Dore (1983, 1987), by contrast, intimates that the Japanese system of corporate governance may rely on entirely different processes which Gerlach and Gilson and Roe only allude to. Based on qualitative empirical research in Japanese companies, Dore suggests that the extensive Japanese business

---

[3] Large industrial groups, such as Mitsubishi, Mitsui, Fuyo.

networks are sustained by 'relational contracting' among business partners. This he argues is based on 'goodwill', which he defines as 'the sentiments of friendship and the sense of diffuse personal obligation which accrue between individuals engaged in recurring contractual economic exchange' (1987: 170).

Although Dore extends these ideas in his more recent work which deals with comparative forms of capitalism (1996, 1998, 2000), he does not fully develop 'relational contracting' in terms of its implications for the way that Japanese companies are governed in practice. I would suggest that this concept could well be a valuable addition to the corporate governance debate, as it anticipates many of the concepts associated with 'trust-based' forms of governance discussed in the previous chapter. For example, he suggests that the effect of 'relational contracting' is that it generates a diffuse sense of obligation to individual trading partners. The result of this he likens to Durkheim's (1893) discussion of the non-contractual elements of contract: the consciousness of an obligation imposed by society enforces basic rules and principles, ensuring honesty and the keeping of promises. In the case of Japanese business networks, Dore proposes that 'society' is replaced by trading partners. He suggests that the stability of the relationship between trading partners is key, where both sides recognize an obligation and try to maintain it, and real personal relationships are essential. In this interpretation, like those of Gerlach (1992), Gilson and Roe (1993), and Clark (1979), cross-shareholding is incidental and it is the relationships themselves which are important for governance.

In summary, a somewhat stylized version of the main perspectives on the corporate governance role of Japanese shareholders is as follows. Most economic commentators tend to assume that shareholders in Japan have been prevented from fulfilling their 'natural' governance role, and that this is destined to change as equities increasingly replace debt finance on company balance sheets. However, some empirical analyses suggest that cross-shareholding and the associated *keiretsu* system is relatively resilient, and that these may be associated with alternative governance mechanisms. Finally, there is a suggestion that shareholding itself may not be relevant at all to the way that governance functions in Japan, and that it is the relationships between business partners that is crucial. As there is no strong consensus about how, if at all, shareholding is relevant to the Japanese system of corporate governance, I suggest that this, as well as the associated business relationships, is worth exploring empirically in more detail.

2.3. THE ROLE OF THE MAIN BANK

The main bank system is widely perceived to be an important component of Japanese corporate governance arrangements, playing a significant role in the monitoring of company managers in lieu of shareholders (Watanabe and Yamamoto 1993; Monks and Minow 1995; OECD 1996). In this section, I shall briefly trace the development of work on the main bank, drawing attention to various different explanations of the company–main bank relationship and its governance role.

Unlike the US, Japanese banks are able to hold company shares (up to a maximum of 5 per cent of total company equities), which is considered to give banks some incentive to monitor their clients. But more importantly, economists argue that the high gearing of Japanese companies has meant that bank lending takes on many of the characteristics of more risky equity finance, which obliges banks to monitor client companies (Sheard 1987, 1994). Also, the nature of Japanese bank lending appears to be important in this context: the premium charged by lending institutions above the official discount rate does not appear to reflect fully company risk (Corbett 1987); although 60–70 per cent of loans are collateralized, they are collateralized against general rather than specific assets; explicit debt covenants (e.g. limiting shareholder payouts or restricting investment decisions) are rarely made, instead banks generally ask corporations for extensive ongoing access to company financial information when making a loan (ibid.).

The intervention of main banks in the management of financially distressed clients, including for example the well-known restructuring of Mazda by Sumitomo Bank (Pascale and Rohlen 1983), is perhaps the most commonly cited 'evidence' of the potential influence of main banks being actualized. Also a number of empirical studies appear to confirm that main banks do play an active role in supporting client companies during financial distress. For example, Suzuki (1980) found in a detailed analysis of 52 companies facing financial distress that the main determinant of recovery was the strength of its relationship with the main bank, defined in terms of the amount of outstanding loan, the extent of bank equity holdings, and the existence of employee transfers between firm and bank. Equity ratio, interest cover, and cash flow coverage by contrast were uncorrelated with recovery. Also Hoshi *et al.* (1990*a*) found that firms with close ties to main banks invest and sell more than 'independent' firms after the onset of financial distress.

Nonetheless, the role of the main bank in monitoring and assisting client companies is something of a 'puzzle' for economists. There is no official or legal relationship between corporations and a main bank; relationships are informal and non-exclusive. Also, individual banks rarely provide the majority of funding to particular clients: a study by Corbett (1994) shows that the main bank tends to provide only 20–30 per cent of total loans to an individual company. Furthermore, 83 per cent of bank lending takes the form of short-term loans (JETRO 1991), the majority of which are 3–4-month loans against bills. This type of lending is particularly safe for the bank in that interest is paid in advance in the form of a discount, and their liquidity (via a secondary market) reduces the need for explicit monitoring. Longer-term loans tend to be accompanied by the requirement for compensating balances, which although not legal have been seen as either collateral or a means of raising the effective loan rate (Corbett 1987). Nonetheless, in the case of bankruptcy the main bank bears a disproportionate share of bank losses (Sheard 1992, 1994). For economists this appears counter-intuitive: if a bank's actions were based on the economic assumption of self-interest, one might expect that it would take advantage of any monitoring or informational advantage to minimize its own losses.

One explanation for this apparent puzzle, which forms part of Nakatani's (1984) analysis discussed in the previous section, is that the main bank is a risk-sharing institution, receiving high premiums in good times and in return guaranteeing clients when they face difficulties. Nakatani finds that firms which he classes as independent of a main bank relationship have higher rates of profitability and sales growth than a sample of firms with well-established links with main banks, but that they also have higher rates of profit variability and lower levels of employee compensation. This, he interprets as a mutual insurance scheme in which profit and sales are sacrificed in return for risk sharing and external stability. It is 'an ingenious solution to the problem of the non-existence of contingent markets for "management risks"' (p. 229). This explanation depends on the absence of 'free-rider' banks taking advantage of the insurance provided by other banks, but it is usually suggested that in a fairly closed market, such as the Japanese banking sector, it is possible to overcome this potential problem through the concerted action of banks participating in the system.

Another competing rationalization of this main bank puzzle is that a main bank acts as a delegated monitor on behalf of all the banks lending to a firm (Sheard 1987, 1994). In turn other banks act as delegated monitors of other companies, this cooperative monitoring reducing duplication of effort. As a result the main bank itself does not benefit directly as it has to bear the costs of monitoring, but the system as a whole is more efficient: 'The main bank confers a beneficial externality on the other non-monitoring banks. It is prepared to do this because it is the recipient of beneficial externalities from the same banks when it lends as a non-monitoring bank' (Sheard 1987: 15).

The main bank system is such a distinctive feature of the Japanese commercial system that it has become the subject of quite extensive theoretical study in the field of the economics of financial intermediation. Horiuchi *et al.* (1988) suggest that the main bank's primary function is the creation and integration of costly information on borrowers which is not available to the capital markets. In this context, main banks may be a substitute for screening and monitoring institutions such as bond and credit-rating agencies—banks have detailed information on companies, so their lending behaviour signals to the market the company's strength (Sheard 1994). The nature of long-term transaction relationships in Japan improves the quality of this information, creating the main bank–company relationship which allows banks to provide loans to companies and also signal other banks and companies as to the soundness of individual companies.

Hoshi *et al.* (1990*a,b*) support this interpretation, showing in a series of empirical studies that bank-oriented finance has been an effective means of capital allocation in Japan. They find that companies with well-defined main bank relationships improve their access to capital, which they propose is principally because of the quality of the information available to them. This suggests that Japanese companies are thereby able to take on higher levels of debt finance with lower levels of attendant risk than counterparts in the US.

In spite of the various competing explanations and analyses, there is a broad consensus that banks have played a more prominent role in the Japanese financial system than is the case in many other developed countries, particularly the US. Moreover, it is widely believed that the main bank has been important for corporate governance in Japan, as it is in a position to monitor company management in lieu of shareholders, and is able to intervene quickly and effectively in the case of financial distress. For economists the main bank–company relationship is often summarized as being a system of 'contingent corporate governance' (Jones and Tsuru 1997; OECD 1996): 'When performance is good, corporate affairs are left to the incumbent management. When it deteriorates, the main bank, using its power as a lender and shareholder, intervenes in the management of companies to supervise downsizing and reorganization where necessary' (Jones and Tsuru 1997: 2).

Recently, many economists claim that as bank debt diminishes as a source of corporate finance, the ability of banks to monitor their client companies is being reduced (Hoshi *et al.* 1990*b*; Watanabe and Yamamoto 1993). The OECD (1996) concludes that 'with financial deregulation in the 1980s, many firms have been gradually shifting their financing to capital markets. As a result, the discipline exerted by banks has been weakening' (p. 143). Kester (1991) identifies the revision of the Foreign Exchange Control Law in 1980, allowing companies to issue unsecured foreign bonds, as the watershed in this financing revolution. The patterns of corporate finance in Japan at first glance do appear to be changing, with bank lending declining significantly, as shown in Fig. 2.1.

Furthermore, it does appear that since the late 1980s Japanese companies have been switching to direct financing in favour of debt. Borio (1990) shows that Japanese gearing ratios have for some time been converging with those of other countries (see Table 2.4).

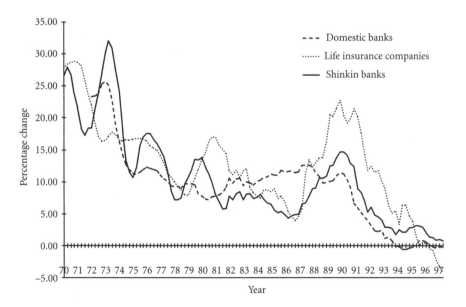

Figure 2.1. *Loans and discounts outstanding for financial institutions*
Source: Compiled from Bank of Japan data (1998).

Table 2.4. *International comparison of corporate gearing ratios*

		1970	1980	1987
Japan	Gross	0.86	0.65	0.59 (1986)
	Net	0.68	0.84	0.42 (1986)
UK	Gross	0.51	0.63	0.48
	Net	0.21	0.25	0.04
US	Gross	0.45	0.50	0.51
	Net	0.21	0.25	0.24
Germany	Gross	0.72	0.81	0.77
	Net	0.74	0.84	0.76

Source: Borio (1990).

Given the increased availability of market-based capital in Japan, questions are often raised about the desirability of a system which is argued to constrain investment by limiting companies' access to capital (e.g. see Kang and Stulz 1997). Weinstein and Yafeh (1998) posit that companies closely associated with main banks have enjoyed lower growth rates and pay relatively high interest rates, which they claim suggests that banks use monopoly power to squeeze client profits through interest payments and inhibit their growth through conservative investment policies. Banks are argued to have had undue power because of underdeveloped capital markets. 'In the absence of contestable capital markets, large banks with close ties to industry siphon profits and restrict investment, and thus may inhibit rather than encourage growth' (p. 27).

I would suggest, however, that closer analysis of the financial data indicates that arguments based on general patterns of finance may be misleading, and the significance of these patterns for corporate governance may need to be appraised more carefully. For example, the assertion that capital market finance is *replacing* bank debt as a major source of corporate finance is misleading: figures show that although there is an increased *proportion* of capital market finance in company total *external* financing, this has not come about as a result of increased capital market flows, but is instead the result of a sharp drop in bank finance against relatively stable capital market flows during the 1990s (see Fig. 2.2).

One alternative explanation for the financing statistics is that Japan is making a (painful) transition from a developing economy to a mature economy, which involves a decline in fixed capital formation and financial investment, resulting in a reduced need for external finance (OECD 1996). Absolute levels of capital market finance remains stable, while retained earnings grow. As a result, claims about the weakening of the company–main bank relationship as a result of a capital market revolution are argued to have been exaggerated:

It is difficult to be certain, though, that [capital market induced changes] translated directly into weaker monitoring performances by banks . . . It would be an exaggeration . . . to say that the main bank system has collapsed or that it may disappear in the future.   (OECD 1996: 178)

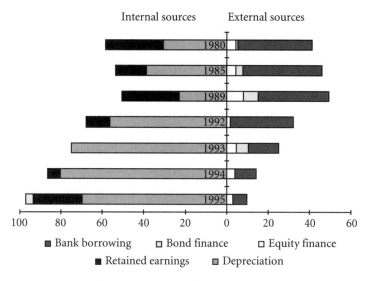

Figure 2.2. *Changes in corporate finance of TSE listed companies*
Source: Hojin Kigyo Tokei Nenpo (Annual Corporate Statistical Report) 1997.

Aoki *et al.* (1994) also challenge the prevailing view that the main bank system is breaking down. They suggest that the main bank system is not necessarily decreasing in importance simply because of the financial reforms which have taken place since the 1980s. They argue that it is increasingly recognized that links between banks and companies are systematized and are at many different levels, and as such the 'main bank' should no longer be simply defined as the bank with the largest proportion of borrowing. Instead the main bank system 'refer[s] to *a system of corporate financing and governance* involving an informal set of practices, institutional arrangement, and behaviours among industrial and commercial firms, banks of various types, other financial institutions, and the regulatory authorities' (p. 3: italics in original).

This conceptualization of the company–main bank relationship is, they suggest, more complex than earlier models based solely on lending arrangements, and generates a host of new questions about the nature of the relationship. Their observations draw attention to the caveats appended to many of the earlier economic analyses of the main bank system, which acknowledged the paucity of qualitative research on the main bank system, and conceded that there may be other explanations of company– main bank relationships which might offer no direct benefit to an individual main bank. Possibilities which have been cited include implicit norms, enforcement by Ministry of Finance and Bank of Japan, or that banks may gain preferential access to other lucrative financial business with main clients, including foreign exchange and clearing business (Sheard 1994). Hoshi *et al.* (1990*a*) acknowledged that intervention by main banks in the management of poorly performing firms might take place not only to improve the performance of the poorly performing company, but also because of reputational worries about the firm as a whole, personal loyalty to other members of the group, or a reluctance to admit a mistake in extending credit to the company. However, such issues have generally been left outstanding in the literature, and remain to be explored.

2.4. THE ROLE OF EMPLOYEES

There is an extensive research literature on Japanese employees and employment practices, which have been viewed as a crucial element of the competitive advantage of Japanese firms during the postwar period of rapid economic growth. In this literature, there has been some discussion of the positive implications of employment practices for corporate governance, in terms of the strong participation in company decision-making that they engender. By contrast, most recent analyses of the Japanese corporate governance system tend not to address any possible governance role that employees might play; if they are mentioned at all it is to argue that Japanese companies may have prioritized the interests of employees at the expense of shareholders, but that now, given the pressures associated with globalization, this is destined to change. In this section I shall explore these contrasting interpretations of the role of employees in Japanese corporate governance.

During the 1970s and 1980s, when the economic success of Japan became a focus of attention around the world, the relationship between a company and its employees was frequently discussed as a key component of Japan's national competitive advantage. 'Enterprise welfarism' and 'welfare corporatism' are among the terms which were coined to distinguish the system adopted by many Japanese companies; important elements of this system included guarantees of lifetime employment, seniority wages and promotion, the development of firm specific skills, enterprise unions, labour-management consultation, and the provision of company housing, medical, recreational, and dining facilities (Matsumoto 1991).

Abegglen (1958) and Hazama (1964) are often credited with popularizing the idea that the employee-centred Japanese company had its roots in pre-industrial, that is (household) forms of organization, where characteristics such as duty and mutual obligation, loyalty to the group and consensual decision-making were important. In this vein, Nakamura (1981) explicitly discusses the governance characteristics of pre-industrial social organization, which he argues subsequently served as a model for modern Japanese society in general, and companies in particular. He suggests that participative village governance systems developed during the Tokugawa period (1600–1867) enabled the development of a deep understanding of the social and political processes and problems of a small community. During this period Japan was commonly divided into small villages, where commoners had to govern their own affairs, including the assessment of taxes, the administration of social, political, and fiscal matters of the village, the allocation of water rights, the conciliation of village disputes, and so on. By the end of the Tokugawa period, villages had become relatively stable communities, with well-structured and relatively small (*c*.200 members) populations. What emerged in these communities as a result, was a form of governance based on consensus, using democratic and participatory means to resolve village issues, with a great deal of local autonomy and personal involvement in affairs.

Some other researchers have attributed aspects of Japanese employment practices to distinctive Japanese cultural characteristics, often emphasizing the importance of Confucianism and Buddhism in informing the values, attitudes, and patterns of behaviour particular to the Japanese, including interdependence, a respect for elders, a common sense of security, a lack of personal ego, group identity (Nakane 1970). However, there has been some reaction against what are seen as culturally deterministic analyses of the Japanese corporate system (Gerlach 1992); most research on the Japanese firm and corporate system since the mid-1980s has attempted to reveal the economic rationality of the Japanese firm, and reconcile this with the particular cultural and social setting of Japan (Aoki 1984; Aoki and Dore 1994; Yamamura 1997).

Studies in this tradition have emphasized that cooperative and paternalistic labour relations have not always been common in Japan, and that before and immediately following the Second World War there were often violent labour disputes. These were deemed to be counterproductive by government and companies set on economic recovery, and are argued to have resulted in the deliberate introduction of measures to create a less volatile labour force (Okazaki 1994; Fingleton 1995). For example, the suppression of an external labour market made it difficult for Japanese employees to find alternative employment; by paying employee salaries according to age (Ministry of Labor 1997), an employee effectively loses the present value of his future earnings if s/he leaves or if the corporation fails; as Japanese pensions are generally paid out of company assets, rather than from independently funded schemes (Ministry of Labor 1993), employees face the possibility of not receiving a pension if the company goes bankrupt. Such features are argued to have been developed in order to 'incorporate' (Whittaker 1998) employees into the company, deliberately aligning their interests with the long-term vitality of their company in order to produce more stable labour conditions.

Another interpretation takes the view that regardless of the initial causes or motivations for their introduction, current employment practices are a reflection of the fact that the Japanese company is perceived to be primarily a social organization, not simply a mechanism to accumulate capital. As such, Japanese employees are perceived and perceive themselves to be participants in their companies, not contracted labour who are deliberately tied to the company in various ways. Dore (1973, 1983, 1987) is perhaps best known for developing this 'community' model of the firm, which he opposes to the 'company law' model common in the UK and the US. A similar conceptualization of the Japanese firm is also discussed by Matsumoto (1991), who suggests that the Japanese firm is a 'venue where corporate employees combine various elements and the necessary capital for corporate activities'. Itami (1994) also argues that the Japanese firm is a 'human-based enterprise', as opposed to the American model of the firm as a collection of material resources.

The strong identification of Japanese employees with their firms is argued to be consistent with many widely recognized features of Japanese business: for example, by concentrating on expanding market share rather than improving profitability, Japanese companies have been able to offer more opportunities for employees; productivity enhancement is willingly pursued as employees know they, as well as the providers of capital, will receive an important share of any gains made; high levels of investment in training and R&D can be safely made as corporations realize that they will reap the long-term benefits. Many studies have made reference to the high levels of participation of employees in Japanese companies, embodied in group decision-making, joint employee-management consultation teams, and the practice of consensus building, which are associated with this distinctive employee-centred corporate system (OECD 1977).

Research on Japanese industrial relations is one area in which the relevance of these features for corporate governance has explicitly been explored. For example, Whittaker (1998) discusses the governance implications of participative 'corporate community' type industrial relations, alongside passive or confrontational industrial relations (which are less common, but which also exist in Japan). In companies with participative industrial relations, workers are argued to have a voice which is reflected in corporate policy, which suggests they play an important role in the governance of their companies. This governance role is institutionalized, for example, in labour-management consultation processes, which are not only common in Japanese firms, but appear to be growing even though union activity itself may be declining (in 1972, 62.8 per cent of companies with a union had a labour-management consultative committee, in 1984 the proportion had risen to 70 per cent, and in 1994 the figure was 80.7 per cent (Japan Institute of Labour 1997)). The list of issues which are open to consultation are broad, including management policy, production and sales plans, changes in company organization, rationalization, recruitment, lay-offs, wages and bonuses, training, and education (Japan Institute of Labour 1997). Moreover, the level of communication among employees on these issues is high, and is carried out through morning assemblies, workshop meetings, union newsletters and magazines, as well as widespread suggestion and self-appraisal schemes.

The idea that employees may play an active part in the governance of Japanese companies has also been explored by some economists (Garvey and Swan 1992; Imai and Komiya 1994). For example Garvey and Swan (1992) present a model of Japanese corporate governance as a nexus of financial and employment contracts. They argue that a system where managers recognize the interests of workers is economically efficient when firm performance depends on employee cooperation as well as individual effort, but giving 'voice' to employees is efficient only when there is monitoring by creditors, not shareholders.

However, in general, most studies have tended to explore the *implications* of Japanese employee-centred firms for the system of corporate governance, not the role that employees themselves might play in the governance of their companies. Where employees are mentioned, it is often in the context of companies having promoted the interests of employees at the expense of shareholders, which, given the pressures associated with globalization at the end of the 1990s, is argued to be less and less viable (Monks and Minow 1995; *The Economist* 1995; Aoi 1997; Sherman and Babcock 1997).

In summary, there has been a strong tradition of research on the role of Japanese employees, although the implications of the strong employee focus of Japanese firms for corporate governance have often only been addressed implicitly. However, recent economic analyses tend to assume that the prioritization of employee interests in Japanese firms has been an obstacle to effective governance by shareholders, and often suggest that the system is in the process of breaking down as shareholders begin to re-assert their power and authority. Given these contradictory postulations about the role of employees and employment practices for the Japanese corporate governance system, and the questions about its resilience, it seems that empirical research that explores the role of employees within the Japanese corporate governance system would be invaluable.

2.5. THE ROLE OF SENIOR MANAGEMENT

The OECD (1998*a*) claims that at the heart of systems of corporate governance is the board of directors, as it is 'uniquely positioned as the internal corporate mechanism for holding management accountable to shareholders' (1998*a*: 22). In this section I review existing research on the Japanese board of directors, and on the governance role of Japanese senior management generally. Given the limited scope of this research, in some instances I draw on recent institutional and media analyses of Japanese boards and their relevance for the Japanese system of corporate governance.

Recently, in the context of growing interest in corporate governance, greater atten-tion has been paid to the role and practices of the Japanese board of directors, especially the extent to which it represents shareholders' interests (Monks and Minow 1995; CalPERS 1998; OECD 1998*a*). Much of this recent interest is prescriptive rather than inquisitive. For example, institutional investors such as CalPERS have devised specific recommendations for Japanese boards based on their expectations of the role a board should fulfil:

Best Governance Practices in Japan Should Include Elements that Strengthen Management Accountability to Corporate Owners through the Director-Shareholder Relationship.... Japanese Corporate Boards Should Consider the Interests of, and Strive for Accountability Toward, All Shareholders. . . . Corporate Boards Should Include Directors Who are Truly Independent from the Corporation and its Affiliates. . . . The Size of Japanese Corporate Boards Should be Reduced to Enable Effective and Efficient Decision-Making Regarding the Company's Strategic Plan and Executive Performance.   (CalPERS 1998: capitals in original)

CalPERS primary admonition is that Japanese boards of directors need to improve their accountability to shareholders, and one of the main ways of achieving this is to increase the number of independent directors. Currently, approximately 25 per cent of Japanese company directors do come from outside the company (OECD 1996), as shown in Table 2.5.

Table 2.5. *Origins of listed Japanese company directors*

	1984	1989	1994	Average 1984–94
Company Directors				
Internal	74.2	75.6	73.1	75.1
External	25.8	24.4	26.9	24.9
Other Companies	17.1	16.3	18.3	16.7
Banks	5.4	5.4	5.8	5.4
Government	3.3	2.7	2.8	2.8
Senior Executives				
Internal		60	66.1	
External		40	33.9	
Other Companies		29.7	22.7	
Banks	7.1	6.3	6.8	6.8
Government	4.7	4.0	4.4	4.5

Source: Toyo Keizai Kigyo Keiretsu Soran, quoted in OECD (1996).

The 'problem' is that most of these external directors come from related firms and friendly banks, and therefore it is believed that they cannot exercise independent judgement or be representative of shareholder interests (Monks and Minow 1995). It is assumed that as a consequence, Japanese boards of directors are largely unaccountable, for example

By Western standards the often geriatric 'insider' boards of big Japanese companies, with their largely ceremonial meetings, are woefully devoid of checks and balances. (*Financial Times* 14 February 1997)

Viner (1993) endorses this view, arguing that in contrast to American boards where accountability is guaranteed by virtue of the majority of independent directors, the Japanese board is totally ineffective in ensuring any form of corporate accountability. He goes on to argue that American institutional investors are leading a revolution in corporate governance which will redefine accountability for the Japanese corporation, in particular forcing companies to take on more independent directors.

The ability of the president to collude with the directors—who are themselves senior managers appointed by him—in order to conceal serious irregularities, is particularly strong in Japan where the absence of any outside supervision provides a cloak for every dagger. (Viner 1993: 114)

But Viner's view is disingenuous, as there seems to be no evidence that Japanese boards conceal improbity (nor, for that matter, that US boards are particularly representative of shareholder interests). Also, the method of director appointment in all OECD countries, with the exception of Germany, is in practice by invitation of the CEO. Moreover, it is arguably easier for shareholders to nominate candidates to the board and to dismiss them in Japan[4] than it is in the US or the UK (OECD 1996; Clark 1979).

The argument that Japanese 'insider' boards are entrenched is also not supported by some recent empirical research. For example, Kaplan (1994) examines the relation of top executive turnover and remuneration (including salary and bonuses) to earnings levels, changes in earnings, stock returns and sales growth during the 1980s in a sample of 119 large Japanese companies, and compares these with the US. Although top executive job turnover and compensation in Japan do not appear to be directly related to stock performance, they are more sensitive to negative earnings in Japan than is the case in the US. This is argued to demonstrate that Japanese top executives are no more entrenched than their US counterparts. In a separate study, Kaplan and Minton (1994) examine the determinants and implications for company managers of the appointment of main bank and affiliated company directors to the board between 1980 and 1988. They find in a series of regression analyses that both such appointments increase with poor stock performance, with bank directors being appointed after earnings losses. To explain this finding, they suggest that bank and inter-corporate relationships may act in a similar way as, and substitute for, US style market driven 'management control' mechanisms, although they offer no support for this postulation.

Abe (1997) extends these findings, using a larger sample than Kaplan (1994) which includes all of the listed companies on the Tokyo Stock Exchange except finance and insurance companies, covering the period 1974–90. She hypothesizes that if disciplinary pressure exists to replace poorly performing managers, then managerial turnover will be negatively correlated with turnover. Her findings are that Japanese managers are penalized for poor performance, but that turnover decisions are based more on long-term performance measures than short-term ones.

Although these studies do show that Japanese managers are not as entrenched as some economics-based analyses assume they should be in the absence of shareholder monitoring, they are not conclusive about the way that the governance mechanism actually works. Kaplan and Minton explicitly recognize that what they are showing is a correlation between executive turnover and appointment of external directors, and not necessarily a causal link. They propose some other possible factors that might explain the correlation of external appointments and company performance; for example, firms with high debt may tend to appoint bank directors and also tend to have poor stock returns. Accordingly, they extend their analysis and find that appointments of outsider directors increase also with quantitative measures of the intensity of the relationship between a company and its main bank (including the size of borrowings, the concentration of shareholdings and the number of affiliated group firms). Their interpretation of this finding is that it is not necessarily the directors themselves who are playing a monitoring role, but that the exchange of directors signifies the close monitoring role played in general by a company's main bank or

---

[4] A motion to dismiss a director can be filed by a shareholder controlling 3% of a company's issued stock (Commercial Code, Article 257).

associated companies. Notwithstanding, there is no direct evidence to support this claim—it remains a suggestion to explain an otherwise puzzling result for them.

Their difficulty in interpreting their results stems in part from the dearth of detailed empirical research on the senior management of Japanese companies, especially their corporate governance role. Current knowledge about the governance role of Japanese senior management has mainly been informed by the work of economic historians. They argue that the period of rapid industrialization following the Meiji restoration was instrumental in the way that Japanese company senior management subsequently developed. The merchants and former *samurai* who initially controlled commerce, having been given various grants, concessions, and subsidies to compensate for the dismantling of the feudal system, quickly found that they did not have the skills, knowledge, or experience to manage these new enterprises (Fruin 1992). Instead, they were obliged to rely on a new breed of university-educated and sometimes Western experienced administrators to run the corporations they established: although according to the letter of the Commercial Code they were not legally entitled to do so, supervisors, technicians, and bookkeepers quickly began to take decisions in place of the technical 'owners' (Yonekawa and Yoshihara 1987).

In this way the board of directors, although supposedly a body representative of shareholder interests according to the Japanese Commercial Code, is argued to have become divorced from any significant interaction with shareholders. It became a self-perpetuating oligarchy, drawing its membership exclusively from the ranks of employees, developing into what is perceived by some to be a senior management committee representing employee interests. The extraordinary and relentless pace of economic and technological development in Japan has further concentrated power into the hands of senior executives (Yui 1984).

Some descriptions of Japanese senior management roles have been written (Kono 1984), and there are some expositions of the role that Japanese senior management play in individual companies (Dore 1973; Clark 1979); for example, Dore contrasts the board of Hitachi with a British equivalent as follows:

The Hitachi board, then, is like a council of elders of the corporate community (whose closed nature is illustrated by the exclusiveness of the loyalty its directors must owe to the firm). The English Electric board is a collection of men appointed for their capacity to contribute to the direction of the company in the best interests of the shareholders. (1973: 223)

Beyond these historical and company specific analyses, however, empirical studies of the governance role of Japanese senior management are few and far between. There are some statistical data available on the composition of Japanese boards. For example, *Romu Gyosei Kenkyujo* (1988) provide information for firms with 100 or more employees, which shows that the Japanese board comprises a number of different levels of director: the average board is composed of one president, 0.9 vice-president, 0.4 *kaicho* (retired president/chairman), 1.9 *senmu* (senior managing director), 4.4 *jomu* (managing director), 7.8 *torishimari* (director), 0.9 other full-time directors, 1.9 full-time *kansa* (statutory auditor), and 2 part-time *kansa* (although according to the Commercial Code statutory auditors are not members of the board).

More recently, Itoh and Teruyama (1998) have reported a survey that distinguishes different attitudes and behaviours between these different levels of directors. For example, senior directors are concerned as much with investors and share price as they are with employee conditions, while non-titled directors tend to focus more exclusively on employees, especially those in the particular operational areas which they represent. Statutory auditors in large firms also tend to be focused on the welfare of investors as well as employees, although in smaller firms auditors tend to be concerned with loyalty to and cooperation with senior directors. 'Short-tenure' directors (which Itoh and Teruyama suggest tend to be externally appointed directors) tend to focus on stock price and the credibility of the firm in the eyes of stockholders and banks, and are far less concerned with employees. Although Itoh and Teruyama acknowledge the limitations of their study, their study certainly does go some way towards 'opening the black box' (Tachibanaki 1998: 57) of top management in Japan, which up until now has tended to be treated as a monolithic entity.

In summary, empirical research on Japanese senior management is limited, but recent economics-based interpretations tend to view the Japanese board of directors as entrenched. There is some recent evidence, which shows that Japanese company directors are not as entrenched as economic theories suggest they might be. However, as current understanding of the Japanese board is so limited, it is difficult to explain why this is so. Given the growing interest in corporate governance issues, empirical research on the governance role of Japanese senior management would seem to be worthwhile.

3

Carrying Out the Research

3.1. WHY CASE STUDIES?

In the previous chapter I presented an overview of earlier studies that inform existing views on Japanese corporate governance. I suggested that as research on Japanese corporate governance *per se* is a relatively new area, current knowledge is embryonic and not particularly well grounded. The range of conflicting opinion that characterizes current conceptualizations of Japanese corporate governance is arguably the product of difficulties associated with attempting to interpret the Japanese system of corporate governance at a distance from the phenomenon itself. Without some closeness to corporate governance practices and processes themselves, it is difficult to be certain about the significance of various issues for the way that companies are governed in practice.

The lack of empirical knowledge about corporate governance related practices in general, has been noted by several commentators (Pettigrew 1992; Hill 1995; McNulty and Pettigrew 1999). For example, Pettigrew (1992) articulates what he sees as the major drawback of the lack of empirical research on boards of directors:

... great inferential leaps are made from input variables such as board composition to output variables such as board performance with no direct evidence on the processes and mechanisms which presumably link the inputs to the outputs. (p. 171)

As such, Pettigrew makes the case for more 'process studies' of managerial elites, not necessarily as a replacement for other research, but as a complement. He suggests that:

... by tilting the study of managerial elites in a process direction, new answers may be possible to previous baffling questions, new questions will emerge not posed by prevailing approaches, and new forms of knowledge can arise to inform existing empirical patterns. (p. 177)

Such a 'process study' would seem to be invaluable given what I have said about the current state of knowledge about Japanese corporate governance; it seems important to conduct research which allows some proximity to the sense that participants in the corporate governance system make of their own experiences, rather than simply add to speculation about how governance might or should operate, based on inferences from broad statistics interpreted through different theoretical frameworks.

With these concerns in mind I chose to carry out detailed empirical studies of the everyday governance practices in a number of Japanese companies. I felt that exploring the governance processes of a very limited number of Japanese companies would be inappropriate, as there are likely to be many differences between various types of companies. Therefore, I pre-selected a number of attributes which might have some influence on companies' governance practices and processes, and used these as a basis for the selection of companies for the study to ensure I was examining as broad a cross-section as possible.

My first precept was to ensure that the sample covered a range of companies from different industries; Japanese manufacturing companies have traditionally been the mainstay of research on the Japanese firm, so I considered it important to include companies from other industries as well. Second, I aimed to ensure that companies of varying size, in terms of number of employees and turnover, were represented, as larger companies may have different, institutionalized practices than smaller, more flexible organizations. I also wanted to ensure that there was no bias towards highly performing or under-performing (from the shareholder perspective) companies, and as a result a third criterion I used to select companies was return on equity. The fourth criterion was the ratio of exports to total sales, in order to guard against selecting predominantly domestic or predominantly international businesses. Fifth, I aimed to select companies with different proportions of foreign shareholdings, as there is a possibility that international investors may influence the governance practices of companies in which they have a large shareholding. The sixth selection criteria were the date of establishment and date of listing, as longer-established companies might have different and more inflexible business practices than newer companies. Finally, existing research on the Japanese firm suggests that companies associated with *keiretsu* groups may have different governance practices from independent companies, therefore I aimed to include as far as possible an equal number of *keiretsu* and independent companies.

Public companies listed on the first section of the Japanese stock exchanges provided the main case material for this study, but to ensure a broad compass I also included one second section company, one company listed on the Over The Counter (OTC) market, and one non-listed company. The majority of the companies studied were based in Tokyo, but there was a possibility that companies in other parts of Japan might have slightly different practices; hence I aimed to include a number of companies with head offices outside the Tokyo Metropolitan area.

3.2. ACCESS

The principal fieldwork for this research was carried out in 1998–99, when I was based at the Development Bank of Japan (DBJ), Tokyo, with some follow-up visits in 2000. On the basis of the criteria identified above, profiles of suitable companies were built-up using the *Toyo Keizai* and DBJ Company Financial Databases. Specific companies were targeted and then approached, at first by writing to the company president explaining the background to and goals of the research. Initially I approached twenty companies, in the hope that approximately twelve would be willing to participate in the study. In view of the commercially sensitive data that I might come across during the course of the research, I pre-emptively guaranteed company and individual anonymity in the initial approach letter.

Three companies were recruited to the study as a result of the initial written approach. Three companies politely replied that they could not participate at the current time, six companies replied that they would need more information before arriving at a decision, and seven companies did not reply. I followed up all of the companies, including those which initially refused or did not reply, with telephone calls or further correspondence to try to persuade the companies to participate. In most cases I asked personal contacts and colleagues at the Development Bank of Japan to provide introductions to the target companies. With some considerable perseverance seven more companies were recruited to the study in this way.

This type of access can be termed the 'front-door' approach. Its advantage was that it offered the best chance of obtaining detailed and trustworthy data, and the organization of interviews was greatly facilitated (Gronning 1997). Also it was easier to observe everyday practices within the company and to understand relationships, which helped to contextualize the research. Furthermore, I found that as the research was felt to have been sanctioned by the company, employees were comfortable in providing me with relevant background information, including for example board agendas, internal memorandum, organizational charts, salary scales, decision-making (*ringi*) documents, and so on. The potential demerits of the front-door approach are argued to be that it may entail restrictions or conditions placed on access (Gronning 1997). In each of the ten companies which offered me this kind of access no conditions were imposed at all, although as discussed earlier I did pre-emptively guarantee all of the companies anonymity, in view of the potentially sensitive data that I was collecting.

Ten companies were recruited to the study through the 'front-door' approach, but this did not give the appropriate cross-section of companies initially envisaged. Therefore, I used another approach to recruit companies to the study, which entailed finding and making contact with employees of target companies directly, rather than formally involving the company itself. Four more companies were eventually recruited to the study in this way: in most cases initial approaches were made to the investor relations department, and then further contacts were gradually built up on a person-by-person basis within the company. Contacts were also established at two further companies, but insufficient data was gathered from them to be included in the main research. The merit of this 'back-door' approach is that respondents were not selected by the company, and when sensitive issues were being discussed they seemed to be more candid, knowing that what they said was likely to remain confidential (Gronning 1997). The practical disadvantage was that it is very time-consuming to recruit interviewees in this way.

In total, fourteen companies were recruited to the study. The sample included some of the largest public companies in Japan, as well as some small, entrepreneurial companies which at the time of the research had recently been or were in the process of being listed on the Japanese Stock Exchanges. Some of the companies were highly profitable, some were making losses. Some were 'global companies', exporting around the world, while half of the sample were purely domestic concerns.

A breakdown of the fourteen companies appears in Table 3.1, in which most of the relevant company data appear (the data have been jumbled to protect the identities

Table 3.1. *Profiles of companies researched*

Sector	Section	Adj. sales (¥ million)	Employees	Exports (%)	Foreign shares(%)	Founded	Listed	ROE (%)
Computer	0	1,900,000	50	0	0.0	1921	1949	neg.
Construction	1	1,500,000	80	0	0.0	1926	1949	1.8
Education	1	1,050,000	150	0	0.0	1931	1949	2.0
Electronic	1	650,000	875	0	3.4	1934	1952	2.8
Food and drink	1	550,000	1075	0	10.0	1937	1958	3.8
Household	1	425,000	1100	0	10.0	1939	1962	4.0
Machinery	1	250,000	1450	0	12.0	1946	1983	5.0
Oil and coal	1	200,000	2250	3	15.0	1948	1985	5.1
Packaging	1	190,000	4000	10	17.5	1949	1995	5.6
Pharmaceutical	1	95,000	7500	20	18.0	1955	1997	6.3
Publishing	1	40,000	11,500	25	21.0	1958	1998	7.1
Real estate	2	15,000	12,125	40	30.0	1979	1998	7.2
Software	3	4000	20,500	55	45.0	1981	2001	13.0
Wholesale	4	2600	22,000	70	100.0	1983	n/a	17.2

of the companies; each row of data does not refer to a particular company). The first column refers to the section of the stock exchange under which the company is listed. Most companies were listed on the first section of either the Tokyo or Osaka stock exchanges: these are designated '1' in the table. One company is the subsidiary of a major foreign corporation; as it is 100 per cent owned by a foreign shareholder it is not listed, and is designated '0' in the table. One company was in the process of listing its shares on the OTC section of the Tokyo Stock Exchange, and is designated '4' in the table. One company listed its shares on the OTC section of the Tokyo stock exchange while the research was being carried out, and is designated '3' in the table. Three of the samples did not have any foreign shareholders. One company was a core member of a former *zaibatsu* (pre-Second World War industrial conglomerate), while a further six were affiliated to *keiretsu* groups.

3.3. DATA COLLECTION

There are many possible pitfalls with using interviews as a means of collecting reliable and valid data. For example, there is the potential incongruity between a respondents' attitudes and their actual behaviour (LaPiere 1934–35; Briggs 1986), the instability of respondents' attitudes (Gritching 1986), the misinterpretation of questions by respondents (Belson 1981), differences in the phrasing of questions eliciting entirely different responses (Butler and Kitzinger 1976), and differences in interpretation of questions in different cultural contexts (Briggs 1986). These difficulties were particularly pertinent for a British researcher, exploring a topic which was, during the course of the research, the subject of wide media coverage in Japan. To minimize the possibility of these potential problems distorting the data collection, before approaching the main case study companies I undertook seven pilot interviews with businessmen and bankers.

The pilot interviews did demonstrate a tendency for respondents to answer questions in general terms, often referring to specific media reporting and anecdotes of corporate governance related issues, rather than providing spontaneous information about their own ideas and experience related to corporate governance. For example, almost every person I interviewed initially recited how the slimming down of the Sony board was clear evidence of how Japan was indeed changing its governance practices!

In order to guard against these very anecdotal and non-specific discussions, I decided to identify 'critical incidents' (Chell 1998) for each company being studied, to provide a focal point for interviews. Having selected the companies, broad data relevant to the governance of each company was gathered from a variety of sources. Media reports, company accounts, stock exchange data, IPO documents for the newer companies, and information from the internet was sourced, and data from the DBJ industrial financial database and *Toyo Keizai* databank was analysed to provide financial data going back to 1957 or the company foundation date if later. This was a very time-consuming exercise, requiring detailed and lengthy analysis of company data, which is not reported here. Using this information I was able to compile reasonably comprehensive information on each of the companies being studied. This comprised detailed financial information (including sources of finance, important business and shareholding relationships, the development of shareholding structures over time, and key financial ratios), as well as broad qualitative information about each company including major strategic issues, new product developments, scandals, and so on.

Based on this information I was able to identify and apprise myself of the details of relevant 'critical incidents', which could be used to provide a central focus for the interviews concerning each of the fourteen companies being studied. In three cases companies had been the subject of 'scandals' which had featured in the media, three were in the process of, or had recently undergone, Initial Public Offerings, three were undergoing major organizational changes, and five had experienced significant events affecting the operation of the whole organization (e.g. major falls in profitability or withdrawals from foreign markets).

The critical incident technique encouraged interviewees to provide context-rich data, relevant to the company and relevant to their own experience within the company. Also, it helped to ensure that interviews concerning a particular company had a common reference point and referred to specific events which could be cross-referenced and examined from different perspectives, as well as allowing documentary sources to be checked to assess factual statements. The disadvantage of the approach was that it is a highly time-consuming process, requiring a lot of background information to be collected and then assessed.

For each company, interviewees were selected in order to provide a comprehensive cross-section of views. Respondents comprised company directors, managers, and employees, as well as 'external' parties including *keiretsu* partners, main banks, securities companies, and so on. Usually the pre-interview company research enabled me to identify relevant internal and external interviewees, but occasionally during the course of a programme of interviews with a particular company other people or groups would be suggested who would subsequently be approached. In the majority

Table 3.2. *Interviewees*

Directors (50)	Employees (33)	Investors (48)	Outside groups (22)
President (6)	Union (7)	Main bank (12)	Lawyers (2)
Senior director (11)	Finance (4)	Other bank (10)	Professional assoc. (6)
Finance director (9)	IR (10)	Trust bank (4)	Employment agency (6)
HR director (6)	HR (6)	Insurance company (3)	Auditors (2)
Other director (10)	Other (6)	Foreign bank (6)	Media (2)
Auditor (8)		Securities company (2)	Government (6)
		Foreign shareholders (1)	Advisers (6)
		Analyst (10)	

Values in brackets indicate the numbers.

of cases the company itself would arrange internal and external interviews, but occasionally (and always for the companies approached through the 'back door') I would contact interviewees independently.

One hundred and seventy-three interviews were carried out with 153 different employees (some were interviewed two or more times); the respondents have been categorized and are shown in Table 3.2. For each company I aimed to interview a cross-section of company directors, and if I was unable to interview the company president I would ensure that I interviewed the company's former president (usually the chairman or senior adviser). I also interviewed company auditors, union representatives and employees of different ages, seniority and from a variety of different departments, including personnel, finance, and investor relations. I also interviewed a range of each company's investors, including banks and foreign and domestic shareholders, as well as analysts, rating agencies, and other relevant external parties.

There is a view that interviewees selected by companies may be 'vetted' employees (Gronning 1997) as the gatekeepers might be concerned with presenting a particular image of the company as 'they will have practical interests in seeing themselves and their colleagues presented in a favourable light' (Hammersley and Atkinson 1995: 66). I did not get any sense that this was the case, as interviewees selected by companies were just as forthcoming as interviewees I approached independently. However, cases where respondents were interviewed more than once in different locations seemed to indicate that interviewees were more guarded, but also more precise, about the issues they discussed while in the work environment.

I confirmed to all of the respondents in person that nothing they said would be attributable either to them or to their companies. I also explained that although the purpose of my study was to explore the Japanese system of corporate governance, the particular focus of the interview would be on their day-to-day roles and experiences rather than more general ideas or opinions about how corporate governance worked within their company. Interviewees were also told that I did not expect them to answer questions if they felt they did not have the requisite information and experience upon which to base a reply, which is argued to provide better data with higher validity (Andrews 1984).

Some interviewees, especially senior directors and company presidents, often began interviews with what seemed like prepared speeches, about how corporate governance practice was being 'revolutionized' in their companies, or in Japan in general. However, the critical incident technique usually allowed interviews to move beyond this more rhetorical form of discourse fairly quickly. Compared with the pilot interviews, interviewees appeared to be much more comfortable talking about their work and experience in the context of a particular 'critical incident', rather than general (received) ideas about corporate governance. Interviewees seemed to be more 'engaged' with the subject-matter than had been the case with the pilot interviews, given that they could discuss specific company issues with which I was familiar, and was able to respond to, having carried out detailed company research. During the course of the interviews I asked if I could view internal company reports, investor relations (IR) presentations, and other documents including board agendas, policy documents where it seemed they would provide more detail about or clarification about particular issues raised during the course of interviews. Usually interviewees assented to this request.

3.4. DATA ANALYSIS

As discussed earlier, the interviews were loosely structured around four main themes, namely the roles of the main bank, shareholders, employees, and senior management. Within these main themes, questions focused on sub-themes and issues which had been highlighted by my review of existing research on corporate governance generally, and the governance of Japanese companies in particular. This ensured appropriate data collection to allow the comparison of economic and organizational approaches to corporate governance. However, as the data collection process progressed these themes were inevitably modified and developed. As such the distinction between the data collection and the analysis process was not clear-cut: there was an element of 'creating, testing and modifying analytic categories as an iterative process' (Symon and Casell 1998: 5) throughout the whole research process. By the end of the fieldwork I had 173 interview transcripts, containing a mass of data loosely constructed around a myriad of amorphous themes and sub-themes.

The consequent analysis of the interview transcripts was carried out using a 'template approach' (Crabtree and Miller 1992; King 1998). First, a rudimentary template was constructed around the themes which had initially informed the interviews and which had emerged during the fieldwork. The template then served as a basis to begin coding the interview transcripts, imposing some order and structure on what was a large amount of quite complex data, and ensuring that the key issues of the research were addressed. However, in the process of the coding the template itself was revised in the light of ongoing analysis. This flexibility allowed the generation and development of new ideas and themes which emerged from the data, enabling new insights to be explored further. This approach to analysis is different from grounded approach (Glaser and Strauss 1967), which is prescriptive in its recommendations for data collection and analysis, and appears more appropriate for research where it is necessary to build an entirely new theory 'grounded' in the data (King 1998). It is also different from content analysis, in which a coding scheme is developed and then applied to a text in order to generate quantitative data which can be analysed statistically (Weber 1985).

Given the large amount of interview material, it was decided to use computer software to help archive and manage the data. QSR NUD∗IST was chosen for this task, as it provides a variety of tools which help to link and shape ideas and themes without losing the complexity and context of the data. It has been suggested that computer-aided data management software may introduce methodological bias and distortion (Coffey *et al* 1996); however, this criticism appears to be based on a misunderstanding of the capabilities and functions of such software (Kelle 1997). QSR NUD∗IST is a tool which allowed interview transcripts to be carefully broken down, ordered, and then explored from a variety of different perspectives. It is essentially just a data management and text retrieval tool, not a program which in any sense analyses data itself. The software facilitated the indexing and cross-referencing of material, and was flexible enough to allow the revision and modification of coding as the analysis progressed. I was able to move between and cross-reference interview transcripts quickly and easily, and identify themes which were, for example, common to the majority of companies or only to particular types of companies.

The analysis I present in the next four chapters follows the structure of the review carried out in the previous chapter, exploring in turn the importance of shareholders, the main bank, employees, and senior management for the system of corporate governance. Each chapter is structured around the sub-themes which emerged from the analysis. Some of these sub-themes are inter-linked, and some overlap, but in the following four chapters I present them independently of one another, and reserve discussing their interrelation and implications until Chapter 8. In order not to lose sight of the individual meanings discussed by the respondents, I have relied heavily on direct quotations. This may not be to the taste of every reader, but I have done so because as well as acting to clarify and contextualizing the themes, they also give an impression of the content and tone of the original interviews. Unless I explicitly note otherwise, I have only cited from interviews where they are representative of a generally held view. Furthermore, where relevant macro-level data exist, the case study findings are related to broader changes taking place in Japanese industry.

4

Japanese Companies and their Shareholders

4.1. INTRODUCTION

In this chapter I present my analysis of the interaction between the companies that I studied and their shareholders. As discussed in Chapter 2, it is generally claimed that Japanese shareholders have had their ability to monitor managers and hold them accountable circumscribed; however, the growth of foreign holdings of Japanese equities, and the poor economic performance of the Japanese economy during the 1990s, are contributing to the collapse of the traditional system of stable shareholdings, and bringing about a reassertion of shareholder rights. Such views have been disputed by some recent research, which suggests that alliance structures associated with cross-shareholdings might be more complex, significant, and durable than is generally assumed.

The arguments I present here tend to support the observation that Japanese managers are not held accountable by shareholders, nor do they feel particularly accountable to them. Also, this does not seem to be changing, in spite of the introduction of many new practices which are affecting the way that shareholders relate to companies in Japan. This appears to be because the concept that managers *should* be accountable to shareholders simply is not meaningful or relevant to most Japanese managers. Nonetheless, a sense of responsibility towards investors on the part of many company managers I interviewed was discernible, especially among more senior company directors. Where these investors were also long-term business partners (i.e. companies with cross-shareholdings), the sense of responsibility and obligation appeared to be much stronger and more profound. However, in such cases it does not appear to be the shareholdings themselves that are generative of this sense of responsibility.

4.2. CHANGES IN CORPORATE FINANCING

When the fieldwork for this research was carried out, Japan was in the process of reforming many aspects of its financial system as part of the Japanese 'Big Bang' deregulation programme. Also the Asian financial crisis had recently unfolded, which was having a seriously deleterious effect on many Japanese financial institutions: a number of them collapsed during the period of field research. As a consequence, issues relating to deregulation, financial disorder, and economic change generally, figured strongly in many of the interviews I carried out. In this section I will discuss some of the financial issues that were perceived by interviewees to be most significantly affecting the way that companies interacted with the capital markets, and with shareholders in particular.

Institutional Changes

The 'collapse of financial communism' was how one top Japanese government official described the series of financial failures that occurred in November 1997 (*Time*, 8 December 1997). The declared bankruptcy of Sanyo Securities on November 3 was widely regarded as demonstrating that the government, for the first time ever, was prepared to let a major firm fail. Shortly afterwards, on November 17, Hokkaido Takushoku Bank collapsed. One week later, on November 24, Yamaichi Securities, Japan's fourth largest brokerage house, collapsed with liabilities totalling $24 billion. As well as admitting pay-offs to corporate racketeers, the chairman of Yamaichi testified to the Diet's Upper House that Yamaichi had set up five dummy companies in 1991 to conceal the losses suffered by 'preferred' clients, a practice known as *tobashi*.

All interviewees acknowledged that as well as creating a crisis of confidence in the Japanese financial system in general (the effect of the crisis on company–bank relationships will be addressed in the next chapter), these collapses were having a significant impact across Japanese industry in a number of less obvious ways. For example, the director of one Japanese bank claimed that the collapse of Yamaichi had enabled one particular US investment bank unprecedented access to new Japanese securities business because it had hired many former Yamaichi employees. This had given the bank a depth of experience and access to networks that it had not previously been able to enjoy, which in turn was enabling it to become, for example, the lead manager in a number of Initial Public Offerings (IPO), which previously, the bank director claimed, would have been impossible.

Also certain deregulation measures, such as the recently introduced book-building system for issuing shares, were widely believed to be enabling foreign financial services companies to compete more strongly against domestic competition, which previously had been difficult given Japanese securities companies' distribution power. (Book-building is a practice by which a securities company underwriting a public offering of shares builds a book of orders from customers placed on the basis of a provisional price and other terms offered by the underwriting securities company, and decides on an offer price on the basis of demand.) For example, the manager of a Japanese securities company noted that:

In the old days, until autumn last year, there was a tender offering system in underwriting, and a company like [ours] has many clients so we could buy the shares and distribute them. But since the autumn last year the so-called book-building system has been introduced, that is you only need a certain number of large institutional investors, so foreign institutions are in a much better position.

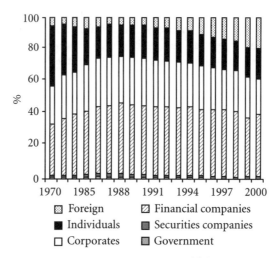

Figure 4.1. *Japanese share market value owned by type of shareholder (%)*
Source: Bank of Japan.

Changes to the share issuance system was also acknowledged by a considerable number of interviewees to be compelling companies to disclose more about their operations than they had done in the past. The director of a foreign investment bank told me:

Before book-building was introduced, companies did not really need to disclose much, as they relied on companies to distribute their shares. But since last October companies have needed to deal with institutional investors on an individual basis, so IR [investor relations] has been increasing. This is a considerable change.

The most frequently discussed change though, was the growing importance of foreign shareholders in the Japanese stockmarket. Figure 4.1 shows graphically how important foreign shareholders have become in the Japanese stockmarket since the beginning of the 1990s.

Although the proportion of shares held by foreigners has increased significantly during the 1990s, reaching almost 19 per cent by value in 2000, many interviewees suggested that the relative power of foreign shareholders was even greater than such proportions suggests. For example, one investor relations manager explained that after discounting non-traded '*mochiai*' [mutually held] shares, foreign investors' influence far outweighed the proportion of shares they held on paper, which tended to give them some sway with company managers:

. . . global investors are taking stakes in most companies; when you take out the effect of *mochiai* the actual stakes are nearer to 40 per cent. So these investors are now pressing managers to move in the right direction.

The president of another company affirmed that foreign investors were becoming more influential in his company, not by virtue of the absolute amount of equities they held, which remained fairly small, but in terms of the volume of traded stock which was surprisingly high:

Actually I don't have the exact figure, but [our] foreign shareholders are now around 5 per cent of the total, but if you look at the volume and trading, the foreign investors' share is more than 50 per cent.

More junior interviewees who dealt with investors on a day-to-day basis in the companies I studied confirmed that foreign investors were far more proactive than domestic shareholders had been in the past, and provided plenty of examples of how this was happening in practice. In particular, foreign investors were said to be demanding substantially more information from companies in which they had invested than domestic shareholders had ever done, especially about projected profits and future strategy. For example, one investor relations manager claimed:

My main target is the foreign institutional investors; they want to know the financial information, strategy and much more, so I have to help them. . . . Foreign investors, equity investors want to know about the future, they want to know the future performance projections, and what our strategy will be. So what we do now, is just after the announcement of the semi-annual results we do a roadshow in Europe and the US [but not in Japan], giving all the future information and strategy.

All in all, it was widely claimed that the Japanese financial system was undergoing significant, and even fundamental, change and this was clearly changing the way that all Japanese companies, to a greater or lesser extent, were dealing with their shareholders. For example the senior adviser of one of the companies in the sample (with fairly extensive overseas operations) maintained:

There is a great change in Japanese style capitalism from the main bank sponsored system to an institutional investor capitalism. . . . We welcome foreign institutional investors—as they can accelerate [our] transformation into a truly transnational company which meets the so-called global standards.

International Accounting Standards

Contrary to the commonly held view outside of Japan, during the 1990s the Japanese Business Accounting Deliberation Council (BADC) and the Japan Institute of Certified Public Accountants (JICPA) have worked hard to bring Japanese accounting practices, which have traditionally been aimed at providing relevant information to creditors (Someya 1996), more into line with current needs which emphasize the need to provide timely information to shareholders. During the late 1990s many accounting changes were introduced in Japan, including consolidated financial statements, cash flow statements, tax-effect accounting, retirement-benefit accounting, and current-value accounting for financial assets, none of which had previously been considered particularly relevant given Japan's bank-focused system of corporate financing.

As a consequence, all of the companies I studied claimed to be reviewing, or beginning to make major changes to their accounting practices at the time the fieldwork was being carried out. The companies that were clearest about the way that their accounting systems were going to be changed, or had already made most progress in reforming their accounting practices, were those which were active internationally, as they had already had some experience with accounting practices in other countries. For example, a manager in the finance department of the largest exporter in the sample, with extensive overseas operational facilities, claimed that the company had been strongly influenced by its experiences in the US:

. . . we have been exploring for a long time the best [accounting] systems for [company name], and since we took over some US-based businesses we have learned a lot about US style business and management style. And [our president] visits the US at least every, well quite frequently, and he meets with US management and he discusses what are the best systems for [us] for the future. So we have accumulated many ideas. Of course, we don't think that the US system is the best—we know we have to create the best system for [company name], a Japan-based global company.

Nonetheless, all companies, domestic or international, broadly welcomed the changes that were taking place. It was widely acknowledged that as Japanese financial markets were progressively deregulated, and companies made greater use of market-sourced finance, they would need to adopt different standards of disclosure that would protect minority shareholders and foreign shareholders in particular. For example, a senior director of one domestic company with global aspirations also claimed that to achieve its aims, the company would need to adopt quickly internationally accepted accounting standards:

[Company name] is trying to expand globally. For that, we need to adopt the International Accounting System. And we want to enrich IR [investor relations]. We need to demonstrate that [company name] is a good company to the shareholders in the world. To do this, we need to build a satisfactory company, which projects itself well to the outside world.

The majority of interviewees claimed to be strongly in favour of the adoption of 'global standards' of disclosure (although few were able to explain precisely what they meant by global standards: when pressed, some interviewees talked about US GAAP as the '*de facto* global standard'). Furthermore, they recognized that such changes to Japanese accounting standards would require companies to think far more about their shareholders than had been the case in the past. Where there was resistance to greater corporate disclosure, this was usually claimed to be based on practical concerns, about say tax implications, rather than opposition to the idea of disclosure to shareholders *per se*. A senior representative of the accounting body responsible for accounting changes in Japan captured the sentiments of many company managers and directors I interviewed, when he said:

They are concerned about the cost of consolidating, and the other dissatisfaction is the tax issue—for financial purposes consolidation is OK, but for tax purposes taxation on the basis of consolidation has not been introduced, it's still on an individual basis. However, it seems to me that in terms of accounting generally, there is a significant change in the attitudes of business people.

Investor Relations

One of the most frequently discussed changes in the context of deregulation and changes to the financial system, was the introduction and development of investor relations departments. Many interviewees, especially directors and employees working in company finance departments, were keen to describe how investor relations was transforming the way that Japanese companies were interacting with their shareholders.

The company with the largest number of foreign shareholders in the sample had the longest established investor relations department; this had been introduced after the company had issued American Depository Receipts (ADRs) on the New York Stock Exchange in the 1960s. Apart from this company though, 'IR' as it was consistently labelled was a very recent phenomenon; three of the companies had established an identifiable investor relations department within the previous three years, three had only just put together an identifiable investor relations team, and five claimed to be in the process of 'developing' their activities (the remaining two were not public companies and therefore claimed not have any need for Investor Relations). These ratios are broadly in line with a survey by the Japan Investor Relations Association, which found that in 2000 one in four Japanese listed companies had a dedicated IR division.

For those companies in the sample that did have an investor relations department or team, there was considerable variation in type and levels of activity they carried out. For example, one of the (medium-sized) companies appeared to have a very busy and proactive investor relations department, which was constantly monitoring media and analyst reports on the company, and providing carefully crafted, relevant information to the market on an hour-by-hour basis. By contrast, the second largest company in the sample by turnover, which had extensive overseas operations and a significant proportion of foreign shareholders, had no official investor relations team, and activities were carried out on an *ad hoc* basis. A senior manager of this company confirmed:

No, we don't have an IR department. But we do have a sort of team responsible for relations with investors and, I think I am a member, one of the members. But I think we are just on the first step to disclose and to present and to meet analysts, and accept visits from shareholders, or financial institutions, or analysts.

In general, it seemed that for most companies I studied, although there was considerable discussion about the importance and growth of investor relations in Japan, it was a novel activity, which tended not to be particularly systematized. A (Japanese) corporate analyst from an American investment bank summed this up, telling me:

... I will visit companies every one or two months when I am writing a report. Normally I will meet the IR staff, but sometimes they don't have an IR specialist, so I will meet the

General Manager of the financial division who carries out the IR activity. Even with technology companies I think that less than 50 per cent have a specialized IR division. In the case of most Japanese companies they call it the '*IR shitsu*', a room, much smaller than a department.

4.3. ENDURING ATTITUDES TO SHARES AND SHAREHOLDING

Although many aspects of company activity relating to shareholders do appear to be changing, in this section I want to present a number of themes which seem to show that at the same time, certain underlying attitudes to shareholding and shareholders are not being dramatically transformed.

The 'Immature' Market

Most of the interviewees who had worked overseas were keen to emphasize how, in spite of considerable deregulation, many aspects of the Japanese stock market and issues related to the trading of equities had not fundamentally changed. Among the words commonly used to describe the Japanese market were 'immature', 'primitive', 'archaic', and 'odd'. One example of the backwardness of the market that was regularly cited by foreign analysts and bankers related to the introduction of stock option plans, introduced following a revision of the Commercial Code in 1997. Instead of using them to incentivize key employees (which, they argued, was the 'proper' use of stock options), many companies had apparently granted options equally to all of their employees and directors, often with exercise prices very close to the market price prevailing at the time the options were granted. Various analysts claimed that this demonstrated either how intransigent, or how primitive Japanese companies were.

Japanese investors and domestic analysts were also frequently castigated as illustrating how immature the Japanese stock market remained. In one case for example, a (Japanese) investor relations manager who had worked for many years in the US reproached Japanese investors and analysts, suggesting that compared with the United States the Japanese market was not well developed:

Analysts in Japan are not really very bright. For me most analysts and stockholders are very immature in Japan. They don't see the price chart; they don't try to get all the company information. They just don't know how to buy stock in general. In the States people study the company very carefully. When the [stock] price dropped [here in Japan] stockholders were telephoning us to ask what particular sentences meant that they had read in the newspapers, is [company name] really facing bankruptcy. This is a very typical attitude in Japan—interest rates are exactly the same whatever bank you use, so the general company does not have to compare each bank, so basically they are immature. I sometimes wanted to say to people who called us, 'If you don't know that then perhaps you shouldn't be buying stocks', 'before you buy stocks you need to understand'.

The idea that risk was not fully appreciated by Japanese investors or analysts was another recurrent theme of many foreign analysts' discussions about the deficiencies of the Japanese stock market:

But [Japanese] investors, especially individual investors think that each company has passed through particular conditions. In the US professional investors invest in small venture companies as they are in the best position to judge the risk and return—individuals steer clear, but in Japan the driving force of the OTC market is individuals. The risk factors are neglected.

In many ways, the criticisms that Japanese analysts and domestic investors are relatively unsophisticated, and do not understand risk, are justified. In contrast to the US and the UK, the Japanese government has for a long time actively protected Japanese investors, by intervening in the markets when they have declined dramatically. The most aggressive government intervention in the markets took place in 1964 and 1965, when considerable declines in the value of the stock-market threatened the survival of the country's brokerage firms. These declines were countered by the launch of two funds that bought 2.5 and 3 per cent, respectively, of the stock market by capitalization.

Protectionist policies such as these have continued up until the present day, apparently serving to create the impression among many Japanese shareholders that equities are essentially a risk-free investment, guaranteed by the government. Analysts too have not had much incentive to evaluate stocks carefully. As a result, many non-Japanese bankers I interviewed claimed that Japanese investors, analysts, as well as company directors, had, in many cases, effectively decoupled company cash flow from share price: according to one foreign banker, 'Only now are domestic companies realizing the link between share price and cash generation of the company'.

Share Price Indifference

A general indifference to share price was apparent in the majority of the companies I studied. An analyst, referring to one of the companies in the study, commented that the only occasion when the directors of a company appeared to take notice of their share price was when they compared themselves against other companies in the same industry:

Historically some companies have seriously watched their share price, but mainly in order to look at the difference between them and their competitors. For example, [name] and [name] have watched each other very carefully. They don't actually worry about their own valuation, but simply the difference between them.

In only one company (the company with the largest proportion of foreign shareholders) did it appear that there was a general awareness among employees and directors of the company's current share price. For the majority of other companies, the finance director would usually be aware of his company's share price, but no other company employees, and almost none of the other directors interviewed, appeared to believe that the share price was directly relevant to them or their company. One company president said he was reasonably certain that members of the financial affairs division monitored the share price closely, but that he could not be sure, and anyway, it was not particularly relevant to know the share price on a day-to-day basis. Instead, he claimed, it was the actual performance of the company that was more important for him and his fellow senior directors, in particular the level of sales, productivity, profits, and the number of new products being introduced. Most other directors I interviewed confirmed that measures such as these were far more relevant for them than the company's share price.

In every company I studied, I was told that share price was rarely discussed at board meetings, apart from in relation to some other issue such as the introduction of a stock option plan or a rights issue. On being asked why share prices were not seen to be an important issue for his company's board of directors, the senior managing director of one company suggested:

. . . as for equities I don't think we have a trading account—all the shares we hold are basically *mochiai*. . . . they are just there—of course there is some monitoring of the total price, but you cannot sell them.

Overall, it seemed to be the case that many company directors (as well as employees) simply doubted that a company's share price was a useful or relevant indication of the company's intrinsic performance. Many likened the stock market to a casino, let alone an efficient means of valuing even the financial worth of their companies: the volatility of many company stock prices in the absence of changes in corporate fundamentals was often cited to substantiate this view. One company president summed up this general attitude to shares when he told me:

Well, share price is very important but that's not controllable, or not a short-term controllable factor, that's the reason why we don't discuss much about the share price.

Mochiai

Shares were frequently discussed by interviewees in the context of *mochiai*, that is mutual shareholdings which cemented relationships with business partners. All companies in the sample confirmed that they held *mochiai* shares, and all made a clear distinction between investment and *mochiai* shareholders. Also, all of the Japanese institutional investors I interviewed claimed that they kept *mochiai* and investment shares apart in separate accounts, and that entirely different departments would manage these two different accounts. Even the trust banks where I carried out interviews, which hold shares on behalf of other companies, held separate accounts for each client's investment shareholdings and *mochiai* shareholdings. The latter were also often labelled 'political' shares, and again it was confirmed to me that the prices of these shares were considered unimportant:

There are two different departments to book investment shares and *mochiai* shares, and they are booked in different ways. Also the examination department is different. Trading shares are evaluated everyday, and are subject to a loss-cut rate, and are marked to market at the end of each trading day. Political shares are booked at the original price, and loss-cut is irrelevant.

For the companies that had an investor relations team or department, none claimed to have any responsibility for *mochiai* shares. The investor relations department was concerned exclusively with what were called 'active' investors, while *mochiai* shares were usually managed by a business relations manager, either in the finance department or often in the corporate planning department. For example, an investment relations manager in one of the largest companies I studied told me:

[As an IR manager I look after] the investment side, and the cross-shareholding side is handled by our business relations people. The purpose of cross-shareholding is to get the business, so those sections have the responsibility for these shares. Mr. [name] who you met is the business-side, and he looks after the business relations with those companies.

The concept of *mochiai* appeared to be important to the way that shares were perceived generally by interviewees: that they were not solely considered to be financial instruments, but were also important symbolic tokens, that by being exchanged with another company served to embody a relationship or affiliation. Many interviewees were keen to make this explicit. For example, one company president explained that he did not consider the company that held the majority of his company's shares to be 'real shareholders', as the shares that they held were symbolic. Although he regularly communicated with this company, they had never been interested in the performance of his company, and had never discussed the share price: the only topics they ever discussed related to new products or technology. The shareholding, he claimed, 'only signify the good relationship between them and us'.

Even the Japanese institutional investors I interviewed claimed that a large proportion of their shareholdings were not considered financial investments, but were a part of their business relationships. One major Japanese life insurance company acknowledged that even at the time of the research, the reason it bought equities in companies was as much to cement sales with companies and their employees, as it was to achieve returns on the investments. Also, a senior manager in the credit analysis department of one of the Japanese institutional investors claimed that the extent of the relationship with a client continued to influence their share purchases:

We do not consider relationships with companies when we invest in domestic bonds. But when [we] invest in equities, which the [relationship management] division decides, we consider our relationships with the companies even today.

As in the preceding example, most interviewees confirmed the durability of *mochiai* shareholding. For example, a trust bank manager, with responsibility for share registration, maintained that in spite of some of the apparent widespread selling of equities in Japan during the period of research, this did not represent the breakdown of the cross-shareholding system:

There are some companies which are winding down their cross-shareholdings and which want to have their general shareholders meeting on some day other than the special day in June. The media prefers to report these companies, but if you look more closely I don't think that the winding down is really that significant. Certainly there is a review going on as to how these shares should be kept; until say ten years ago this cross-shareholding was absolutely rock-solid, and now we are seeing some being taken out, but they are usually replaced by some from somewhere else. So it is a kind of re-structuring, and as this continues of course there is some change, but fundamentally cross-shareholding remains.

A company director also confirmed that for his company the *mochiai* system was not being dismantled, simply that there had been considerable pressure following the economic crisis to reassess relationships with business partners; as a result the *mochiai* system was being overhauled:

... the shares that we keep are in fact becoming new *mochiai* shares, in that we will keep these shares in order to cement our relationships with our core business partners.

It was apparent that the selling of *mochiai* shares in a company was widely understood by interviewees to signify the end of business relations with a particular company. As such, for companies with which there was an ongoing business relationship, *mochiai* shares were unlikely to be sold, as this typical comment illustrated:

[Selling shares] is looked upon very badly by the companies. The actual amount of the shares that we hold in each company is not particularly important, but by selling the shares it would be very bad for our relations with the companies. ... It is a fact that we do business with those companies in which we hold shares, and when we sell the shares of the companies which we have selected there is no chance that we will do business with these companies again.

The apparent resilience of cross-shareholding in the minds of the majority of interviewees contrasts sharply with the widely held view, discussed in earlier chapters, that this practice is declining and is likely to disappear entirely in the future. For example, based on its findings from a detailed study of shareholding patterns (see Table 4.1), the NLI Research Institute (2000) concludes that 'Japan's cross-ownership structure is being dismantled with the objective of bringing Japan's corporate system into conformity with global standards, and reducing the price risk of shareholdings'. In its 2001 report, however, the NLI Research Institute retreats from this view, and acknowledges that many companies are still apparently reluctant to sell off shares involving important corporate relationships: rather than disposing of shares on the open market, many companies have been contributing cross-shareholdings to retirement benefit trusts, which enables the shares to be removed from the company balance sheet while at the same time retaining the voting rights associated with the shares. Furthermore, NLI refers to the Japanese Fair Trade Commission's report 'State of Corporate Groups in Japan' (2001), which finds in a survey that 58.1 per cent of companies expect to reduce but not eliminate cross-shareholdings, 37.2 per cent expect to make no change, and 2.3 per cent expect to increase cross-shareholdings. Such survey findings seem to support the interview findings from my research, and confirm that the general attitude toward cross-shareholding among Japanese companies and banks has changed less than raw statistics might suggest.

Knowing your Shareholders

All of the companies in the sample appeared to be concerned about who their shareholders were: in each company, I was told about the tools and procedures that were regularly used to monitor the ownership of their company's stock. For most of the larger companies I studied, the finance department retained the services of agencies

Table 4.1. *Cross-shareholding ratio and long-term shareholding ratio*

| | By value of holdings | | | | | | By number of shares | | | | | |
| | Long-term holding ratio | | | Cross-holding ratio | | | Long-term holding ratio | | | Cross-holding ratio | | |
	Observed	Estimated	Change	Observed	Estimated	Change	Observed	Estimated	Change	Observed	Estimated	Change
1987	47.87	45.81	−0.87	21.47	18.33	−0.40	45.19	43.36	−0.59	18.11	14.75	0.18
1988	47.70	45.70	−0.11	21.00	17.90	−0.43	45.40	43.59	0.23	17.97	14.74	−0.01
1989	46.80	44.84	−0.86	20.30	16.88	−1.02	45.31	43.46	−0.13	17.79	14.48	−0.26
1990	47.58	45.58	0.74	21.42	17.97	1.09	45.78	43.90	0.44	18.62	15.19	0.71
1991	47.52	45.51	−0.07	21.32	17.76	−0.21	45.48	43.62	−0.28	18.60	15.09	−0.10
1992	47.63	45.69	0.18	21.21	17.73	−0.03	45.23	43.39	−0.23	18.39	14.96	−0.13
1993	47.04	45.20	−0.49	20.77	17.48	−0.25	44.23	42.48	−0.91	17.96	14.64	−0.32
1994	46.71	44.88	−0.32	20.70	17.35	−0.13	43.50	41.82	−0.66	17.67	14.37	−0.27
1995	45.16	43.36	−1.52	20.32	16.94	−0.41	41.79	40.16	−1.66	17.16	13.86	−0.51
1996	43.75	42.01	−1.35	19.52	16.20	−0.74	41.18	39.57	−0.59	17.10	13.87	0.01
1997	42.06	40.42	−1.59	18.19	15.03	−1.17	39.61	38.08	−1.49	16.41	13.21	−0.66
1998	41.27	39.90	−0.52	16.02	13.22	−1.81	38.23	36.86	−1.22	15.39	12.43	−0.78
1999	38.01	37.87	−2.03	10.87	10.53	−2.69	34.93	34.70	−2.16	11.70	11.22	−1.21

Source: Nippon Life Insurance Research Institute (2001).

to keep track of who their shareholders were, even though it was acknowledged that it was often difficult to know who the ultimate beneficiary was. These agencies tended to carry out shareholder survey for their clients on a quarterly basis. The smaller companies, which tended to have fewer share transactions, claimed to check their shareholders even more frequently than this: for example, one company asked its securities companies to provide it with details of all share transactions on a weekly basis.

In addition to paying a great deal of attention to who their existing shareholders were, most companies also claimed to try to select their shareholders wherever possible. This was especially the case for the smaller companies in the sample, which tended to have fewer shareholders. For example, the president of one of the recently floated companies claimed that it had just failed to select all of its shareholders itself, and so had been forced to go to an Initial Public Offering (IPO):

> . . . before the IPO we already had 175 shareholders. I mean we were trying to get 200 before the IPO as 200 is the lower limit of being public, so we could go public without having all the hassle of the public offering. We weren't able to achieve that, but it was very close.

The president of another one of the smaller companies I studied, which was planning to float on the Japanese Over The Counter (OTC) stock exchange in 2001, said that he was aiming to select a majority of shareholders himself, and also sell as many shares as possible to the company's employees. Only after a large proportion of shareholders had been selected in this way, he said, would the remaining shares be sold on the market.

Controlling the allocation of shares was, however, not just an issue for the smaller companies in the sample. The finance director of one of the longest-established companies in the sample acknowledged that many large-scale share transactions still tended to be carried out in closed sessions, rather than through the market:

> We have a finance directors group [*keiretsu*] meeting regularly, so we know the faces and can have conversations at these meetings. Sometimes I might sit here, and he will sit there, and I will have the need to make *mochiai*, so while we are chatting the deal is done. When they have a need to sell our stock they will come to us, discuss their situation, and we will consider their proposal. This might happen when their business results are extremely bad, and they have a lack of cash.

The finance director of another large, well-established company told me that many of the financial instruments that the company had recently begun to use were creating novel problems for him in terms of keeping track on the ownership of the company's shares, and was requiring considerable forethought:

> There is a need to think about *mochiai* when we offer CBs [Convertible Bonds] or WBs [Warrant Bonds]. When they are converted the number of our outstanding stock becomes large, so our shareholding becomes very unstable, so *mochiai* is necessary. We are a member of the [name] Group, and also we are transacting with dealers and suppliers, so when they have the same needs as us we can make *mochiai*.

4.4. ADAPTING THE 'GLOBAL STANDARD'

In the previous two sections I have suggested that while there were many changes taking place which were affecting the way that companies in the sample interacted with their shareholders, underlying attitudes to shareholders within companies seemed to remain unchanged. In this section I explore in more detail certain company practices related to shares and shareholders, which seem to confirm that in spite of myriad changes taking place in the financial environment, these are not necessarily generating an intrinsically new approach to shareholders or shareholding.

Delivering Shareholder Value?

In the majority of companies I studied, improving the Return On Equity (ROE) was discussed as an important element of fulfilling a company's obligation to shareholders. For example, a senior director in one medium-sized company claimed that his company had first begun thinking about shareholder returns generally, and the return on equity specifically, in 1996. From that point onwards he claimed that it had become a widely used buzzword within the company. In only seven of the fourteen companies I studied, however, was I told that they were considering the introduction of ROE as a specific measure of corporate performance. Moreover, in four of these seven companies there were no explicit plans about how and when an ROE target might be introduced. For the remaining three companies which had introduced specific ROE targets, none appeared to have implemented a specific strategy to achieve them. For example, one company had missed a target published in the previous year's annual report by a considerable margin, but the explanation given by the company president suggested that ROE was not really considered a primary performance measure:

. . . the environment is very tough for us at the moment, but as far as ROE is concerned I knew that from the time that I set the target of improving the current 3 per cent up to 10 per cent that it was very ambitious and a tough target to meet. But our ROE was too low to start with, so I thought that I should at least set a two-digit figure and make it a stretch target for us. By having such a target we can start thinking what will be necessary, what is required to achieve that target, and then in changing our business practices and way of thinking we can try to concentrate our resources in areas where our return on investment is higher and concentrate on the more profitable areas of business. [But] because of the very tough business conditions and the state of economy in this country the target date may have to be put off by one or two years, but we will keep this target ROE figure as it is, without lowering it, so that we can modernize everyone in this company.

Looking at average ROE figures for Japan, especially compared to the US (see Fig. 4.2), it is clear that Japanese companies have not been particularly successful in improving their returns to shareholders, in spite of the widespread rhetoric about ROE and shareholder value.

One reason for the low ROE may be the reluctance of many companies to buy back and retire their own shares, which became possible in 1994 after the Commercial Code

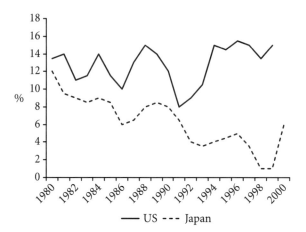

Figure 4.2. *Average return on equity in Japan and the US*
Source: Averages for NRI 400 (Japan) and S&P 500 (US).

was revised. Several of the companies in the sample had altered their company articles to allow them to buy back shares, but the majority of interviewees who discussed share buybacks thought they were unlikely to be widely used given the economic climate at the time. Only one of the companies I studied had actually bought back its own shares. A finance department employee told me that the main reason that this had happened was because the company chairman had been a member of the government committee that had recommended the changes in the law that allowed share buybacks. The low incidence of share buybacks among the companies I studied accords with a survey by the Japanese Life Insurance Association (1998), which found that between 1995 and 1998 only 285 companies bought back and retired shares, although 1462 companies altered their company constitution in order to do so.

For many, it was claimed that share buybacks were not feasible because company stability was more of a priority. For example, one company explained its large cash holdings thus:

Well, under the current economic circumstances we have to keep a lot of money, a lot of cash, but in the future if the Japanese economy recovers we might consider buying back our own shares.

In another company, the finance director claimed that the company was aiming to improve the return on equity, yet in his next sentence he stated that his main objective was to increase the amount of cash on the balance sheet 'for safety'. The potential incongruity of these two goals did not appear to be recognized.

In sum, interviewees used the language of 'shareholder returns' and 'ROE' relatively frequently, and yet the financial and business strategies of companies did not appear to be changing very much: in particular shareholder returns continued to be valued below company stability. This seems to indicate that for many interviewees, the idea that a company's primary purpose is to generate returns for shareholders, was not really meaningful, a theme I will return to in later chapters. This fundamental difference in understanding was made plain to me by one company president, who recounted that only after having appointed an international advisory board was he beginning to realize the full implications of what focusing on shareholder value 'really' meant:

My memory of the first one or two international advisory board meetings is very very vivid and clear. . . . We, as typical Japanese executives, tried to present the growth strategy of our own business, and the international advisors from Europe and the United States . . . raised various questions. As we discussed our strategy they began to ask how would that affect the value of the company, how would it enhance the value of the company, or what would the likely reaction of shareholders be. If we talked about investment then they immediately asked what would the return on investment be. When we tried to present our profit and loss picture they immediately asked what about the balance sheet. These were the types of questions raised, and then I slowly began to realize what shareholder value really meant. It meant returns, returns, returns.

Listening to Shareholders?

Many company employees claimed that investor relations activities were transforming the way that shareholders communicated with, and were able to influence their companies. For example, one investor relations manager claimed that his department was able to transmit information from investors and analysts to the president or the board of directors fairly efficiently:

We pay great attention to information about the company which we hear from external sources, and if necessary we feed this back directly to the president or directors or departments concerned, or else circulate copies of the articles.

Also in one of the longest established companies, an investor relations manager maintained that he was able to facilitate a valuable dialogue between investors and board of directors:

Also we have very good communication with the board, and we can pass on information very well between the markets and the board. They [company directors] listen and our [company] strategy is influenced by what we say.

Nonetheless, such claims were not echoed at more senior levels of the companies I studied. The majority of company directors appeared to be unaware of what 'the market' thought of their company. For example, the president of one of the larger companies in the sample said to me about one recent action the company had taken:

I think the market approved of the management attitude, but I don't know what factors the market respects or rates highly. That I don't know exactly.

Indeed the majority of directors interviewed asserted that they were not really interested in the opinions of analysts, investors or the market concerning their company *per se*. For example, one finance director reported that he only agreed to speak to analysts because they could provide useful information about competitors and the industry in general. Most analysts I interviewed, from both domestic and foreign financial institutions, confirmed that company directors only seemed to tolerate their demands for information because they were expected to provide information about competitors and the company's industry in general.

In most companies, I was told that investor relations activities had initially been established to handle enquiries from foreign shareholders and analysts, and in the majority of companies that had an IR team this was what it continued to do exclusively. For example, in one company 98 per cent of its shareholders were domestic, but I was told that *all* of the queries that the investor relations department had received in the past year had come from foreign shareholders. Comments such as 'domestic shareholders hardly ever have questions about the company directly' and 'Japanese shareholders hardly ever speak' were very common in most of the companies.

In the main, company directors I interviewed often seemed fearful of foreign shareholders and analysts. For example, one company director discussed how his company's investor relations department would respond to enquiries by foreign shareholders, using vocabulary which suggested some apprehension about the demands of foreign shareholders:

I think it depends on the kind of attack they receive. For example if they try to force them to buy back shares, or . . . if they suggest some policies, they try to explain why and what the company is doing. So they are reacting according to the attack.

The manager of a trust bank also alluded to the anxiety of Japanese managers about foreign shareholders, when he described the reaction of his clients when they first received enquiries from an American institutional investor some four years previously:

For example four or five years ago no one knew about [US pension fund]—they first saw the letters sent by [US pension fund] to the companies and they thought it was another *sokaiya* [corporate extortionist]. Honestly. They thought they were racketeers trying to get money out of Japanese companies.

The descriptions of relations with foreign shareholders contrasted strongly with the descriptions of company interaction with domestic shareholders, in particular cross-shareholders. For example, in one company where there was a strong and well-established investor relations department, I was told that there was no communication between the investor relations department and (domestic) cross-shareholders:

[Our] largest thirty or fifty shareholders are cross-shareholders, and in fact they are not really interested in [our] performance or [our] announcements. If [we] make an announcement then I will get the relevant materials together and give them to the proper section, and then they decide whether they give it to the shareholding company or not. And in actuality, they do not usually give it [unless] they are specifically asked by the company about our performance or announcements, in which case then of course they will explain. In that sense regarding the cross-shareholders, there isn't any investor relations.

Furthermore, it appeared that domestic shareholders generally did not expect to have regular communication with companies over and above generally available company information. Even domestic institutional shareholders interviewed did not expect that a company would make any special disclosure to them:

[We] analyse the companies by using disclosure information and news. [. . . We] attend the annual shareholder meetings of main companies only to show our existence as a stockholder.

In sum, although many companies claimed to be listening to shareholders far more than had been the case in the past, this really meant responding to the demands of foreign shareholders, but not shareholders in general. Moreover, this appeared to be in practice an unfamiliar and even worrying development for many directors of the companies I studied. For example, one investor relations manager recounted to me the reaction of his company's president the first (and last) time he attended an analysts meeting:

Analysts who have worked for American banks, they do not hesitate to ask any type of question. [Our company president] attended one meeting with analysts, and when he realized what analysts wanted to know he couldn't answer properly because I think it was painful for him—he didn't have an answer.

Providing Shareholders with Better Information?

From the perspective of company 'outsiders', the supposed increase in levels of share-holder communication was widely seen as inconsequential: for example, most analysts and foreign bankers in particular were cynical about whether the establishment of investor relations departments was enabling them to get better access to company information, even if the amount of available information had gone up. The con-sensual view of analysts and foreign institutional investors seemed to be that most of their interaction with companies, and company investor relations departments in particular, was fairly superficial:

There is an impression that statements have been carefully prepared in advance, and if I ask specific questions they don't seem to really be listening. I wonder if there is a sense that the company is like your home, it is private property, and outsiders are not really welcome unless they have been invited in.

Indeed, many analysts claimed that companies withheld most of the potentially useful information. One analyst explained that this was not just because IR was a relatively new activity, and departments still had to find their feet, but principally because the investor relations job was not well regarded by most companies:

. . . whether or not all information is passed to the person is one problem, and then another problem is whether they are disclosing all of the important information or not, but the main problem is whether IR is recognized as a serious job—in the case of some companies this is a big problem . . . frankly some IR sections don't really know what is going on in their companies.

There seemed to be a general impression among analysts and other interviewees in the financial services industry that the growth of investor relations was associated with the increased protection and vetting of company information, rather than any increase in flows or quality of information. Some claimed that this was associated with the particular way that IR had evolved in Japan. For example, one analyst claimed that in many cases, investor relations departments had developed from the teams, which all of the larger Japanese companies I studied had, to deal with *sokaiya* (corporate extortionists) and 'black journalists' (corporate blackmailers). He gave as an example the investor relations department of one of the companies I was studying:

In the case of [company], the IR people are part of the PR [public relations] section and are in charge of black journalism—in other words the head of this section knows very well these kind of things, and always he is mainly concerned with the actions of each director or the president or top management.

The day-to-day activities of those responsible for dealing with shareholders seemed to bear out the suggestion that investor relations was more concerned with protecting the company from shareholders, rather than facilitating greater information flows to shareholders. Many investor relations' employees frequently described their role as one of filtering and protecting company information. For example, one investor relations' manager, recently employed from a securities company, described his job as involving simply the gathering together of all internal company information and deciding which could be communicated to the outside world, and which should be kept confidential. At another company, the manager of the investor relations department emphasized to me that the role of his department was not to respond to, or enter into any dialogue with, investors or analysts, but simply to prepare documents that would be sent out. When asked how he knew what information investors required, I was told that organizations such as JIRA (the Japan Investor Relations Association, founded by Nomura Securities and The Nikkei newspaper group in 1993) regularly held seminars, and the company also sought advice from a securities company: it never entered into a dialogue with its shareholders.

In one company the public relations department had taken on the role of managing investor relations two years before. Its main achievement, according to the director of the department, had been the production of a more colourful annual report:

Until the department was set up the annual report was very plain, with no photos, no graphs, no colour, so the first thing we did was try to improve the appearance of the annual report. Essentially, it had been the responsibility of the *somu-bu* [President's Office] in liaison with the treasury department, but we are still not entirely happy with the current format.

Another investor relations department director acknowledged that their most valued adviser was a specialist public relations company:

Yes, we have a lot of information about stock price movements, and famous analysts' comments. More important for us though is the help we have from our PR company.

Such descriptions seemed to be in line with the general impression of outsiders that the establishment of investor relations does not signify a fundamental change in attitude to shareholders, but is more about managing flows of information to an increasingly powerful special interest group.

4.5. INVESTORS AND PARTNERS

In this final section, I argue that managers are not deliberately preventing shareholders from becoming more involved with companies, but simply that the concept that they are agents of shareholders, or could in any way be held accountable by (short-term) investors, is beyond their comprehension. But I also want to draw attention to the slightly different behaviour and attitudes of company managers and directors to cross-shareholders. In particular, I note the high levels of communication and general interaction that seem habitually to take place between a company and its main cross-shareholders.

Responsibility to Investors

As discussed in earlier sections, in general the companies in my sample did seem to be willing to introduce new practices to make themselves more 'shareholder friendly'. In every company, to a greater or lesser extent, it appeared that there was some desire to understand and accommodate the expectations of foreign shareholders. The following comment was fairly typical in this respect:

... if we expand our investors we have to disclose fairly and properly and we accept the burden to answer the requests by investors. Different investors means different questions, different requests.

Measures including the development of investor relations activities, the introduction of international accounting standards, the introduction of ROE targets, and so on were being widely considered, and to some extent implemented. However, as I have discussed, and as the language of the comments above suggests, these developments did represent a novel departure for most of the companies I studied, and there was a sense of unfamiliarity and unease with many of the evolving practices. For example, in the case of one company which had some financial difficulties and was under pressure from foreign investors to close some of its unprofitable business units, the president explained to me the dilemma he felt:

From the financial efficiency point of view we should close some business, in fact I think it's quite a lot of businesses, but once we do, no the company is responsible for employees and suppliers and . . . If one business continues to be at a loss for five or four years then perhaps we should close that business, but if it is breaking even, then it is a very tough decision.

It seemed that there was a general feeling among company interviewees, that the claims of foreign investors for greater participation or voice in the affairs of the company should, to some extent, be accommodated. However, the idea that the claims of shareholders had, in any sense, priority over the claims of other company participants, was not meaningful to them. Company interviewees consistently told me that they valued investors, but this was at best on the same level as they valued employees and customers. For example, one senior director gave me his idea of what his company board members valued:

Most of us do not think that shareholders are the only owners of our company. I think the company is owned by shareholders, workers and customers.

Taken together with the other arguments I have presented in this chapter, it seems that although many changes were taking place, these were not taking place because managers felt more *accountable to* shareholders: the concept that shareholders could possibly be in any sense corporate owners, or that their rights took priority over the claims of other company participants, was simply not comprehensible to most managers. Yet at the same time, they did appear to feel a genuine sense of responsibility to investors, recognizing them as important and valued company participants. For example, one interviewee told me that although the company had recently decided to focus to a greater extent than in the past on increasing its stock price, it was because the president felt a responsibility to investors who may have lost money:

In the long term the President has decided to catch up the stock price, we don't want anyone to lose money if they have bought at this price.

In another company, the finance director explained that the company recognized investors needed more information about the company than they had done in the past, and as a result it had a responsibility to improve its investor relations activities:

Investors can know our company, and then they will be relieved when they invest their money in our shares. If they don't have enough information they will always be worried.

In sum, it appeared that managers perceived shareholders to be important participants in the company, to whom they had some responsibility, but this was as investors and not as company owners. For example, the president of one of the recently floated companies in the sample told me:

I think it is important to help them [shareholders] understand what kind of company we are, and we have a responsibility to explain.

Closeness to Cross-Shareholders

As discussed earlier in this chapter, investor relations department employees claimed to have very little communication with domestic shareholders. Nonetheless, in every company I studied I was told that outside of the investor relations department, communications with cross-shareholders were frequent, and usually wide-ranging. For example, the president of one of the medium-sized companies I studied claimed that he and his fellow directors had 'very frequent meetings, formal, or informal meetings every day' with colleagues from a (larger) business partner.

The frequency and significance of communications with cross-shareholders was particularly evident in those companies which were part of well-recognized *keiretsu*. In these companies, interviewees usually told me about monthly 'senior management' meetings attended by the core members of the *keiretsu*. The purpose of such meetings was most frequently described as information sharing, rather than the discussion of individual company performance. For example, one senior director told me:

> At the senior level though there is the [name] group meeting each month, where our presidents and senior management get together. At these meetings we mainly discuss general economic information, and give details of any major news or deals.

In addition, I was told that there was frequent and regular communication between employees at all levels of *keiretsu* affiliated companies and banks, including regular formal and informal meetings, social events, work on joint projects, and so on. A director of one company discussed the relationship with other members of the *keiretsu* thus:

> Informally, we have many individual relationships, they are like colleagues, and in that respect it is a very good system.

Such close and intimate relationships were not limited to *keiretsu* companies though. For example, the finance director of one company, not part of a recognized business group, told me:

> Every month, not me but one of the directors visits [our biggest shareholder] and explains what has happened that month and the monthly results, and listens to their comments. He visits the president, the chairman, and the executive vice presidents so that all of them have the opportunity to ask questions. This is the Japanese way of communicating. As for [the second biggest shareholder, a life insurance company] and other institutions I myself visit twice a year, because in this country we don't have quarterly reporting, so we explain and invite questions from them, and normally not only the person in charge of the relationship but the president and several key executives will attend.

And at another company, again not part of a *keiretsu*, the senior managing director told me that he and his colleagues all continued to maintain close personal relationships with colleagues in an associated firm, although given the number of business scandals which had appeared in the media they had recently become a little worried about how this was perceived. As such, they were very careful to make sure that all of the meetings had a written agenda and were minuted.

Relationships with cross-shareholders often involved close working relationships at many different levels of the organization, and the sharing of staff, expertise, and information. For example, a sales manager in one of the medium-sized companies, again not part of a *keiretsu*, described how beneficial the relationship was with one of its (larger) suppliers as the two companies were able to share sales information:

> ... we have many advantages in our relationship, as they are the number one [company in their industry] and they have a broad network of sales, and [their] sales people visit these customers on a very frequent basis and we can share their information. ... We share information to find the best way of approaching potential customers.

In one of the smaller companies in the sample, the president claimed that the principal reason he was forging a closer link with one particular (large) company was that he would be able to share the technological expertise of the partner:

> Up until last year this company was very independent, and the business remained very narrow, but I have decided to change. We should have a full alliance and support from [company

name's] total technological resources and power. So I am changing from a fully independent company to a more closely allied company, especially in the R&D fields. Our R&D resources are limited, but [company name] has a huge . . ., some of those they don't want to utilize for their own purposes, for [name] fields. This kind of technology may be important to us, so I asked to transfer them to this company.

In sum, in most of the companies I studied, the relationship with cross-shareholders went beyond the simple exchange of equities, and frequently involved exchanges of staff, information, and technology. In two cases where companies had financial problems, the closeness of the relationship with cross-shareholders was made very apparent, as the partner companies contributed advice, staff, and some limited financial support in an attempt to help them survive. However, as the examples in this subsection show, the cross-shareholdings are not themselves generative of the close relationships between a company and a partner. Instead they seem to be an expression, or embodiment of the relationship itself. In the next chapter, I will explore this idea in a little more detail, as I examine the nature of the relationship with most companies' biggest cross-shareholder, the main bank.

5

The Company–Main Bank Relationship

5.1. INTRODUCTION

In this chapter I present my analysis of the relationships between the companies that I studied and their main banks. As discussed in Chapter 2, the conventional economic explanation of the company–main bank relationship is that it is a monitoring arrangement, which has developed in the absence of active corporate monitoring by shareholders; recently, as companies have begun to rely more on capital markets, this monitoring role should be diminishing. However, there is some recent research which disputes this interpretation, and suggests that the company–main bank relationship might be more than simply a monitoring mechanism; as yet, however, this avenue of research has not been well developed. In this chapter I discuss my findings, which support the idea that the company–main bank relationship is more complex and durable than is traditionally supposed by economists. Moreover, I suggest that the company–main bank relationship does play an important governance role in the cases that I studied, but this is not attributable directly to the financial relationship between the two organizations.

5.2. TRANSFIGURATION OF THE BANKING SECTOR

All of the interviewees who discussed the role of the main bank asserted that the bank–company relationship was undergoing rapid change. In particular, a shift in the balance of power between banks and client companies was frequently discussed. For banks, this was often discussed alongside worries about the increasing difficulty they were experiencing in placing staff who were approaching retirement age with their clients, which had not been the case in the past:

Previously we were very strong in comparison to the companies, but lately the situation has completely reversed. Now the companies have better credit ratings than most banks, so we do not have the power to send our retired people to the companies. They are much more likely to say no and refuse us.

At another bank, a director described a similar situation:

In the past we had a huge market to provide our senior people to customers, based on our power over the companies. But now the balance of power is changing, and it is much more difficult to send our senior [retiring] people to the companies.

As for the companies, this shift in power in their favour was occasionally referred to explicitly; more frequently, examples of behaviour were given which illustrated that companies were enjoying a more equal position *vis-à-vis* their banks. For example, even the second smallest company in the sample felt able to make demands which it claimed would not have been possible in the past:

We just told them if you want the business give us the service. If you want cash come and pick up our cheques. So the bankers that run around the town, the bankers who come to us, they're able to get a lot of cash from us and we're a huge . . . a relatively large importer in this area and we do a lot of foreign exchange. We can do that to them now.

Bank Lending, Internal Finance, and Access to Capital Markets

The most frequently given reason for this perceived shift in the balance of power was the diminishing ability of Japanese banks to provide debt finance to companies. During the period of research, the Japanese economy was undergoing what was repeatedly referred to as a 'credit crunch'. The capacity of Japanese banks to provide finance had been seriously compromised following the write-off of loans that had gone bad following the collapse of asset prices in the early 1990s. This was exacerbated by further write-offs of loans to Japanese and foreign companies which had turned bad during the Asian crisis of 1997–98. All of which were being further compounded by the need for all banks to reduce their loan portfolios in order to meet universal capital-adequacy ratios laid down in 1989 by the Bank for International Settlements (BIS). The considerable weakening of banks' ability to provide finance was a significant enough change that it had been labelled by companies, *kashishiburi gensho*, the 'unwillingness to lend phenomenon'.

Many company interviewees claimed that as a result of the weakness in the banking sector, the reputation of banks had fallen considerably from previously high levels. For example, a senior director in one of the large companies in the sample felt that it was the banks who bore a lot of responsibility for many of the problems the company was experiencing. He cited a list of his company's non-performing investments, unrealized losses, and failed projects, all of which (he suggested) the main bank had originally encouraged the company to undertake. For their part, most bank employees interviewed did appear to be contrite about bank lending practices in the 1980s, before the collapse of the bubble economy, which they acknowledged in hindsight had often been imprudent:

We always had a risk assessment model, it's just that we did not pay any attention to it during the bubble. As long as we had collateral we would just try to lend the maximum that we could. In effect every company was assessed as having the same, or more specifically no risk attached to their borrowing. We always charged the same prime rate to every company, as long as there was some guarantee in terms of property or shares. . . . Now we have to be much more careful.

Partly as a result of Japanese banks' diminishing lending capacities, many companies in the sample claimed to be increasingly meeting their financing needs from internal funds. The finance directors of all the larger companies and most of the medium-sized companies in particular stressed this change in financing practice: for example, the finance director of one of the larger companies reported that 'we paid back almost all of our bank loans: that's the reason why the bank's status has reduced'. Although this was less true for the smaller companies in the sample, which generally relied more on bank finance than their larger counterparts, they also professed to be in a stronger financial position *vis-à-vis* their banks than in the past. For example, the finance director of one of the smallest companies in the sample claimed to be managing its cash flow far more carefully than he had ever done in the past, in order that it would not have to rely on bank finance.

In addition, almost all of the company directors interviewed claimed that new opportunities to source finance from the Japanese and international capital markets was another potentially important factor serving to balance the power of the main banks and companies. For example, one company president explained that he was planning to use convertible bonds for the first time to raise money for the company. Another company had, for the first time, begun to recruit into its finance department a limited number of mid-career staff from banks, expressly to work on new means of raising money from the capital markets. He acknowledged that the number of employees being hired in this way was very limited, and that they tended to come mainly from failed or failing financial institutions. Nonetheless, it was a significant departure from traditional practice where financial experts might be seconded to a company from its main bank, but would ultimately remain employees of the bank.

Financial analysis that I carried out showed that in practice only the larger companies in the sample were actually sourcing funds directly from the capital markets, and even this was limited. Statistics from the Japanese Ministry of Finance (see Table 5.1) confirm that in general, during the late 1990s Japanese companies have generally relied on internal sources of finance, rather than increasingly tap the capital markets. Nonetheless, from the interviews carried out, it does seem that new corporate

Table 5.1. *Japanese companies' sources of finance 1996–2000 (100 million yen)*

Classification	1996	% change	1997	% change	1998	% change	1999	% change	2000	% change
Total funds raised	483,481	100.0	483,189	100.0	407,744	100.0	377,095	100.0	432,093	100
External funds	29,237	6.0	62,494	12.9	32,393	7.9	−97,943	−26.0	−105,163	−24
Capital increases	37,942	7.9	22,337	4.6	14,241	3.5	27,629	7.3	44,637	10
Bond issues	−11,396	−2.4	434	0.1	36,168	8.8	−11,337	−3.0	−33,974	−7
Long-term borrowings	−22,119	−4.6	−7,552	−1.6	46,322	11.4	−27,143	−7.2	−113,093	−26
Short-term borrowings	24,810	5.1	47,275	9.8	−64,338	−15.8	−87,092	−23.1	−2,733	−0
Internal funds	454,244	94.0	420,695	87.1	375,351	92.1	475,038	126.0	537,256	124
Internal reserves	47,327	9.8	10,156	2.1	−40,155	−9.8	73,110	19.4	120,667	27
Depreciation expenses	406,917	84.2	410,539	85.0	415,506	101.9	401,928	106.6	416,589	96

Source: Ministry of Finance.

financing possibilities have, to some extent, enabled companies to feel a little less reliant on their banks, which in turn has served to modify the relationship between the two.

Foreign Competition and Bank Restructuring

Many interviewees suggested that the changing financial landscape and associated problems being experienced by Japanese domestic banks were providing foreign financial institutions with an unprecedented opportunity to win business from Japanese companies. Most foreign bankers interviewed confirmed that they were taking advantage of the weakness of Japanese banks to try to secure more high-value business with Japanese companies:

Of course our aim is to put more pressure on the Japanese clients to work with us, for example since we are willing to provide them with funding we also want more export driven business which is the high return business. So if we see an opportunity like this credit squeeze, we do have a stronger ability to negotiate better terms on the lending product itself, but also if we decide to lend we are able to put pressure on them to give us more attractive business. Because a lot of these companies have to rely on foreign banks to cover exports, as the Japanese banks do not have the expertise or even the willingness, and at the same time the company does not have the capacity which it used to have, they need help from foreign banks so we are in a better position to dictate the terms.

Moreover, some foreign banks reported that they believed their chances of encroaching on Japanese core banking services had also improved as a result of being able to recruit well-qualified Japanese staff, which they had not been able to do in the past:

When it comes to Japanese we have certainly seen a major change over the past two years, now we can hire top graduates who are on the top of our wish-list who want to join us. Three years ago this would have been impossible. So because we are a financial institution and graduates know you are well-paid, and that in a foreign institution it is more likely to be based on meritocracy than seniority, young people are becoming more willing to join us. We feel that we are now getting good young people.

There appeared to be a broad consensus among bank interviewees that given the new financial environment, and this very real competition from foreign financial services companies, Japanese banks would increasingly need to focus on commission-based financial products and services instead of the loan business which had been the traditional mainstay of Japanese banking:

Well, we are increasing our commission business at the moment, like domestic cash settlements. We didn't charge for this before, but now we do. Before we could earn a lot from loans and deposits, but we cannot at the moment, so now we charge.

This change in emphasis towards specialist financial services was widely acknowledged to mean that certain aspects of banks' internal systems required adapting. The most frequently cited changes included the restructuring of internal departments and the modification of recruitment and training practices. One of the banks, for example, had reorganized itself into five functional groups: henceforward, employees would be assigned to one particular group, and would only be promoted within that group to encourage greater specialization. Recruitment and initial training processes had been modified within the bank in order that new employees had the opportunity to determine which of the particular groups they were best suited to, but once they had been allocated to a particular group, it was likely that they would stay within it for the rest of their careers.

Many bank interviewees suggested that changes such as these were resulting in the creation of a stronger external market for financial staff. Many claimed that increasing numbers of their colleagues were moving between banks, which had not been the case before. Consequently, it seemed that banks were being forced into drastic new thinking on salary structures, so that specialist staff could be attracted and retained:

... in this department you must pay a lot otherwise you cannot keep good people. For clerical staff we should probably pay lower wages. So now we have divided the bank into four profit centres, so it is easier to pay different wages. Our department, as well as the dealing and international banking departments now have higher salaries.

In sum, the changes taking place in the financial environment were widely regarded as permanent, and all of the Japanese banks where I carried out interviews were restructuring their operations, reducing their focus on the provision of debt, and repositioning themselves as financial services companies. Some employment practices were being significantly revised, and the majority of banks were considering, or were in the process of merging or allying themselves with other financial institutions. By the time the fieldwork for this research was completed, most of the major Japanese commercial banks have indeed merged, and the financial services environment now looks very different from what it did when the research project began (see Table 5.2).

Table 5.2. *Major Japanese banking groups, 2001*

Group name	Merging banks	Date announced	Combined assets (March 2000)
Mizuho	Industrial Bank of Japan Dai-Ichi Kangyo Bank, Fuji Bank	20 August 1999	$1.36 trn
Sumitomo-Mitsui	Sumitomo Bank, Sakura Bank	14 October 1999	$934 bn
United Financial of Japan	Sanwa Bank, Tokai Bank, Asahi Bank	14 March 2000	$980 bn
Mitsubishi Tokyo Financial group	Bank of Tokyo Mitsubishi, Mitsubishi Trust, Nippon Trust, Tokyo Trust	19 April 2000	$871 bn

5.3. THE CONTINUING IMPORTANCE OF RELATIONSHIP BANKING

In spite of the numerous references to changes in financing practices, shifts in the balance of power between banks and companies, and the major restructuring of most Japanese banks and the banking industry itself, interviewees maintained that where there was a strong relationship between a company and a bank, the commitment of one to the other was unlikely to be undermined completely.

Steadfastness of Relationship Banking

None of the interviewees reported that their banks were completely abandoning traditional employment practices. In particular, although the long-term viability of the lifetime employment system was questioned by some interviewees, there seemed to be a consensus that it was important for the establishment and maintenance of long-term relationships with clients. The challenge for the banks was how best to reorganize themselves so that they could offer specialized financial services but at the same time maintain and develop client relationships:

Lately we have had to hire specialist dealers and traders in forex or derivatives. The dealers have a special salary scale with maybe ten levels and are paid with a bonus scheme. The main staff though continue to be employed through the traditional lifetime employment system, and this has not changed . . . we still need generalists who know all the businesses, and who will be promoted to the higher levels of the organization.

At another bank a similar situation was recounted:

Basically, we continue to operate the seniority system in the bank, and it is very successful for the relationship style of banking. Now though with competition from other banks and the need for specialists we have also begun to hire from other banks, and change the way that we pay salaries. If you look at the operational changes we now have commercial banking and investment banking divisions. Specialists will mainly work in IB divisions, and if there is job rotation it will be within the two business areas rather than across them. Of course, there will be some exchanges, but not so much.

The commitment to relationship banking on the part of banks was also seen in a strategy being explored by three of the banks interviewed, which entailed partnering or merging with other banks (including foreign ones) which had particular financial skills, so that they could sustain and build upon their relationship advantages:

Our assets are our customers, and of course, we have to know about new technology but the most important thing for us as a commercial bank in Japan is to maintain the relationships with our core customers. We can work with the US banks—they need the relationships, but we need the technology.

Comments such as this suggest that the commitment to the maintenance and development of client relationships was a considered, strategic decision, based on a realization that non-Japanese banks tended to enjoy a competitive advantage in financial technology, but did not have the distribution channels that domestic banks had built up over the years. In another bank, for example:

It's more difficult in the capital market—we have set up our own trust companies and so on, but you cannot compete with companies like [US Investment Bank] or [European Commercial Bank]. In capital and equity-related markets we have no real competitive edge. If it is large issue in the Euromarket we have to leave it to [Japanese Securities Company] or [US Investment Bank].

In addition to acknowledging the superiority of foreign banks in certain specialist areas, a number of senior bank officials interviewed claimed that new financial technologies, although important, quickly became commodities, and as such were unlikely to change fundamentally the way that they did business. For example, one bank director told me how his bank had entered the derivatives market in the early 1990s, which had initially been a very profitable area of the business. Very quickly though, it had become an intensely competitive market, resulting in margins being cut significantly. More recently, he told me, the same had happened in the area of securitization, where the bank had invested heavily only to find margins being cut drastically as other banks entered the market. As a result, the bank had decided that rather than try to continually update their product and service portfolio to compete against foreign banks, instead they would concentrate on maintaining and improving their relationships with their core clients.

In sum, the commitment to relationship banking did not appear to be a reactionary adherence to traditional ways of doing things, but was a proactive commitment to what was seen as an important business practice. As one banker succinctly put it:

. . . in terms of the technology US banks are far away from us, much more advanced. But the relationship is very important, and unless they know the real needs of the companies the technology only remains technology.

Company Commitment to Relationships

The commitment to relationship banking on the part of the banks appeared to be reciprocated by the companies. In spite of the frequent comments about the balance of power being adjusted in the relationship, and some disillusionment with banks associated with recent loan debacles, the relationship with the main bank appeared to be durable and still highly valued by companies. Most company directors and finance department employees explicitly acknowledged that the long-term benefits of relationship banking outweighed any short-term advantages that came about from using whichever financial service company happened to be the most competitive or cheapest at any given time. If anything, it appeared that the uncertainties associated with the turbulence in the Japanese financial environment was strengthening the bond between companies and their main banks, and that communication levels were increasing rather than declining. For example, one bank director said:

Well, in my case there is no change—we continue to have a very steady relationship with our clients, and it is not likely to change, and there is no reason to change. Companies will probably want to keep the relationship even more as the climate becomes even more difficult.

This was corroborated in most of the companies I studied. For example, the finance director of one company claimed that even though the amount of finance provided by the bank had diminished, they continued to maintain their relationship:

Our day-to-day contact is still the same, even though the volume of transactions has been reducing. If we can find some merit in doing a transaction with them, we will do the transaction with them. Before [name] bank had maybe 30 or 40 per cent of the transaction volume, but this has reduced quite a lot.

In some cases, maintaining a good relationship with a bank was justified as a rational insurance policy: even though a company might be able to raise money relatively easily through the capital markets at that point in time, in the future it may become more difficult. However, in the majority of cases it seemed that the partnership with the main bank had more than a simple insurance value. For example, the comments of one company finance director, concerning the useful advice that the main bank could provide, suggested a more profound, dependent association:

We had just an overdraft and big loan, and two accounts. Now [our main bank] has introduced us to [their newly established investment bank subsidiary], and they are trying to advise [us] that it is maybe better to get money and different instruments from the capital markets, so they tell us we must study.

Indeed, with the exception of the largest, global company in the sample, every company which had carried out capital market financing had done so through their main banks, which seemed to demonstrate a continuing commitment to and trust in their main banks on the part of the companies.

Furthermore, apart from the large global company in the sample, none of the finance directors or senior company directors expressed a strong preference for capital-market financing over bank debt. As discussed earlier, many referred to the capital market as a valuable potential source of finance for their companies, but most maintained that in practice they would only raise money on the capital markets as a last resort. For example, the finance director of one very large international company captured the commonly held view when he claimed that he had recently issued bonds only because 'the capacity of banks to lend money is shrinking'.

Finally, some of the remarks that company finance department employees made about their dealings with foreign banks seemed to confirm a strong commitment on the part of companies to the relationship with their [Japanese] main banks. For example, one finance department employee noted that 'We do not use [foreign banks] in the same way as we use Japanese banks'. Another finance director said 'firstly we ask Japanese banks to do something, but if they can't do that, answer our request, only then do we ask American banks or European banks'. This attitude may explain why in spite of their best efforts, it appeared that foreign banks were unable to encroach on the core banking services provided to companies by the Japanese domestic banks. For example, according to one foreign bank:

Of the domestically active companies where we provide lending support they are mainly foreign multinationals. When it comes to the global trade finance business most clients are domestic [i.e. Japanese] companies—they are the large trading houses and the large manufacturers, and on the structured trade finance side also it is the large trading houses and independent importers of commodities like oil. So our Japanese clients are really *only* on the trade finance side, where very few of the Japanese banks can match our expertise.

Shared Histories

Another feature of many interviews, which suggests the continuing importance of the relationship to each party, were frequent references to a shared history between a company and its main bank. For ten of the fourteen companies studied, all of which had been established more than twenty years, the shared history between the main bank and company figured strongly in interviewees' discussions of the relationship.

Important elements of the history of a particular relationship tended to be remembered in a consistent fashion by both bank and company employees. Such stories often made reference to the importance of the partnership between company and bank during the struggle to build up the business in its early years. For example, one banker in his mid-thirties recounted in detail the story of the foundation of one of their client companies back in the 1920s:

The founder was from a very poor village in Toyama, the eldest child of six whose family were tenant farmers. From the age of thirteen he made *sake* [Japanese rice wine], but at the age of thirty-one decided to come to Tokyo. In the short term he was a manual labourer [but after considerable hardship and] the Tokyo earthquake [his] business grew phenomenally.

The historical links with the main bank were even discussed by the subsidiary of the American company in the sample, which had been established in Japan before the Second World War:

[This company] has existed for sixty years, and World War II was a very bad event for us, but we continued to operate even under that situation. We didn't have any assets, so it was hard for us to get money—we were not listed so we could not approach the markets. So at that time there was one bank which co-operated with us, so I maintained the relationship. So not because I'm in a *keiretsu* or anything like that, but for historical reasons; it's nice for me to have that relationship, if for example, I have problems.

The history of the relationship between a company and its main bank not only appeared to constitute a central, symbolic reference to the interdependence of company and bank for those directly involved in the relationship, but also was an important symbol of the bond between a company and its main bank to the wider business community. When I questioned a company employee about why he felt a story he had just recounted to me was important, he replied:

This is a pure Japanese way of thinking. The market knows why we have this relationship with this particular bank, because they also know the history. [The main bank certainly] knows what it did at the time. Each person in the department carries this information to their successor; when I got this job two years ago the first message I got from my predecessor was that we need to keep this relationship. I don't think it will be broken, certainly not in the next twenty or thirty years. I don't know how to explain it, it is a very harmonious relationship.

The importance of the historical ties was also illustrated by the case of one particular company which discussed its continuing relationship with Taiyo Kobe bank, even though this bank effectively disappeared in 1992, following its merger with Mitsui Bank to form Sakura Bank. Although the company was very large and listed on the first section of the Tokyo Stock Exchange, the company accounts were not held at Sakura's head office, but at the Otemachi sub-branch, which was formerly the main Tokyo office of Taiyo Kobe Bank. Day-to-day communications continued to be with the Otemachi branch rather than the head office, and interviews with company employees as well as the bank staff themselves showed that the relationship was still perceived to be with Taiyo Kobe bank, and Sakura in name only. On this evidence, the recent wave of bank mergers in Japan may not have such a profound effect on company–main bank relationships as many predict.

Mochiai and the Business Relationship

The durability of relationship-based banking came across strongly in discussions with interviewees about the changes taking place in Japan to the system of cross-shareholdings between banks and client companies (often referred to as '*mochiai*', as discussed in the previous chapter). Interviewees in all of the banks studied confirmed that during the period of the research they were disposing of large quantities of shares they held in some companies.

We are currently analysing our shareholdings in various companies, and have decided to select those companies where we don't have much chance of providing loans, and sell these shares. This is about 10–20 per cent of the shares which we hold.

As discussed in the previous chapter, a number of factors, including the introduction of mark-to-market share valuation, compliance with BIS capital-adequacy ratios, and new regulations concerning the total value of stocks that banks can hold have meant, in the context of a declining stockmarket, that banks have had to drastically reduce their shareholdings since the mid-1990s. As well as the banks, all of the larger companies and the majority of medium-sized companies claimed to be disposing of many of the bank shares that they held. For example, one of the larger companies studied spoke of selling the shares of fifteen of the thirty banks which they held. Another company discussed reducing the number of bank shares it held even further:

In the future we will do this, they want to reduce and so do we. We have already sold some banks shares with whom we don't have a lot of business . . . Now we borrow money from around twenty-five banks and insurance companies in Japan, so a lot here. I want to reduce that figure to ten—five and five, five banks and five insurance companies. We have already reduced the number significantly these last three years.

Notwithstanding, it seemed that the large-scale disposal of mutually held shares did not represent the breakdown of the cross-shareholding system between companies and their main banks, but, as indicated in the previous chapter, a careful *re-evaluation* of core business relationships. The reason that companies had too many shares on their books was consistently blamed on over-aggressive expansion during the late 1980s, when most banks entered into mutual shareholding arrangements with as many companies as possible in the hope of doing business with them. This was widely perceived, by both bank and company employees, to have been a disastrous strategy. Now, with BIS capital-adequacy ratios and new accounting requirements acting as catalysts, I was told that since 1997 a concerted effort to reduce shareholdings had begun. Statistics from the Bank of Japan appear to confirm that this is a reasonably accurate portrayal of bank shareholding patterns over the past twenty-five years or so (Fig. 5.1).

Where there was a business relationship between a bank and a company, however, all interviewees who addressed the issue emphasized that cross-shareholdings would remain. For example

... for those core companies which we do want to continue doing business with we definitely would not reduce the share holdings.

The forcefulness of many interviewees on the importance of cross-shareholding seemed to confirm how important it was to the business relationship. Every

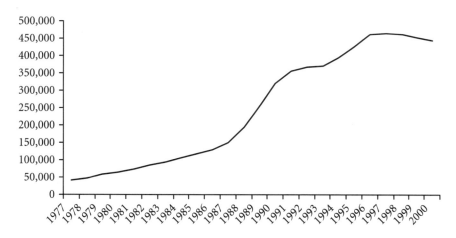

Figure 5.1. *Total shareholdings of Japanese banks (100 million yen)*
Source: Bank of Japan.

interviewee who discussed cross-shareholding emphasized that it represented a political investment in a broader business relationship, and should not be perceived as a financial investment in the shares themselves. For example, one company director explained:

This is a political investment, not an economic investment. An economic investment means that people buy stocks with a view to the price increasing, but a political investment means you want to keep the relationship with the company.

Even with the rapid changes in the financial environment, interviewees claimed that both banks and companies continued to distinguish explicitly between political shareholding which cemented business relationships, and those which were held for investment, even holding the shares in different accounts and managing them in different departments:

... we do of course [now] monitor our share holding as a whole, as we are allowed to use 45 per cent of the value of these shares for the BIS capital adequacy ratio. But we have separate departments for the two types of shares, political and investment, and of course they are counted separately on the balance sheet.

It was consistently maintained that the system of cross-shareholding was simply a way of facilitating business: in specific terms, it was claimed that as well as demonstrating commitment to a relationship, it also enabled companies to minimize external instability so that attention could be focused on the business itself.

In sum, far from witnessing the beginning of the end of the cross-shareholding system during the period of this research, it seemed that if anything the disposals of mutually held shares represented the consolidation and re-concentration of the system, as illustrated by one bank manager:

Well, you hear in the paper and rumours that companies are selling our stocks and abandoning our cross shareholdings. But this is not the case—currently we have relationships with more than 2000 blue-chip companies, almost every listed company, but we have internally selected 10 per cent of these 2000 as core companies, specific companies for us. These shares we will keep.

5.4. CONTEXTUAL KNOWLEDGE AND COMPETITION

In the previous sections I have suggested that in spite of changes to the balance of power, the relationship between Japanese companies and their main banks appears to be resilient, if not strengthening. However, this raises some important questions. For example, do companies conceive the relationship with the main bank to be anything more than a simple insurance policy against future financial difficulties? Are the relationships exclusive, anti-competitive pacts? In this section I try to throw some more light on the nature of the relationships between the companies studied and their main banks.

Company Definition of Main Bank

All of the companies in the sample affirmed that there was one particular bank with which they enjoyed an especially close relationship. For most of the company interviewees, the particular factor which was most commonly identified as distinguishing a main bank from other banks that the company used, was the range of banking services that the main bank offered. Settlement services, the administration of employee accounts and other cash-intensive transactions in particular (sometimes referred to as the 'day-to-day' or 'messy' banking activities) often defined which bank was perceived as a company's main bank. For some of the larger companies I studied, the main bank would sometimes even have a small branch or room located on the company's premises, where employees could pay bills or carry out small transactions. Also, the offering of tailored products to employees of core company clients was generally the prerogative of the main bank:

For example [this mortgage product] is not a public product, it is only offered to companies with which we have a strong relationship. That means it is a very strategic product, but the sums involved are not large. This kind of loan is not collateralized, but it is kind of welfare. Most companies don't have loan products for their employees, but this is offered as kind of a service to the company. It's a service to the company itself.

Although, in general, the main bank was the preferred lender, many of the company interviewees made it clear that the volume of loan business itself was not the central element in defining which was the main bank:

Last year, we finally paid back all the money that we owed [our main bank], but, even before that we pretty much didn't need their money, we needed them for settling payments or receiving payments.

The extent to which a whole raft of services, rather than just being the main lender, are important in distinguishing the main bank was particularly evident in the case of one particular company, the construction company, which claimed not to have a main bank. The finance director explained that as the company relied mainly on long-term finance, it did have a particularly close relationship with a long-term credit bank. However, the company president and all of the directors interviewed explained that this could not be called a 'main bank', as it did not provide the company's settlement and other cash intensive services, it did not provide general financing advice, and it provided no services to company employees.

Only two other companies in the sample were hesitant to use the term 'main bank', yet in both cases employees did affirm that the companies had close relationships with particular banks. One of these companies was the youngest company in the sample, and had just undergone an Initial Public Offering (IPO). The company president and financial director claimed to dislike the term 'main bank' as they associated this term with traditional, staid Japanese practices which ran contrary to the modern image they wished to project. The other company which was loathe to declare itself as having a main bank was the most international in terms of exports and equity ownership: '[Name] is the closest that we would have to a main bank, but we don't really call it that.' The hesitancy to refer to a main bank was apparent throughout many of the interviews within the company, but was surprising given that the relationship between this company and its main bank was widely known in Japan. For example, although a member of the finance department was strongly critical of the financing capabilities of this particular bank, he went on to say:

We don't have the same kind of relationship with them that other Japanese companies have with their banks. But they do process our payroll cheques, and we have a long history with them. . . . of course we discuss our performance [with them] every term, and also well, they need deposits, at that time we cooperate with them, so we have that kind of relationship.

It appeared that the reason the company hesitated to use the term main bank was that they too associated the term 'main bank' with traditional, outdated Japanese practice. Even though the relationship had not changed significantly, the term was something which was out of keeping with the modern, global company image they wanted to project.

Hence, although some companies may have prevaricated in using the term 'main bank', each company acknowledged one particular bank with which it enjoyed a particularly close relationship, but palpably this was based on more than just a debt transaction.

The Importance of Communication

Extensive channels of communication appeared to be an important element of the company–main bank relationship. For example, one bank director, in charge of the relationship with one of the larger companies studied, reported:

The relationship [with the main bank] is very important. At the moment, our communications take place at many levels. Our president will meet with [the company president and finance director] maybe twice a year, and my boss is the managing director, and he will also see them twice a year. I myself will meet with [the company president and the finance director] four times a year. My counterpart at [the company] is another Mr. [name], who is the head of the finance department, and I meet him maybe once a month, and probably call him twice a month. My deputy, the head of 'Team 6' will maybe visit four times a month, and the staff will call maybe ten times a month, on the phone or visiting.

For the smaller companies, contact with the main bank was often carried out through more junior members of staff, but this still remained extensive and frequent: an employee at one of the smaller companies reported that 'on a day-to-day basis our finance department and the bank exchange phone-calls and faxes all the time'. One bank employee with experience abroad confirmed that in his experience the nature of the contact between a main bank and client was quite different in Japan than in the US:

I'm not sure about the UK, but I was stationed in the US for five years, and as far as I know the contact is far more frequent [in Japan] than is the case in the United States. And in the US you usually use the telephone, but in our case we visit very often.

Another bank director described to me the kind of interaction that typically took place when it sent an employee to assist at a small or medium-sized client:

. . . banks send people to the companies, and they manage the companies, and the people sent from the banks come to the banks regularly and discuss how the company should be managed and financed, and how the debt structure should be, and how the cash flow is working.

Given the perceived importance of the relationship with clients in the eyes of the banks, those who have responsibility for managing the relationship appeared to be very carefully selected. I was told that generally someone chosen as a relationship manager would be a relatively young employee who had been identified as a potential 'high-flyer'. They would be a good all-rounder, with a broad knowledge of the bank's operations and the variety of products and services that the bank offered. One bank director told me that the reason that selection was taken so seriously was that the job was somewhere between an adviser and a salesman. For the very large companies in the sample, permanent assignments of relationship managers by the banks appeared to facilitate the high levels of communication, and were important to the quality and depth of information that the banks appeared to gather:

There will be two junior members of staff who will spend each day with [the company], going from section to section to understand the needs of the company. If the opportunity arises for financing we will get the information and then fill in the form with our senior executive, and get permission for the loan if necessary. Lately, if it is a question which involves tapping the capital markets we will make an appointment for a specialist to visit the company with the representative from the corporate lending department. The information is not only financial. I will give you a story: if our officer finds out that the daughter of the president is twenty-five he will return to the bank and try to find a suitable husband among the bank staff or perhaps at another company. This is the kind of very detailed information which we try to get on the company. The kind of information which we are able to get in this way is very comprehensive: for example, if we see that the company is doing something in a particular way or has decided to finance a project in a particular way we are in a very good position to be able to advise them of an alternative or better way of doing it.

For some of the foreign bankers I interviewed, the effort that was put into developing these long-term relationships by Japanese companies was perceived to be strange. For example, the director of a foreign bank berated the behaviour of some of his Japanese staff:

I think that the problem we face with some of our Japanese [employees] is that they have too strong a focus on the relationship, and what I have to tell them on a regular basis is that 'You are a relationship manager, you should serve your customer as well as you can, but it's a relationship, and the customer should not get all of the benefit and we get none'. That is still very strongly engrained in many Japanese minds, and the case where the salesman of a retail store will go and wash the car for a customer, basically do everything possible to make a sale, it's good to have such an attitude but only if they realize that the reason to do it is to make money for our bank. It would probably make more sense to explain the detail of the product in more detail, rather than spend the time washing the car.

Yet in terms of building up a long-term relationship, regular interaction between employees and business partners appeared to make very good sense to the Japanese participants, and seemed to be considered not only useful, but central to the relationship. Indeed when competition between banks was discussed, the quality of products or service was usually not considered to be the main issue; instead the quality of the information generated as a result of interpersonal relationships appeared to be considered crucial to generating a competitive advantage for the bank. For example, one former relationship manager described his daily routine with one of the companies in the sample:

In the relationship department there is generally one manager for each large client. For example I used to visit [company name] every day, starting at the 22nd floor and working down to the 1st floor. I would have very good information about what was happening, and would visit every division. The company was very pleased to give me information. [. . . Banking is] very competitive. We want to get the most business.

Knowing the Company

Extensive knowledge of the company by the bank seemed to be a central feature of the relationship between a main bank and a company. Many interviewees confirmed that banks in general tended to receive far better information than shareholders:

Just after the result announcements the IR people will visit the banks, and sometimes the main underwriters, but the banks sometimes get additional materials, which are more precise. Investors tend to get only the basic information.

All of the banks confirmed that as main banks they aimed to get as much detailed information about their core clients as possible. This always went beyond financial information: I was told that detailed information on inventories, new technologies, products in the pipeline, staffing issues, and so on, as well as 'external' information such as position *vis-à-vis* competitors and the current reputation of the company and its products, was regularly gathered. There was a consensus among the bankers interviewed that as a result of this detailed contextual knowledge, they were far better placed than other external parties to process company information, in particular being able to understand financial data in the context of all the other information they knew about a company:

Of course, you can tell a lot from official documents, but you really do need a lot of inside information, to see how the company is moving. And being a main bank we don't have a problem getting this kind of information.

Yet the detailed and wide-ranging information gathered by a company's main bank did not appear to be used to exercise power or control over the company. Instead banks tended to justify the time and energy they spent gathering this detailed knowledge on the basis that it was a service of considerable value to the companies themselves. One banker, for example, made this explicit:

Companies at a general level don't have that much interest in the kind of information we can provide, they are always thinking how they can carry out their business most effectively. So we must understand what the company is doing now, so we need information about what the company is doing now, and based on that we can make proposals and presentations. That point is very important, and that is how you can distinguish a main bank. If we don't do such things they don't say our bank is a main bank.

Bank interviewees rarely talked about serving the bank's own interests; by contrast they repeatedly discussed serving the best interests of the customer. The following type of comment was fairly common:

We have an investment banking group within the bank who are professionals in securitization and capital market finance, and I believe it is my duty to talk to our customers and get information about what they need, and when I return to the bank I discuss with the professionals how we can use our capital market expertise to give the companies what they want. It is important to understand exactly what the companies need; the investment banking people have the technology, but they don't know precisely the customer needs—this is most important for us.

Cooperation and Shared Goals

From the perspective of the company, the extensive sharing of information with the main bank did not appear to be something that was felt to be a burden. On the contrary, many company directors perceived the close interest shown by the main bank to be an advantage to their business. For example the president of one company claimed:

. . . we are very intimate, and they are very interested in our business, and they give us important information for the business itself. Their objective is to make our business more effective.

Moreover, the extensive sharing of information appeared to create the conditions for a high level of service from the bank. For example, one bank was offering one of the companies studied a range of quite detailed (and costly) introductions and advice at the time it made a particular tranche of project finance available, at no extra cost to the client:

In this case we have provided a link with the Ministry of Transport and JNR [Japan National Railways], and regarding the loan procedures we have had to get some recommendation papers from the MoT [Ministry of Transport] and JNR. Also now they have bought the land, they are looking at a cinema complex for tenants, and two companies are being considered, but [our client] cannot decide which is better, [company A or company B], so our international department is giving them some information.

In many of the medium-sized companies studied, the main bank appeared almost to resemble a division of the company, rather than a separate provider of financial services. This included regular exchanges of staff between companies and their main banks, junior company employees being seconded to the main bank to learn about finance, and junior bank employees being temporarily transferred to companies to learn about and assist the company: 'when we need financial specialists for some business field we ask our banks to send people for two or three years' commented one company finance director when questioned about training in his department. Such staff exchanges did not appear to be diminishing. Indeed, their importance was sometimes claimed to be increasing because of the dramatic changes taking place in the financial environment.

Regarding transfers of more senior employees, as discussed earlier it was claimed that this was far less prevalent than had been the case in the past. In my sample of fourteen companies, four of them had former employees of the main bank on their boards of directors. However the reduction in numbers of main bank staff being taken on at a senior level by client companies was usually attributed to the general economic climate, rather than problems with the company–main bank relationship itself. Indeed, in each of the cases where a company had received a bank director, I was told that the exchange was mutually beneficial:

We had two senior directors who came from the bank. It was our president who requested to send good people to our company, and also probably the bank wanted to send the people to know our company very well.

A more detailed illustration of the perceived mutual benefits of such staff exchange was the case of one of the smaller start-up companies being studied, where two employees of the main bank had been loaned to the company. Both of the salaries were paid by the receiving company, but were topped-up by the bank. One had been appointed as a director of the company on a permanent basis, the other on a two-year contract working as head of the finance department. Both visited their bank on a monthly basis, and retained strong social contacts at the bank, but they appeared to be firmly committed to the success of the company as if they were permanent employees. According to the director of the bank who had arranged these staff transfers it was a straightforward, mutually advantageous arrangement. It was the first time that the bank had made a loan to this particular type of company, so by seconding employees the bank was able to learn about the company's specific financing needs and way of operating. From the company's point of view, it had only limited financial expertise within the company, so the two employees who had been seconded were able to bring invaluable skills and knowledge.

Limits of Interdependence

In spite of the extensive access that companies granted to their main banks, there also seemed to be tacitly understood limits as to the type and level of information that banks would be allowed to procure. The medium-sized and smaller companies in particular appeared to be protective about their most sensitive commercial or financial information, as for example the finance director of one such company revealed:

... we accept one [main bank] employee, I don't know where he is, and our employees go to [the main bank]. I think it is beneficial for us to understand what they are doing so ... our company employee is paid by us. But I wonder how we would treat the [main bank] employee if we received him in our [finance] department, to do our audit, to carry out our business like other employees [laughs]. They could get all the information!! No, we would not let them get sensitive information. Yes when we get a [main bank] trainee we put him in a plant, or the quality control department, so they don't have access to sensitive information. [The main bank] is the only bank with which we exchange our employees, but we do not exchange all our information.

From the banks' point of view, all confirmed that they were interested in the ability of the company to repay loans, and if they were given access to detailed financial information they would of course welcome it, but in general close scrutiny of company finances was generally limited to the initial credit assessment before a loan was made, and thereafter relied mainly on basic checking of financial statements every six months, and a quick review each time any short-term credit lines were rolled over. In one case, answering a question about how carefully a particular main bank scrutinized the financial performance of one of its clients, the general manager explained that one of the reasons less senior bank employees were used as relationship managers was that their role was not to monitor companies, but simply to gather information:

You must remember that the staff who look after the companies on a day-to-day basis are young and generally inexperienced, and their role is just to get information, but the companies don't disclose everything.

Also, there was no evidence of any explicit monitoring of clients' share prices by the main bank, even though they often owned significant proportions of the total equity (for most of the companies in the sample this was often 5 per cent, the maximum permissible under the Japanese Commercial Code):

We do check the prices of shares as a whole but not really individually. If a company's share price is low we will not directly talk to the company about this—in this sense we are not like [foreign] institutional investors who if the share price is low can sell or try to get the management to do better.

Indeed, it appeared that just because a bank held shares in a company, this did not entitle them to any special right to intervene in the management of the company. For example, according to a manager in one bank:

Two or three years ago I was asked by a clerk to advise the top-level of management from the point of view of a large shareholder, as the clerk had a complaint concerning the management of a company, and he wanted to say something to them but he was not allowed to say it to them, so he asked me if I could complain on his behalf as a shareholder.... I reported to my boss, but we couldn't say anything.

These preceding examples seem to indicate that the relationship between a company and its main bank is not based on the power of one party over the other; on the contrary, both parties seem to be concerned with acting in ways which avoid being perceived as taking advantage of a powerful position. In this respect, the frequent references to the balance of power in the relationship, discussed earlier, appear to signify sensitivity to the potential dangers of abusing a powerful position. By acknowledging and being sensitive to the balance of power in the relationship, each party can act in ways that are in the best interests of the long-term relationship.

A Competitive Financial Market

None of the companies I studied said that the main bank relationship limited their freedom to choose better value services or products from competing banks. In a number of cases, interviewees gave examples of particular projects where the main bank was not involved at all in the financing. In such cases I was told that the company would always select the means of finance that most closely met their specific requirements, regardless of whether the company had a special relationship with a particular bank or not.

Bank employees too, seemed to be clear that however close any relationship with a client was, this would not prevent a company from ensuring that it got the best financing deal. For example, a senior director from a city bank, discussing its relationship with a company being studied which was part of the same *keiretsu*:

Of course, we are part of [name] group, so we have particular relationship with the other group companies, but there is a lot of competition. For example recently a very large financing was carried out by [a non-group] Bank, and the directors here were very surprised. However, large companies very much focus on the efficiency of their financing, [and] our main criteria is to secure the most profitable business, which of course we have to balance against our historical ties with certain companies, especially in the [name] group.

In a similar vein, another bank director said of its relationship with one of the companies being studied:

Even though [we are] the main bank, business is business so we have to compete, and [name] compares our services with other banks very carefully. Yes, whenever they need something they always take proposals from more than two banks and compare. If the conditions are exactly the same they will come to us, but if the other bank is better they will go to them; it's a commercial relationship. It's a kind of first refusal business.

One bank interviewee suggested that it had become particularly important in the context of rapid change that they were able to devise better products than their competitors:

The type of financing is now very different—before it was mainly loan finance, now the big companies have very much more sophisticated demands and financial departments. The big blue-chip companies like [company name] now use many different banks, and are only interested in the high-quality products. If another company has a high-quality product they will use that bank. And of course there are then the capital markets where the companies can raise capital. In the case of [company name], [another bank] had a very good product; so our directors consult with the [company name] directors to understand why that product was preferred, and we may then develop a similar product. But in the end the best-quality products are preferred.

And for the smaller and less well established companies in the sample, there appeared to be some scepticism about banks' motives, suggesting perhaps that the market for specific services and products was even more fluid when the relationship between company and main bank was less well established. For example the finance director of the smallest company in the sample stated:

I mean they are pretty much interested just in having us borrow money, or deal in currencies, and usually they want us to deal in options, swaps, which if you're an importer are not really advantageous . . . They try to sell them in disguise as risk management tools, but pretty much it's usually zero-cost options or trying to raise the interest rate of a deposit, and it usually has a ceiling and a floor and a knockout plugged to it, and I'm not too happy about those. . . . They usually have someone from the head office come down, with the branch sales officers. They try to explain it and sell the product, but I usually don't buy into it.

Overall, the apparently free and open market for financial services and products which were described to me by both company and main bank interviewees seems to indicate that the company–main bank relationship, rather than being fixed and anchored in mutual dependence, is more accurately characterized as an association that is strongly informed by history but relies for its resilience on constant interaction and reinvigoration.

Bank Support During Financial Difficulties

While the research for this book was being carried out, there was a real possibility of one of the companies being studied going bankrupt (it was 'merged' with a competitor in spring 1999). The senior general manager of this company's main bank confirmed it would always become directly involved with the management of a client company in such circumstances, but that this involvement was not motivated only by the financial implications for the bank. He also confirmed that the main bank would always attempt to help a core client to the best of its ability, irrespective of size (interviewees in all other banks corroborated this). However, it was acknowledged that in general, more resources would be committed to larger clients, as the knock-on economic effects were perceived to be greater. For example, one director in another bank who had been involved with several company 'restructurings' following financial difficulties told me:

[When a company is in financial trouble] the main bank will attempt a restructuring and explain it to other banks so that they will accept the plans. For example we would do that for [our client], because if that company went bankrupt the problems with many subsidiaries and employees would have a big impact on the economy.

All bank interviewees who discussed this issue made clear that in times of financial distress the main bank would act for the company, not the syndicate of banks. This is a crucial distinction; economic analyses generally assume that it is the other way around, that the main bank will act on behalf of other lending institutions. Interviewees emphasized that banks rarely discussed company affairs among themselves, or felt any obligation to monitor companies on behalf of other banks: 'We are competitors, so we have no ongoing relationships at all, no, no, no.' Only in the case of syndicated loans would there be direct contact with other banks, and the communication would always be on a strictly commercial level: 'Unless there is some lenders committee we don't negotiate with the other banks. It is always through the lenders committee.'

Hence it seems that when a main bank deals with other banks in times of financial distress, it is acknowledged that it is acting in many ways as the partner of the company. One bank director made this explicit:

If the company's financial situation goes wrong, the company comes to the bank to ask how to finance the cash and how to reconstruct, and how to tell other banks.

In sum, the commitment that banks made to support companies during financial distress appeared to be based not on a desire to protect their immediate investment, but much more on a sense of duty and obligation to the client company.

5.5. ACCOUNTABILITY, OBLIGATION, AND TRUST

Taken together, the points I have discussed in the previous section suggest that although the relationship between company and bank is generally acknowledged by both parties to be strong and durable, its characterization as a relationship founded solely on debt provision, and therefore motivated primarily by the need for the bank to monitor its investment, appears fallacious. This is not to say that there was no financial reporting by companies to their main banks: most company directors acknowledged that they would provide regular and detailed information to their main bank about their financial situation. In many cases, this was seen as an integral part of the unspoken responsibility of a company to let their banks know how their business was going, rather than a contractual obligation. For example, one company president asserted that:

There is no direct pressure, but they are eager to know [how] our situation is with the various businesses.

And directors would often feel it their duty to inform the bank of any out of the ordinary events as a matter of course, as for example this finance director explained:

I can always telephone the managing director of [main bank], and sometimes I go to the bank and give some explanation of our business results, and if some special event occurs I will also give some explanation.

Comments such as these appear to signify a sense of accountability on the parts of these finance directors. However, this is not accountability resulting from being monitored, or being 'held' accountable in any other way. Rather it appears to be an accountability based on sense of duty or obligation to the bank. In the following subsections I try to cast some light on this sense of accountability.

Reliability and Obligation

Many company directors, in particular finance directors, discussed their main bank as the one on which they knew they could rely. Indeed, one finance director claimed that the basic definition of a main bank was that it was 'the most reliable' bank for a particular company. The senior managing director of another company said that the difference between banks in general and the main bank was that he could 'always telephone the managing director'. Another finance director was hesitant about whether to call a particular bank his 'main bank', but he was sure about its reliability:

I don't know whether I should call it the main bank, but I have one bank which I can always rely on. For example last fall [autumn] banks tightened their lending in order to comply with the BIS ratios, so many banks wanted to get their money back, but in that case one bank maintained very good relations with me.

Another finance director also mentioned this sense of reliability, but made it clear that this went beyond simply doing what they had promised, but having confidence that the bank would always act in the best interests of the company:

The advantage is that whenever I face a problem I can personally ask them [the main bank] to help me, and I am *positive* [emphatically] that they will help me. And also, they have a lot of knowledge about M&A and so on, so I can always call them to help me. I want confidentiality, but I don't always want an agreement or contract with them. There is no liability there; there is always I owned you or you owned me, always there is that kind of relationship, but with [bank name] we don't have any of that.

From the point of view of the banks, it was clear that they appreciated that companies relied upon them. Many bank interviewees, at all levels of seniority, claimed to feel a sense of duty to serve their clients. For example, bankers frequently professed 'we have a responsibility to this company', or 'We are . . . responsible to serve any kind of requirement from [company name]'. Moreover, it appeared that fulfilling these responsibilities to the other party was an important, constitutive element of the relationship, as for example this bank director indicated:

A company like [company name] will have problems, not necessarily financial, in the future, and we will give them advice, talk about the Japanese . . . industry, and in that sense our information will be very important. Sometimes we will advise them on their balance sheet, and so on. We will make complicated simulations, and so on. We must keep the quality of our advisory service very high or we cannot remain the main bank.

The director of the construction company I studied gave another example of palpable cooperative behaviour being important or even intrinsic to a successful relationship with a main bank:

[. . .] our main bank sometimes introduces construction jobs, so if they introduce us to some job then we will deposit some money with them, something like that, it's a kind of give and take.

And with the longest-established relationships, interviewees in banks and companies often used the term *otsukiai* when discussing their relationship with each other. This term refers to the ongoing physical acts considered essential to maintain a relationship, including face-to-face communication, visits, drinking together, exchanging presents, and so on. For example, one company discussed the continuing borrowing from its main bank, even when it did not have any particular funding needs, as *otsukiai*:

> ... we decided to borrow some money to finance the tax for operational fee from them, although we hold enough cash flow, to keep ourselves on good terms with them. I am not sure whether it is appropriate to use the word *otsukiai*, which means we borrowed from banks money which are not really used for investment but which is at least *otsukiai* towards them. So we repeat this borrowing and return, borrowing and return from them every year, about 1.5 billion yen whenever we are required to pay tax. But there hasn't been any long-term financing for about ten years.

The enormous value attributed to the business relationship itself by Japanese main banks and their client companies was made particularly apparent by way of contrast with the approach of the non-Japanese banks I interviewed. The latter made it explicit that they were primarily interested in selling products and doing business which would result in generating the highest value business for themselves, and there was never any indication of a felt sense of mutual obligation between a bank and its clients. One extreme, but not unrepresentative illustration of this came in an interview with one young (British) banker working for an American bank, who berated the fact that as the Japanese companies became more sophisticated in understanding the financial products being sold to them by his bank, it was becoming more difficult to 'rip their faces off'.

Personal Relationships and Trust

The sense of mutual respect and obligation between a company and its main bank seemed to be intrinsically bound up with personal, long-term relationships between employees at the respective organizations. For example one finance director claimed to value advice from someone he trusted more highly than anonymous, ostensible 'professionals':

> There is certainly a strong demand [for specialist financial] information, but basically Japanese companies don't trust just anyone. We want information from people we have been dealing with for many years. Rather than spend lots of money for professional advice from the US, we would prefer to hear from our next-door neighbour.

Comments such as these, which pervaded interviewees' discussions of the company–main bank relationship, seemed to indicate that this was not seen as an asocial, mechanistic business contrivance, but was explicitly perceived as a relationship between people. The finance director of one of the companies in the sample, for example, explained that one of the contributing reasons his company was unwinding certain cross-held shares was that the company was unable to maintain the personal relationships that mutual shareholding required, because the number of people working in the financial department had been reduced. This seems to indicate that the carrying out of business between the company and main bank is seen as an intrinsically human act. Moreover, this was suggested to have many advantages for the way that the relationship worked in practice. For example, one finance director claimed that by recognizing the human aspects of the relationship, negotiations could be 'tough' but were implicitly fair:

Of course, they are very tough people. But we can negotiate with them based on reliable human relations, because we know what kind of person he is, because we know what kind of people we are dealing with based on the confidence we have in each other, but in the end business is business. We always have very tough negotiations.

Within such a conceptualization of the relationship, it appeared that a sense of respect towards the other party, and acting in a way which maintained the integrity of the relationship, was critical. For example, once when I asked whether the main bank might sell shares in his company without prior consultation, the finance director of the company was incredulous, emphasizing how important trust was to the relationship:

They *necessarily* [emphatically] give us notice! It is a kind of . . . it is manners, Japanese manners. It is not a contract. The relationship is based on trust for each other, and these are basic manners.

The banks also recognized the importance of acting in a way to maintain and develop trust within the relationship, and this was widely perceived to be fundamental to their continuing position as main bank:

[Our main clients] are coming to us to talk about the future, the US economy and the Dow [Dow-Jones], and so on, so that kind of intangible dependence on the part of our clients is growing. They must be confident in our employees. [We] are not just a bean counter.

Some senior bankers acknowledged that the implementation of new risk-assessment models was being frustrated apparently because of the implications that these new measures had for the trust-based relationships:

. . . because of the traditional relationships, there was never any reason to ask . . . whether the return was appropriate or not. This creates a lot of problems for us now, because a lot of times they do not understand why for us lending is a problem. They just see it as 'Are you afraid to lend to us?', it's like they think we are not comfortable with them, rather than being an issue to do with return.

One bank director claimed that in spite of the introduction of new credit assessment tools, branch managers were still likely to base lending decisions on the strength of the relationship with the client:

[. . .] we have a points system [a description of the credit scoring system and safeguards follows]. . . . but I think the bosses in the branch don't understand the system. I mean if the relationship between the president and the bank is good they will [agree a loan], even if their score is low. Because we have a long-term relationship [with a particular client] the manager will change the system. In fact I think the branch managers do understand the system completely, but they just decide terms and conditions based on their experience.

And during the period of research at least, efforts were being made to protect aspects of the relationship that supported the development of trust within the relationship, in spite of the myriad changes taking place in the Japanese financial environment, as the senior managing director of one bank indicated:

[our reorganized bank structure] is like a mini department store, and you can go to the various sections, or functional departments as we call them ... for the advanced financial technologies. But we have to be equipped with good relationship managers in each section, and they can recommend our clients to go to the various departments. . . . Our business department is still split by companies, not by function. [Foreign bank name] used to have that sort of relationship management, but fifteen or twenty years ago that completely broke down, and now they have derivatives specialists and so on. But now I think they are slowly coming back to relationship management, because it is human nature, human instinct. If you go to the derivative department, probably you have a fear that your discussion might be transmitted to your competitors. With us you always see the same faces, ... it is a matter of trust.

In sum, the company–main bank relationship seems to be a venerable, trusting association, not an arrangement contrived by the main bank to monitor a company and hold its management accountable. This relationship seems to engender a strong *mutual* sense of accountability, through a respect for and a sense of obligation to each other. In this sense the company–main bank relationship appears to play an important corporate governance role.

6

A Community of Employees

6.1. INTRODUCTION

In this chapter I present my analysis of the role of employees in the governance of their companies. As discussed in Chapter 2, there are two main perspectives on the relevance of employees for the system of corporate governance in Japan. The first is that the Japanese company is a corporate community rather than just a production mechanism. The implication of this view is that employees may play a central role in a participatory system of corporate governance. The second perspective, associated with mainstream economic conceptions of the firm, is that Japanese companies have prioritized the interests of employees at the expense of shareholders, which is a sign of poor corporate governance. According to those who subscribe to this latter view, this situation is now destined to change, as shareholders are increasingly able to reassert their 'rights' given the changes taking place in Japan associated with globalization.

The arguments that I present in this chapter strongly corroborate the former view. Lifetime employment and its associated practices continue to be highly valued in the companies I studied. These practices are closely bound up with a strong commitment among employees to their colleagues and their company, which is in turn bound up with strong feelings of personal and collective responsibility among employees for the actions of the company as a whole. This is consistent with a participatory and inclusive form of corporate governance, where employees are committed to and closely involved in ensuring their companies are governed well.

6.2. ADAPTING EMPLOYMENT PRACTICES

At the time the fieldwork for this research was being carried out, the general employment situation in Japan figured strongly in the minds of most interviewees. Many interviewees discussed the pressures being brought to bear on traditional Japanese employment practices, as a result of the economic downturn and the rapidly changing commercial environment. In 1998–99, the unemployment rate had more or less doubled since 1991, albeit from a very low percentage (see Fig. 6.1), and furthermore, the ratio of job openings to applicants had fallen to its lowest level ever (see Fig. 6.2).

Even though Japanese unemployment has remained low compared with most other developed countries, and the ratio of job openings to applicants appears to have simply fallen back to its long-term average, the media, in particular the foreign media, have made much of the rapid decline in Japanese employment levels at the end of the 1990s.

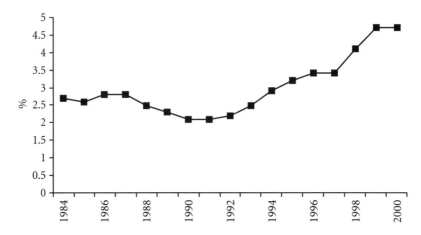

Figure 6.1. *Japanese unemployment rate 1984–2000*
Source: Ministry of Labour, Labour Force Survey.

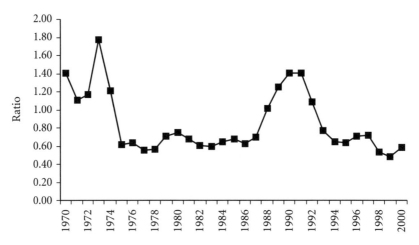

Figure 6.2. *Ratio of job offers to number of applicants*
Source: Bank of Japan.

In particular, the press has been filled with stories predicting the demise of lifetime employment, asserting that economic pressures associated with globalization are forcing companies to adopt more flexible employment patterns. Many interviewees echoed the claims made in these media reports. For example, one senior banker claimed, somewhat dramatically:

In five years I expect there will be a great change in the salary and employment systems. Not only our company, but the nation in general is very keenly aware that they are facing the third wave of change. 130 years ago we Japanese had a drastic change from the samurai world to the modern world. And fifty years ago we experienced another shock as democracy was imported. So the nation is now beginning to realize that what they have to face is the third great change.

In this section I want to discuss three (interrelated) issues which figured most strongly in interviewees' discussions of changing employment practices, namely the problem of high wages, the shortage of specialist employees and the sustainability of lifetime employment and seniority-based promotion systems. I will argue that although in each case some modifications to 'traditional' practices did appear to be under way, none of the companies I studied were abandoning, or were planning to abandon, their underlying commitment to the practices themselves.

Wage Costs and the 'Nenko' System

Many interviewees, from company presidents down to recent company recruits, claimed that their companies were facing serious difficulties as a result of high wage costs: rarely did anyone speak of there being a problem simply with numbers of staff. For example, the president of one company claimed that 'We have enormous salary expenses now, which is an enormous problem'. A director in another company told me 'The main weakness of the employment system is the relatively high average salary'. A manager at another company claimed:

We have 12,000 staff, but I am sure in the US and UK companies such as [company names] also have large numbers. This is not really an issue—the problem is really the wages—we are very highly paid.

Eleven companies in my sample had a *nenko*[1] wage system for permanent employees (the three which did not were all recently established companies), and in nine of these I was told that as a result of wage pressures the system was being reviewed or was in the process of being modified. For example, one personnel director described to me how his company's salary system had recently been adapted, to enable a greater proportion of employee pay to be determined by specific job responsibility and individual 'skill' rather than age, which had been the case in the past:

The salary goes up from 22 to 48 or 52, but after that it actually goes down . . . According to [our company's] standard family model, after you reach the fifties your children move outside the family. It doesn't depend on the actual number of children you have, but is a standardized model which is the basis for everyone's pay. You must have the first child at twenty-six, and the second at thirty. This is the age curve, but we also have a stepped system based on skill or responsibility. Before the ratio was different. Before the age element was far more important than the skill element, but now the skill/responsibility side is growing quickly.

---

[1] The *nenko* wage system is traditionally translated as 'seniority' wage system. This does not refer to a salary determined *entirely* by the age of the employee. It refers to a system whereby the basis for an employee's salary is determined *principally* by length of service or age (in practice these are the same, as all core employees join a company at the same time), in addition to a discretionary amount based on job-specific responsibilities and/or job performance.

At another company the personnel director, a Japanese who had been recruited from an American company, was trying to modify the seniority-based salary system a little more radically:

When I came here the salary base was seniority based, and we started new graduate hiring about fifteen years ago. [The company president] likes people who can help him immediately, but he also wants to train people as he believes that [the company] will be built by new graduates. So basically we are seniority-based, from 22 to 50, but there are some exceptions like me or the [finance director]. Not many, but maybe 20 out of 1000 employees. So what I am doing is trying to change it to be more performance based. . . . Now I am looking for a [consultancy] firm which can give me some idea about the appropriate salary split between seniority, performance and responsibility which is universal between say sales and the accounting department. I think pay will be 70 per cent by position, and 25 per cent and 5 per cent, but currently I'm not quite sure how to do it.

As well as modifying the basic salary system, some companies were also adjusting their bonus payments to reduce wage costs. All of the companies in the sample paid a biannual bonus, equivalent to an additional three–eight months' salary each year. Although most interviewees emphasized that the biannual bonus had come to be generally regarded as a non-discretionary part of the salary, in three companies which had experienced financial difficulties, it had been reduced. For example, the finance director of one company, which had recently reported a significant trading loss, explained that the company had decided to reduce bonuses that year because of the severity of the problems that the company was facing. In another company, which had recently suffered financial difficulties, the finance director told me how they had permanently revised the way the bonus was paid. The company used to pay each employee the equivalent of eight months' salary as an annual bonus, regardless of company performance, but that year they had been forced to link it directly to business performance. It seems that many other companies have also adopted this or similar schemes that link employee pay to company performance, as in 1997–99 real average salaries declined in Japan (see Fig. 6.3).

The most frequently discussed problem associated with the *nenko* wage system was the high level of remuneration the system guaranteed to older workers, who were often considered by interviewees to be the least productive. Some of the younger company employees in particular claimed that the system of paying older workers, who were in their eyes less dynamic and valuable than they were, was unjust and that effort and productivity should be better rewarded. As can be seen in Fig. 6.4, Japanese workers in their late forties and early fifties do receive relatively high wages and bonuses compared with their junior colleagues, but in fact wages tend to decline after a worker reaches his or her mid-fifties.

The real problem that Japanese companies have faced during the late 1990s, and will continue to face for the next decade, is not so much low productivity among older employees, but simply an abnormally high proportion of (high-earning) employees aged between forty-five and fifty-five in the workforce. Most interviewees believed that companies had no choice but to honour their commitments to workers in these

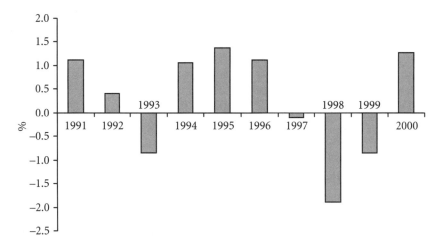

Figure 6.3. *Year on year percentage increases (decreases) in real salaries, 1991–2000*
Source: Adapted from Bank of Japan.

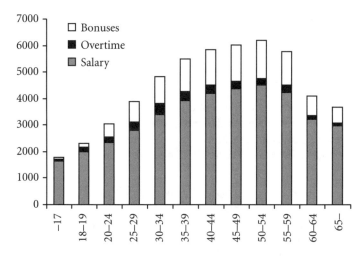

Figure 6.4. *Average Japanese salaries by age (2000)*
Source: Adapted from Ministry of Health, Labour and
Welfare, Labour Statistics (2001).

age-groups as far as was possible. However, this is not to say that the system that guaranteed older workers such high salaries was not being adapted where possible. The director of personnel at one company, for example, explained that it had been decided that the proportion of 'performance-based' pay would be increased for every employee, and the age-related component would be reduced. This would give the company greater flexibility to reduce the overall wage bill if required, but this would be done only in the direst of circumstances: it was more likely that younger employees would see greater variability in their salary payments as a result of the changes, than older employees to whom the company had a long-term obligation.

In sum, although the high cost of employment was recognized as a particular problem in the majority of companies I studied, this did not appear to be bringing about a fundamental change in the way that employees were paid. In all of the companies I studied, the problems were being addressed by exploiting the considerable flexibilities that existed within the wage system.

Skills Shortage and Job Rotation

Many interviewees claimed that given changes in the commercial environment in Japan, there was a rapidly growing need for 'specialist', as opposed to generalist staff. Foreign bankers and analysts in particular frequently referred to the lack of financial skills among Japanese company employees, which they felt were becoming increasingly important given the way the financial environment was evolving. In a number of cases, I was told that there was a widespread lack of understanding in many Japanese companies of overall company risk, as well as the risks associated with the financial products that many companies had begun to use. For example, an American investment banker claimed:

The finance department might understand say interest rate risk, but they do not understand the correlation with foreign exchange risk. The risk management system is not administered centrally, so they don't understand the overall risks they are taking as a company in the market.

There was an especially strong perception among foreign bankers and analysts that the system of rotating company employees between departments prevented the accumulation of financial skills and knowledge that was increasingly necessary in the current financial environment. A director of a European investment bank told me, for example:

[Lifetime employment] is still a problem. I think we spend a large amount of time during transition periods [when a new employee joins a company's finance department] to make sure that the person who is dealing with that unit will properly introduce us, we have to make sure that the new person gets the right message from his predecessor. . . . I think for the companies it is not beneficial at all. It may be good to have general managers with broad knowledge, but you have too many people with a generalistic knowledge within the company, but not enough product specialists.

Many interviewees within companies concurred with this view: it was acknowledged that changes in the commercial environment were creating a need for more specialist employees in certain areas than had been the case in the past. Financial specialists were most frequently mentioned in this context, along with engineers, lawyers, and technologists. As a result, many companies were modifying some aspects of recruitment and in-service training. For example, the director of personnel at one of the larger companies in the sample discussed how his company was recruiting a small number (one person, not necessarily each year) of specialist staff to the finance and legal departments:

We have recognized this issue increasingly in the past few years, so now we have two separate systems: those who are recruited to the 'special manager system' stay within law or finance departments, and are paid salaries in line with what they could earn outside [our company]. Compared with the general staff these are very good salaries.

In another company, a finance department employee told me that because of the changes taking place in his company, he had remained as an employee in the same department for twelve years, and it was increasingly likely that he would stay there for the rest of his career because of the particular skills and knowledge that he had built up. No one else before him had ever stayed in the department for so long, but now a number of more junior employees were also being assigned to the finance department for the long term.

Several of the companies also claimed to be introducing new training courses to satisfy the demand for more specialist staff. For example, the finance director of one company discussed how his department was addressing the need for more expertise by bringing in external professionals for the first time to run company training sessions, and hiring a limited number of experienced outsiders ('lateral hires') with specific skills who could pass on their knowledge to other company employees. Nonetheless, in spite of such modifications, the traditional job rotation system remained the cornerstone of the employment system within the companies I studied. The head of personnel at one company explained how the system worked in his company, suggesting that, if anything, his company felt a need to give employees even broader experience than had been the case in the past:

On average people stay at one division for four years, and at the end the individual is asked for their preferences and the boss is also asked about the person's aptitude, but the final decision is left to the personnel division as it is us who has to coordinate the overall company position. Traditionally there is a tendency for managers to go through particular divisions, but in the future we would like people to have a broader experience. Mr. [name] is a good example—if the person is very good his boss is reluctant to let him go, but the not particularly good are rotated far more frequently.

In one of the high-technology companies, the president told me that he considered it important even for his engineers to be able to experience different departments throughout their careers with the company. Furthermore, in many companies I was told that job rotation was believed to be becoming a more relevant practice given the dynamic commercial environment, as it enabled the company to give specialist employees first-hand knowledge about the whole business in the shortest possible time. Also, the rotation of employees to partner companies, main banks, joint ventures, or subsidiaries was also used to give employees experience and skills which might not be easy to provide within a particular company. For example, the personnel director of one of the largest companies I studied told me that he was able to give some employees broader experience than they might usually get by seconding them to smaller joint-venture companies, where they could experience a far greater range of different jobs than was possible given the departmentalized structure of the parent.

In sum, it appeared that in most of the companies I studied, in spite of limited changes to recruitment and training practices as a result of the recognized need for more specialist staff, the focus remained on developing general, company-specific skills. One personnel director summed up the view of most personnel directors with the following comment:

... we really concentrate on general management skills. We do feel a need to introduce [more specialist] training in the future, but our main aim is to concentrate on *integrating* specialists, as general skills are more important.

Lifetime Employment and the Seniority System

In all of the companies I studied, it appeared to be considered important for the company to have a core staff of lifetime employees. The two most recently established companies did not offer lifetime employment, but I was told that this was only because they lacked the resources or reputation to attract lifetime employees. For example, the personnel director of the most recently established company in the sample told me 'It's very difficult to get long-term employees. Everyone wants to go to the big names like [large electronics company name]'. In the other company which did not offer lifetime employment, I was told that until they could establish a core group of lifetime employees, they were relying heavily on staff seconded from the company which had initially provided much of the finance and technical expertise in setting up the company.

In those companies which did have a system of lifetime employment, I was told that the number of new graduate recruits who would become core, lifetime employees was being reduced as a result of the economic difficulties that most companies were facing,[2] and that more emphasis was being put on hiring part-time or non-core workers.[3] Furthermore, most companies claimed that there had been a small, but steady increase in the number of employees switching company during the course of their career (although statistics from the Ministry of Health, Labour and Welfare suggest that this is a long-term trend which has actually slowed during the course of the 1990s). However, none of these were fundamentally changing the traditional

---

[2] A joint survey by the Ministry of Health, Labour and Welfare and the Ministry of Education found that the percentage of job-seeking college graduates who secured employment in 1999 plunged to 74.5%, its lowest level ever.

[3] The Ministry of Health, Labour and Welfare's *General Survey on Diversified Types of Employment* (2000) in 15,000 business establishments with five or more employees, shows that 'non-regular employees' accounted for 27.5% of all employees in 2000, up from 22.8% in 1994. Part-timers accounted for 20.3% of all employees (73.9% of non-regular employees), representing a 22.8% increase between 1994 and 2000, while the number of full-time workers decreased by 2% over the same period. Other non-regular employees included contract employees (8.4% of all employees), farmed-out workers (4.6%), and dispatched workers (3.9%) (farmed-out workers are employees temporarily working for one firm but contractually employed by another). 61% of firms said that they used non-regular employees 'to reduce labour costs'. 76.1% of non-regular employees preferred to continue working as non-regular employees.

practice of recruiting *core* staff directly from universities or high schools, and aiming to employ them for life. The recruitment practice described to me by the personnel director of the software company was typical of those companies which had lifetime employment systems:

We just follow Japanese industry practice. For technical or engineering recruits we visit professors and ask them to recommend bright students. And for non-technical students the industry practice is that jobs are open to anybody, so we choose students at our discretion.

It was much more difficult for the smaller companies in the sample, who were not prestigious enough to ask university faculty to recommend their best students. However, the focus of their annual recruitment drive was also young graduates, who would be targeted either through advertising within particular universities, or by accessing university lists of graduating students who would be directly invited to attend a *shitsumonkai* (question and answer meeting) where they could learn more about the company.

Once recruited in this way, the careers of core lifetime employees were structured around what was commonly called the 'seniority system'. A senior director in one of the larger companies explained to me his experience of promotion within the seniority framework:

For promotion, seniority is important—age. In my case, when I was selected as director eight years ago everyone else who was selected was more or less the same age. Then those who were three or four years senior were promoted to managing director. Then after three or four years these people become presidents of subsidiaries.

In all of the companies I studied, the 'seniority system' was described in similar terms, that is as a broad career framework, not an inflexible age-based hierarchy. For example, a manager in the personnel department of one of the medium-sized companies depicted the system in her company as follows:

We have different grades. When we join the company, we start at this level [pointing to promotion scales]. And within about your second or third year, you would automatically become grade 2. To become grade 3, it usually takes about 7–8 years. And then there is a big hurdle—in order to be promoted from grade 3 to 4, you have to give a presentation on your achievement for recent years in front of all the directors. Certain people pass and are promoted. And then to be promoted from here to here [pointing again], you have to be really good. So here, here and here [pointing again], there is no seniority system. You have to be really good to be promoted at these higher levels.

In another company the director of personnel described how the seniority system was not felt to constrain employees who demonstrated particular ability or aptitudes:

Basically we have the seniority system, therefore even those have a lot of ability, if they have not gone through the certain path they will not be considered for promotion. A *kacho* [head of section] has to be thirty-eight or thirty-nine. But in reality a person's real ability becomes patently obvious, even at the age of thirty. So Mr. [name] has become *bucho* [head of department], which is usually attained at the age of forty-eight even though he is only thirty-nine.

There were, nonetheless, modifications also being made to the system. As mentioned earlier in relation to salaries, many companies were increasing the emphasis on 'performance' within this seniority framework. One employee, for example, claimed that the recent introduction of targets had made his yearly appraisals appear more transparent:

[Previously] we were told to outline our task for the next coming half a year or something, and at the end of that, after one year we would talk with the boss and say oh you've gone this far and haven't done this enough. But since last year this has changed and we now have the 'target control system'. At the beginning of the year we meet with the boss and outline a concrete target, and we are told what is expected of us by the boss, so compared to before it's more rational and understandable, it's easier to determine from the outside when a person is being accurately judged or not.

In another company an employee explained to me how her company had recently introduced 'challenge sheets' which she felt made biannual employee appraisals more transparent:

What's very different from Western companies is we don't have job descriptions; it's almost impossible to prepare a job description here, so it makes it even harder for us to evaluate each employee's performance. So we now have what we call a 'challenge sheet', it's a type of evaluation sheet we use. In the beginning of the fiscal year, in April, employees sit down with their boss and discuss what is expected during the year. So you make your own goal for that year, you write your goal and what you will do to achieve that goal. And that works as a contract, sort of. And in the mid-year, they sit down again and discuss what has been done and what hasn't been done or what kind of modification needs to be added. And by the end of the year, your boss can evaluate your performance based on your challenge sheet.

In spite of these modifications, the traditional seniority system was not being abandoned in any of the twelve companies I studied which used this system, and the new focus on 'performance' seemed to be a presentational as much as a substantive change. One employee, for example, made it explicit that underneath the surface of the 'changes' which his company had made, certain key aspects remained the same:

We used to have the seniority system and lifetime employment system like everyone else in Japan, but we changed the whole system a few years ago, four or five years ago. Now we say we evaluate your performance, it doesn't matter how old you are or how long you are working in this company . . . well . . . actually this does matter a little, to be honest, as an employee I know.

Many other interviewees shared this assessment of the nature of changes being made to seniority systems in the companies I studied. In the majority of companies, the measurement of performance appeared to be well established, but the idea that an employee's *individual* contribution to the performance of a company could be disaggregated, and then measured or rewarded, was viewed as anomalous. Rather than judging employees by outcomes, it was their effort and motivation that were considered far more important. For example, the head of the sales department in one of the large manufacturing companies claimed that although he had a financial target, failure to achieve this did not affect the way his salary was calculated; *intentional* factors seemed to be more important as a measure of 'performance':

I have a profit budget, but if I don't reach the target there is no penalty. It's relative, the total performance is looked at. We have 50 items to check, if you are sincere, intelligent, competent, and so on. The factors will decide half of the salary, and the personnel department will decide the other half.

In a further four of the companies in the sample I was told that sales staff had clearly defined sales targets, but that it would be impossible to link salaries or promotion directly to achieving these targets. It was claimed that the achievement of targets was not under the control of an individual, but depended on the contribution of other members of the company, as well as factors outside the company's control. For example, one sales director explained to me that he could not possibly reward members of his department on the basis of their individual contribution to company performance as 'we don't have direct control over the market'.

In sum, during the period that I carried out this research there was a growing emphasis on 'performance' as a criteria for career advancement, but 'performance' in terms of capability, motivation, and intentions, not outcomes. There seemed to be a consensus within the companies I studied that it was not only difficult, but unrealistic to judge employees on the basis of their 'individual' contribution to company performance, given the interdependent nature of work and the potential for contingent factors to influence outcomes. Consequently, seniority continued to be used as a basic framework for career progression in all of the companies which I studied, underpinning the firm commitment to lifetime employment.

6.3. COALESCING INTERESTS

In the previous section I suggested that in spite of the evolution of many employment practices in the companies I studied, there was a continuing commitment to the key principles of lifetime employment and its associated practices for core employees. In this section I seek to offer some explanation as to why these principles continue to be embraced so strongly. I argue that in most companies, core employees do not seem to be so much *contracted* to the company, but appear to be perceived and to perceive themselves as intrinsically *constituting* the company. In this sense, the conceptualization of a company and its core employees as separate entities is, in the cases of most of the companies I studied, equivocal.

Becoming a 'sha-in'

A common issue discussed by many interviewees outside of the companies I studied, was whether younger employees had the same sense of loyalty and commitment to their companies and the lifetime employment system generally, as their older colleagues were widely believed to have had. For example, a business journalist told me:

Well, young people do not rely on the companies so much as the older people—they have seen Yamaichi [the securities company, recently bankrupted when the interview took place], and realize that companies have their own life tenure, so they don't want to rely on one company for the whole of their life, so I think it will change.

At two recruitment consultancy companies, I was also told that they perceived a growing dissatisfaction with Japanese employment practices among certain groups of young people. For example, a director of one of the consultancies believed that employees with experience overseas were more likely to be disillusioned with the Japanese employment system:

There is also more recently, as a result of employees going overseas and maybe studying for MBAs, a sense of dissatisfaction when they return to Japan and they are put into junior positions where they rotate whereas if they worked in Europe they would probably become vice-president of marketing or something like that. It's very hard to understand this when you see colleagues overseas in quite important positions.

Notwithstanding, within the companies themselves, the younger employees I interviewed usually appeared to be *anxious* about their employment prospects, rather than dissatisfied with the traditional Japanese employment system. For example, a very recently recruited young employee told me:

I don't know [about how committed I am to this company], because I was only recruited six or seven months ago, last August, I'm trying to assert where I am, and get the feeling whether I can pursue this, whether I really want to pursue this, and, yeah, whether I really care to commit myself to this?

In another company, I asked an employee in his mid-twenties why he had contributed so much time and energy to a particular project:

I am not working wholly for the company, but I'm not doing my job wholly for myself, so I'm somewhere in the middle. Money is important as I have my family, but then I'm not so keen about . . . I never really think I'm doing this for the company, that is not the . . . it is probably more for myself, again not just for the company, but self-satisfaction is driving me.

Slightly older employees though seemed to be much more comfortable with and committed to their companies and the lifetime employment system. Moreover, many of these older company employees explained that they too had felt some frustrations following their initial recruitment, but as time passed they had begun to identify more closely with their company. For example, one employee in his late twenties recounted to me his experiences in this respect:

First there were a lot of occasions when I was very disappointed to be honest, well first of all I was assigned to domestic sales, which was not really what I was looking for, but . . . they told me that it was good for me and my career in [company name] to be familiar with what we are making and selling. If I was assigned to say the personnel department I wouldn't be so exposed to the machines and the customers that this company is heavily relying upon, so I do acknowledge that, but the way the job was done at that time in the domestic market was not sort of, . . . good, I mean there were a lot of situations where I thought it was not logical at all, so I do remember there were a lot of times I was quite disappointed.

An employee in another company, in his mid-thirties, painted a similar picture of frustration for younger employees, but a growing identification with the company as one's career progressed:

Since I joined [company name], I have changed job every three years, but have stayed within the manufacturing division. This is rare, to stay in the same division. Sometimes people are not satisfied with this [job rotation] system, for example my junior employee told me he wants to go abroad [with the company], but he has no chance. But he will not consider moving companies. He is not brave enough to leave. I think the longer one stays with [company name], things are quite good, no-one wants to leave. There is a relatively high salary, good welfare system, holidays, and . . .

In another company, an employee also in his mid-thirties told me:

I thought that it might be the case [that I would not be as loyal to the company as my predecessors], but after spending ten years with [company name] people start feeling a close bond with the company, and want [company name] to be a good company, and many people, I mean men, if they settle down and have a family I don't think many really think of switching jobs—they prefer to pursue their careers and continue where they are and to increase their status by you know increasing the status of [company name].

Comments such as these suggest a recognition among employees that over time, their own personal interests and status are increasingly bound up with the interests and status of the company itself. Although younger employees may not have the same commitment to the company as older colleagues, it seemed that this was not because of a generational change in perspective and values, but because the strong and close bond with their companies was only developed and reinforced over time. In this sense, the Japanese term '*sha-in*', or 'member of the company', seemed to be a more accurate label than 'employee'. One *sha-in* who had been with his company for about fifteen years maintained:

Once you are employed by a company you can experience several jobs within the company through internal rotation, and as you learn more you feel more relaxed and happy with the life you are given by the company, and you concentrate more on building a career within the company without thinking about outside the company. This comfort makes us feel very happy and that we are protected by the company in our day-to-day life, and within that framework you can plan your life.

Establishing a Community of Employees

In the twelve companies which practised lifetime employment, newly recruited staff usually underwent long inductions, which tended to focus on getting to know their colleagues and the company itself, rather than on teaching functional or technical skills. For example, the personnel director of one company told me that the main part of their induction programme involved new employees visiting an island that the company owned, with more senior employees. There they would live in tents, eat, drink, and carry out activities together in order to get to know each other and learn about the company. In the oil company, the personnel director also told me that getting to know the whole of the business system at first hand was an important part of the induction of all new recruits: new employees would visit all of the company's various divisions during the first three weeks of joining, then would work in the refineries for two weeks, and finally would have three or four weeks working in a petrol station. In one of the medium-sized companies, I was told how important the induction of new employees was in creating the bonds between cohorts of employees, which lasted throughout their careers:

And employees meet together once every year, people who joined the company the same year and they make really good friends within the company. These types of ties are very important within Japanese companies. [At the induction for new recruits] we teach them manners, about [company name], what we do, and what we want them to do, what we expect of them, and we have marketing training, a general training, very basic. At the end of the orientation, everyone goes out and sells our products.

In most companies, core employees did not appear to be treated solely as workers, but other aspects of their lives were often taken into consideration. This was evident in the salary systems I have already mentioned, which were *not* designed to provide a gradually increasing salary, but a salary appropriate to an employee's stage of life (see Fig. 6.4, which shows that the rate of increase in salaries tends to accelerate for employees in their late twenties, when they are likely to begin a family, and decelerates in the early fifties when it is assumed that family expenses are reduced). It was also the case that in many companies, accommodation was provided for employees, again appropriate to the stage of life which an employee had reached: for younger employees this might be a dormitory, while for older employees with children this would be a family apartment. In most companies it appeared to be taken for granted that understanding and providing for the needs of employees was a fundamental aspect of being a good employer. For example, one personnel department employee in one of the recently established companies discussed how employees were being encouraged to think about their future 'life-plans':

But when you need help, the company will help you. That's our stance, our attitude. And most of our workers are very young, on average female workers are 29 and for males 31, it's a very young company so we don't have to worry much now, [laugh] but soon you have to think about your parents, who is going to look after them, and you, your children. If you are asked about your life plan, you probably don't have much to say. So we realize that we need to educate our employees. So we provide opportunities for our employees to take a life-plan seminars so that they can start thinking about for example what kind of life insurance they should have and so on.

The concept of employees as '*sha-in*' rather than merely workers, seemed to entail a reciprocal understanding among employees that their own lives were inextricably interlinked with those of their colleagues and the company as a whole. This was apparent, for example, in the company with the most severe financial problems, where employees seemed to be doing all in their power to save the company, to the extent that during the lunchbreak all non-essential electricity usage, including lighting, was stopped to save money. In another company with financial difficulties, an employee said that although the reduction of the company bonus had been a major problem for many of his colleagues, especially those with families, they were willing to make the sacrifice:

They understand because they know the situation of the company, and they are asked for their cooperation in getting through this period. The current situation is very tough for employees, because if we leave it is very difficult to find a new job, and basically we have company specific skills rather than particular functional skills, so movement is very difficult. So as far as I am concerned I would like more of a bonus, but if the company goes down it would be terrible.

With almost no exceptions, none of the core company employees that I interviewed appeared to feel that they were constrained by their companies, or had been coerced into adapting to the company and its culture. On the contrary, in most cases the strong identification and commitment was viewed in a positive light. Comments such as the following were fairly typical:

It is a stage on which to live my life. I want to be active and fruitful. There are three key areas of my life, my family, the company and myself; the company is the biggest part of that, or takes up most of the time. If I am wise I can always be creative and happy.

Another employee in a different company made plain the extent to which he felt his future was bound up with that of his company:

. . . do you know the term 'corporate citizen'? The company invests in us, and this means that the company is financing us, like a school. So I think we have to give back something to the company. All workers are incorporated into the company and have a sense of being a citizen of the company.

Protecting Employment

In the companies I studied, there was a strong commitment to the protection of employment for core employees. This was especially evident in the companies which were in financial distress. According to the senior managing director of one company experiencing particularly severe financial difficulties, it was all but unthinkable to make employees redundant, as this would reflect badly on the company as a whole:

[We] are recognizing this problem [of over-manning], which is very serious for the company. In particular the image of the company will suffer very much, and of course we Japanese have experienced recessions many times before, but the firing of Japanese employees is very important and is probably the worst thing a company can do.

The president of one of the larger companies maintained that the commitment to employees was based on a difference in Japanese 'values':

If we had one thousand workers but only eight hundred are needed, in the US two hundred would be cut and the costs would be saved, which gives better profit to shareholders. But in

Japan, unless one is really squeezed, and the company may go bankrupt—that's different—but usually at the expense of profit we would prefer employment. I think there is a difference in values in Japan. Of course we respect shareholders, but employees are essential.

Given the arguments I have presented in the previous subsections, it seems that this commitment to employment can be explained as more than simply a 'value'; it appears to be both a condition and a consequence of the strong identification and commitment among employees to each other and to the company as a whole. Core employees are not seen simply a factor of production that can be hired and fired at will, but *are* the primary constituents of the company. As such, the commitment to maintaining employment is not simply an anachronistic practice, as it was sometimes portrayed in the international media during the period of research, but is fundamental to the notion of a company as a social organization. For example, a director in one company told me:

I do not think that [company name] will cut staff members unless they do a bad thing like commit a crime. If people stay, or the employee keeps to the rules, there is no chance of being cut. If we did, hmm . . . something about the company would have changed drastically. If the system had changed that much I would have to consider very carefully, I would feel very threatened.

A commitment to protecting employment does not mean, however, that employment was protected at any cost. In one of the companies I studied, a significant number of employees were being strongly requested to leave, and in several other companies older employees were being asked to retire early, but in each case this was only happening after every other possible avenue to preserve the company had been explored. Typically the first strategy employed by companies with minor financial problems was to reduce recruitment. If these problems increased, wage costs were reduced, which I discussed earlier.[4] Only then if the company situation deteriorated further would the existing workforce be reduced. This would be effected by retiring temporary workers and then older workers, or placing them in spin-offs or subsidiary companies. In cases such as this, companies would reduce the terms and conditions of employment, but what was important was that they were able to maintain the employment guarantee, as this personnel director in another company said:

And also we have some service providers which are joint ventures between [company name] and early retirees, for example a [industry] company that is a spin-off from [our] communication department. There are several reasons for these companies—one is lower terms and conditions, one is new business opportunities, for example we do not have the ability to run a travel agency, but if we have one under our umbrella we do not have to pay outside, we can keep all the money inside, but mainly we can keep the employment opportunity.

The pervasive use of such strategies to protect employment was confirmed in August 2001, when an unprecedented number of Japanese electronics companies

---

[4] In the companies which were making the most drastic reductions to wages, the proportionate reduction for company directors and senior management was greater than for general employees, possibly because they could afford it more, possibly because they felt more responsible for the problems of the company.

announced, almost simultaneously, large-scale reductions in their workforces.[5] Many foreign media immediately suggested that such huge layoffs presaged the abandonment of lifetime employment in Japan, as so many of the job cuts were to take place in Japan rather than in overseas operations; the *Wall Street Journal*, for example, wrote that 'a mounting toll of job cuts by major Japanese corporations underscores Japan's deepening economic woes and delivers another blow to its weakening lifetime-employment system' (*Wall Street Journal*, 3 August 2001). However, it quickly emerged that none of the redundancies would be compulsory, and all would be achieved over a period of time through natural attrition, a reduction in new hiring, transfers of staff to subsidiaries, and extensions of early retirement programmes.

Among the companies I studied, it was only in the company with the most severe financial difficulties that the workforce had to be significantly reduced in a similar fashion. In this company, reducing the number of employees was described as a very last resort to save the company as a whole. Even so, employees were not being made redundant, but were being (strongly) encouraged to take early retirement. A senior director at the company told me that they had been forced into this, because the company was now playing a 'survival game' and all other possibilities had been exhausted. In this company, the comments of directors and senior directors seemed to indicate strong feelings of responsibility and a sense of remorse for having let their fellow employees down. For example, one of the senior directors at this company told me:

... through early retirement, in the past eighteen months we have reduced the workforce, twice, about 200 employees have enjoyed a happy retirement [sad laugh]. Simple sudden-death. Sudden happy. I am very worried that morale will be bad. It is very important for our board members to explain and show to [company names] and our employees how our company will go in the next two or three years, we have to do this.

The Family Company

Families, real and metaphorical, were frequently discussed by interviewees in many of the companies I studied, which seemed to echo the notion of the company as a social organization above all else. One Japanese analyst commented on the problems that this occasionally caused for him:

... it is very different and very difficult in terms of asking questions and communicating [with Japanese companies] in general. It is very impolite to ask questions, and they are often dodged—it is very much seen as a family business still, and often they *are* family businesses.

As this analyst intimated, real family influences did appear to be strong in many of the companies in the sample. This was true for all five of the companies which had been founded since the 1950s. For example, in the most recently floated company, the president was a former employee of the electronics company which had originally founded the company as a spin-off. He had appointed his uncle as company chairman,

---

[5] Fujitsu announced a reduction of 16,400 employees, or 9% of its total workforce; Kyocera 10,000 employees, or 20% of its workforce; Matsushita 8,000 employees, or 3% of its workforce; Hitachi 14,700 employees, or 4% of its workforce; and Toshiba 17,000 jobs, or about 9% of its workforce.

and members of his family held the majority of the shares. In another recently floated company, again originally the subsidiary of another company, the founder was the chairman, his wife had been appointed president, his brother was one of the auditors, and his nephew was the finance director. The majority of shares were also held by members of the family. In another large, listed company, originally established in the 1950s, where I was surprised by the relatively rapid advancement of one senior managing director, he explained to me the reason:

Well, it's not very common, because, well, I am a, well [hesitates] a son of the founder, that is the reason why my career is so fast. . . . My father decided, well, all the directors agreed with him.

As well as being important in all of the more recently established companies, the influence of founding families also appeared to be strongly felt in four of the longer-established companies. For example, in one of the largest companies, originally founded a hundred years ago, the founding family held the majority of shares, and the current president was the great grandson of the founder. The president designate was the finance director, who was not a member of the founding family, but he was married to the current president's daughter.

In another three companies, all in the top 200 of the Tokyo Stock Exchange by market capitalization, founding families still appeared to be influential even though they held minority shareholdings. In one of these companies, originally founded in the 1930s and listed on the Tokyo Stock Exchange since 1949, the founding family still held a relatively large proportion of the outstanding shareholding, and appeared to regard the company to some extent as a family company. For example, the president told me:

And in our company, it might be very Japanese system, we have a chairman. He is my cousin. [long pause] We have lunch together and occasionally I say to him, 'Hey, what do you think of this investment' and he says something like 'That sounds good,' or 'Maybe you should rethink that'. After such process, I tell it to the board.

In another of these companies I was told by one of the directors:

. . . here the influence of the founding family is still great. Here, where the [name] family ownership is only 10 per cent or so, still they act as owners.

In the third of these three companies I was surprised to discover that the current president was a member of a powerful founding family, which had apparently no significant shareholding at all. One employee at the company told me:

[Company name] really belongs to the [name] group, and although it is a listed company it is owned by the [name] family, even though they do not have a significant shareholding.

In the nine companies where the founding family was still involved, I was often told that the family influence was reflected in the way in which the company was organized. In particular, company presidents were often discussed as, or saw themselves as patriarchal figures, with the responsibilities that the head of a family would have. For example, one company president, who at the time of the interview had not revealed to me that he was a member of the company's founding family, described his own view of his company thus:

The company is a sort of a family; the president is the father, the directors are the elder sons and possible candidates for his successor. If the second son seems to be more capable, the first son could be removed and given the job of president of a subsidiary for example, just like a real family. The relationship is just like father and sons.

Many other interviewees claimed that the notion of the company as a family was common to many Japanese companies, not only ones where there was a real family influence. For example, the president of one company with no apparent links to a founding family told me that it was usually very difficult for outsiders such as myself to be allowed such detailed access to employees and internal information, because the company was regarded as a family: 'the culture of Japanese companies is family-like, and it is difficult and rare for outsiders to open the door and come in.' Also a Japanese analyst told me that:

[. . .] most corporate executives have not had the opportunity to discuss with people outside the company. The relationships they have is like a family, so they don't need to explain themselves or give the clear, objective information,

In sum, the concept of the company as a family appeared to be quite common, and, in a surprisingly high proportion of the companies I studied, this may have been associated with the real influence of founding families. The idea of the 'company as family' seems again to reflect a particular conceptualization of the company, which is seen much more as a closely knit, long-term social system, rather than a contractually based economic unit which exists primarily to transform material inputs into outputs.

6.4. IDENTIFICATION, COMMITMENT, RESPONSIBILITY

In the previous sections I have argued that in most of the cases I studied, the company seems to be perceived as first and foremost a social organization, constituted primarily by employees. Lifetime employment is closely bound up with this conceptualization of the company, and continues to be practised in the majority of companies I studied. In this final section, I argue that this conceptualization of the company, and the way that companies tended to be organized as a result, are important for the way that the companies I studied are governed. In particular, I argue that the long-term commitment of core employees to their colleagues and the company creates the conditions whereby employees feel a strong personal and collective responsibility for their own actions, as well as those of their colleagues and the company as a whole.

Hierarchies, Systems, Procedures

In all of the companies I studied which had lifetime employment systems, job roles and organizational hierarchies were always clearly defined, and operating and decision-making systems and procedures were very carefully delineated. For example, the director of the administrative affairs department of one company showed me the company procedure book, which carefully detailed how decisions were to be made, and who was responsible for which aspects of the decision-making process:

This is a rule book which says who decides what [flicking through rule book], for financial issues, new products, budgets, account agreements, R&D, product naming, new product marketing, and so on. Small matters are decided on by line managers and plant managers. Then there are directors, the board of directors, the president, and the senior executive committee. [As for manufacturing decisions] this states the maximum amount for the budgets. Small investments can be decided by line managers up to this limit, then plant managers up to here [indicating table of figures], then if that limit is exceeded they are decided by the manufacturing manager. If the amount is still higher, these areas are decided by [name]. He is the head of the manufacturing technology and distribution planning division and he is also a board member, so he is responsible for reporting to the board. All these rules are controlled by my division.

Clear company structures and processes such as these were common, and were often described as crucial for systematizing and ensuring participation in complex decision processes which involved many different parties, especially given the practice of job rotation, which the majority of companies followed. Interviewees frequently discussed the relatively well-known *ringi*[6] procedure in this context, which was used by all of the companies in the sample. The following description of the *ringi* process was fairly typical, illustrating the importance attached to ensuring that all relevant parties to a decision were formally consulted:

In the General Affairs Department, we receive all the proposal papers as a secretariat. Then we deliver them to the appropriate sections. [brings *ringi* document] . . . As you can see, the rules say who decides what. This one is finance; this space is for the finance section . . . this then goes around department by department, and from person to person. These are the proposal for investments. This then goes around other related sections. And, in the case of this proposal, it would go up to the *jomu-kai* [senior management committee], and then be ratified at the board meeting.

In another company I was told about the systematic procedure to ensure that appropriate cross-checking of decisions was carried out, which usually involved several different departments, and even checking that the checking had been carried out properly:

The legal department check whether the plan is within the rules or not; if it is a production department decision for example, they check whether preparation has been done well or not. In my department, we see whether such checks have been done properly. We also check, for example, what the department is going to do with the old machine when they make a request for a new machine. We also see whether the plan follows the general policy of the company. . . . Auditors check after the board have checked; they do not intervene in the decision-making itself, but they check the final decision of the board.

---

[6] *Ringi* is a formal process of consultation involving the circulation of a draft plan, prepared by the person making a proposal, among other departments and executives who are affected by the proposal.

Moreover these procedures seemed to be regularly reviewed and revised to ensure that they were kept up to date, as in this typical example:

Major changes to the rule book are made every ten years, but minor changes are more frequent. This rule book changed last year. Every employee knows about it. The rule book is placed in each division. For example the [name] plant has one in each section. And in the near future, we plan to put it on the company home page so that everybody can see it more easily. . . . We need to look at very frequently, in my case, every day.

I was frequently told that it was inconceivable for employees to circumvent the hierarchical 'due process'. For example, the idea of a junior employee going straight to the company president with an idea was anathema:

No, no [emphatically]. That would cause too much commotion all around the company, no, never. I'd take the traditional way and go to my immediate boss and then convince his boss, and then his boss, which would then be very close to [the President].

In one company I was told that communication with outside parties often had to be delayed as a result of the formal decision-making process being followed, indicating how important it was considered to be:

And, if the timing wasn't good, the plan is held up for another two weeks until the next meeting. In that sense, the workers have to keep the schedule of the meeting in mind and work towards it. It is a problem when we have to make outsiders [e.g. clients, business connections] wait, but we must make sure it is properly circulated.

Although this hierarchical style of decision-making was acknowledged as being somewhat slow, the majority of interviewees claimed that the trade-off of speed was worthwhile given the advantage of ensuring the involvement of all relevant parties, and the careful consideration of all important decisions. For example, the finance director of one company claimed:

It seems to take a long time, but I'm not sure if this is true. It's actually rather effective, because before I bring a matter to these meetings I can consider all opinions and make necessary revisions, so the discussion hours in these meetings is shorter and the decision itself is quick. Also, the people and departments concerned are well informed and aware of what's going on, so information sharing is quite good. Nowadays all employees have e-mail, so I can send information even to the younger people, so the decision process becomes flat. I allow my juniors to send urgent or important messages above me anytime. Well, not passing me completely but 'cc'ing me. Oh yes, in the long-term it's a time-saving process. We have to be careful to make decisions as quick as possible.

There also seemed to be a recognition that this hierarchical, inclusive decision-making process was invaluable in helping to prevent mistakes. For example, one employee who had experience of a different, more individualized decision-making system when he worked at the company's Irish subsidiary, claimed that problems had arisen because of the lack of involvement of employees in decision-making:

Our Irish subsidiary is small, just 50 employees, but in Ireland our president is Irish and I reported to him, and he directed me—almost all the people report directly to him, so decision-making is very fast. However there were some mistakes, as the checking system is not so strong [as our hierarchical system].

Hierarchical structures and procedures appeared to be appreciated by junior employees, as they formalized (and therefore facilitated) communication with senior management. Moreover, it seemed that the strong sense of hierarchy and procedure gave them more confidence in their own positions, allowing them to raise issues without worrying about the effect it might have on their career prospects. For example in one company, an employee in his mid-twenties told me that the fact that there was a clear hierarchy above him made it easier to communicate pressing issues upwards: even if his immediate boss ignored him or did not understand the importance of a particular matter, it was very easy to raise it informally with someone more senior within the organization. In another company an employee told me that it was relatively easy for junior employees to influence senior management, in spite of the apparently hierarchical company structure:

Well, I think it's not as hierarchical as it may look. Myself I do not participate in all decision-making, I do not think I would always make the right decision right now, but if I did have the right belief I think I could join in and would present a good enough reason. Certainly many of my colleagues who are more experienced, they are certainly making decisions at the lower level which would influence the upper level.

In sum, the clear hierarchical structures and formal operating procedures which characterized the majority of companies I studied, appeared to be important for the way that the companies were governed, as they were fundamental to ensuring wide consultation, and the checking and cross-checking of 'corporate' decisions. But interestingly, these were not seen as coercive control structures and processes. Instead they tended to be viewed positively by the majority of employees, as they seemed to ensure that fair and predictable procedures would always be followed, enabling employees at all levels of the company to contribute to and participate in company decision-making, and reducing the chance for mistakes to be made.

Inclusive Dialogue

As well as being involved in everyday business decisions through formal structures and procedures, in the majority of companies I studied it seemed that even the most junior employees were able to participate in and contribute to major decisions affecting the way the company was run.

In eight of the companies in the sample, including all five with more than 7000 employees, junior employees were able to contribute formally to decisions about the way that the company operated through the company union.[7] In these companies, both unions and senior management seemed keen to engage in a constructive

---

[7] In every company union, on reaching *kacho* (section-head) level employees had to give up their membership of the union, so unions tended to represent junior employees exclusively.

dialogue on a broad range of issues. For example, the head of the pharmaceutical company union told me:

The head of the personnel department as well as other departments gather to discuss freely about the most topical problems and their solution with the union. The topics which are discussed here include, for example, how to create a comfortable working place; research, development, production, medical sales, OTC sales. They are discussed in groups.

Although both sides frequently emphasized the goal of a constructive and co-operative dialogue between the union and senior management, this is not to say that there was never disagreement between the two, or a sense of complacency on the part of the union. All of the union officials I interviewed seemed to take their role of representing the interests of (junior) employees very seriously. All of the unions were self-financing, and were autonomous in their consultation and internal decision-making processes (although in all except one case the union was provided with rooms and various administrative facilities and support). As such they seemed to feel, and acted on the basis that, they were not obligated or subordinate to senior management. For example, the following comment by one union leader was a typical description of, what were often described as feisty, discussions unions had with senior managers:

[We] argue against the board about raising wages, bonuses, and miscellaneous benefits. There are other demands such as medical fees, housings, company-owned housing, shorter working hours, changes in the way we conduct our work.

In another company, the president acknowledged that the relationship with the union was not always harmonious, and that senior management was experiencing some problems with the unions in two of their factories:

Yes, our relationship [with the union] is usually constructive but in some factories, that is not [company name] but our group company, there are one or two exceptions.

In spite of differences of opinion and apparently spirited exchanges, especially during the 'Spring Wage Offensive' (*shunto*), it seemed that both senior managers and union representatives recognized that they were not fundamentally separate groups with different or competing interests. This was particularly manifest in a number of companies where I was told that the union was perceived to be a training ground for a senior management position: for example in one company I was told that all the current members of the board had once been union officials, and that it was now becoming a prerequisite for a senior management position to have worked as an official for the company union. In such cases, it appeared to be especially clear to both union officials and board members that although they represented different perspectives, they shared a common interest in the future of the company as a whole. For example, a senior director in one company claimed:

There is a friendly relationship. The board perceives that the standpoints between the two are different, but above all that, both we and they are trying to find a good solution for the company.

In another company, a union official also acknowledged that when he was negotiating with the personnel department on behalf of the union, the interchangeability of roles was often in his mind:

...you could be on the other side anytime, you might be in that person's position in a year. The Japanese labour union is entirely different from the foreign style union.

In recent years union membership in Japan has fallen to record lows (21.5 per cent of the workforce in 2000, down from about 25 per cent in 1989),[8] which the media has tended to attribute to disillusionment with annual collective wage negotiations, and the abandonment of seniority-based salary scales in favour of more individual, meritocracy-based pay and promotion systems. From within the companies themselves though, it appears that this is not the case; instead, dialogue between senior management and employees has become so institutionalized that unions are becoming to some extent redundant. Most junior company employees I interviewed claimed that their company union was in general useful, but was becoming less essential for effective communication with senior management.

In all of the companies I studied, including those without unions, there was a strong, empathetic relationship that underpinned employee–management dialogue. However, in those companies that did not have a union (which tended to be the smaller or newer companies), it seemed that because of the smaller number of employees communication between senior management and junior employees was easier and more informal. In these companies, there seemed to be a strong emphasis placed on ensuring that employees were kept informed about the company activities, and that senior management was kept in touch with employees' views. For example, most companies held daily or weekly 'assemblies' at departmental or (in the case of the smallest companies) at company level, where employees could discuss issues with senior management directly. In one company, when I questioned an employee about the union she told me that she and her colleagues felt a union was not really needed as communication within the company was so good: as well as regular weekly meetings where senior management met and discussed issues face to face with employees, she told me that the company had, for example, a formal system whereby employees (*c*.2250) wrote to the president each year, who guaranteed to read all of the letters and reply where necessary. In another case the company newsletter included a monthly questionnaire which solicited employee views about a wide variety of issues related to working conditions, which the company appeared to take very seriously and act upon promptly. In another company with no union I was told that there were many different forums where employees could come together to discuss work and company related issues:

There are clubs like tennis group and other types of group. We have intranet group forums, and some people use that to discuss some matters or we use the computer to communicate, or for example there is a group of mothers who communicate, exchange information on work

---

[8] Ministry of Health, Labour and Welfare.

or private matters. Managers look through these groups and try to see what people are really thinking.

Furthermore, in those companies without unions, the dialogue between employees and senior management did not appear to be less effective than in companies with a formal union. For example, in one of the companies where there was a large number of female employees, those with children had successfully lobbied senior management to provide day-care facilities:

Lots of women employees were saying we should have day-care inside. And before we moved to [place name], we used to have our office in the [place name] area. It was very difficult to have a day-care centre in that area because the cost of land is very high, and we did not own our own building, so we couldn't do much to build it anyway. So when we decided to move to [place name], we talked for a long time about establishing a day-care centre, and the top management was very supportive.

In sum, with or without a union, extensive employee–management dialogue seemed to be fundamental to the way that the majority of companies I studied functioned. In most of the larger companies, the company union constituted an important channel through which core employees could be constructively involved with decisions which effected the company as a whole. Even in the companies without a union, there were informal and formal procedures and bodies which ensured that employees were able to engage in constructive discussion with senior management on matters related to the company. Most importantly, this inclusive dialogue did not appear to constitute a mechanism contrived by senior managers to make employees feel a sense of 'involvement' or 'participation' in the company. Instead, in the majority of companies I studied, broad consultation and involvement of employees seemed to be a natural and guileless company practice. For example, in one of the largest companies in the sample, the president told me that he considered the regular solicitation of employees' views to be one of his key roles:

Since I became president I have made casual, not well-announced visits to the plants and factories and research centres, and every time I start by making some initial remarks and all the rest of the time, some 30 minutes or one hour, is dedicated to question and answer or free-discussion. That is the time to establish feedback. I encourage them to ask me questions and I like to ask questions of them, that is the best form of communication. I make it a point to make such visits once a month, and I include all domestic and overseas countries. It means quite a few opportunities every year. Each time I begin with ten or so general managers, and then separately with forty or fifty section heads, and so on with each different layer of managerial level I organize a meeting and hear their views.

This seems to demonstrate the importance attached to processes that ensure that employees, who were firmly perceived to constitute the company, had a voice in the way that their company was governed.

Conformity, Complacency, Concealment

In some of the companies that I studied, there were suggestions that the strong sense of corporate community also had the potential, in certain circumstances, to have negative consequences for the way a company was governed. For example, some interviewees claimed that pressure to conform to the majority view occasionally resulted in the avoidance of potentially controversial proposals and decisions, as this comment from a company director illustrates:

Other opinions or suggestions don't tend to reach the board, and some managers tend to rearrange the ideas so they are easy to agree. They are afraid of having the ideas rejected.

In another company, which was in a very profitable industry and able to finance its operations mainly from retained earnings, a number of the directors seemed to be complacent about the company's operations. For example, the finance director told me:

I think [company name] is an excellent company in terms of its company culture: its transparency. So it seems to be rather difficult for problems to happen.

In spite of this confidence, a junior employee told me that as a recent recruit to the company, he had been pressurized into falsifying records in order to make the sales of his division appear better than they were:

Well to be really . . . to give you a concrete example, at that time you know the case of [company name] where they had targets and a lot of pressure to reach that target, well the same situation really existed at [this company] at that time, the pressure was really very very hard, and of course the customers that we are dealing with, if they didn't have any job or good cash flow, they wouldn't dream of buying something this expensive, so it was always very difficult to reach that target, so what happened in those days, and this was not only me, but if I had a hot customer about to sign, if the boss sees the other people's results and thinks that the branch is not doing good enough for him to report to his boss he would then say well give me that paper, in other words he would tell me to pretend that the sale is already done.

As well as providing a striking example of misplaced confidence on the part of a senior company director (or perhaps an attempt to conceal problems from me?), this case demonstrates the potential dangers of a close-knit, cohesive group where there are inadequate links beyond the group. Here it seemed that the manager of a sales department of a particular branch was prepared to act dishonestly in order to maintain the prestige of the department. This was apparently able to happen as staff tended to remain with this particular department for long periods of time: with a strong pressure to conform to the norms of the department, and no clear channels of communication beyond its boundaries, the employee told me that he (and some of his colleagues) had found it impossible to speak up about what was going on in the department. Apparently the company president did discover the problem fairly quickly, and the head of the department was removed and the sales department was broken up and re-formed. More importantly perhaps, the speed of staff rotation between departments was accelerated and verification procedures were strengthened to prevent a reoccurrence of the problem, making it more difficult to conceal malpractice within the confines of a department.

In another of the companies I studied, which had enjoyed rapid growth since its establishment in the 1980s, I was told that the company had had some financing problems, which the president had deliberately concealed from investors and employees. An employee who had discovered the difficulties had left the company, and subsequently made his concerns about the company public (these were widely reported in the Japanese press at the time of the research). A senior director acknowledged that the company had other, similar problems, which no one outside of the senior management group were aware of. In this particular case, it seemed that the company president was able to conceal problems from employees and investors for a number of reasons. Firstly, he was a dominant (and charismatic) founder-president, and the company structure and operating style was one of the least 'familial' of all of the companies I studied. There was no lifetime employment system and a relatively individualistic work culture. There was no strong company hierarchy, and operational systems and procedures were the least well developed of all the companies I studied. As a result, the attributes which I have discussed as being important for engendering a strong sense of identification with or commitment to the company, or formal structures encouraging employee involvement in the affairs of the company, were not in place. Moreover, the company was expanding rapidly, in a fast-moving, high-technology field, and had not needed to establish any relationships with external business partners or financiers. As a result, it seemed to have been possible to conceal the problems the company had experienced from parties outside the company.

In sum, it seems that the strong sense of community has, in some circumstances, the potential to breed conformity or complacency among employees and managers. More importantly, where there is no commitment to the company among employees, or the ability of employees to participate fully in decision-making has been curtailed, it is possible for malpractice to take place within the company and to be concealed. The examples discussed in this section suggest that for employees to fulfil a governance role, it is necessary that the systems I have discussed in this chapter are functioning to involve and commit employees to each other and their companies as a whole, and the mechanisms that allow them to participate fully in internal company affairs are in place.

'Joint and Several' Responsibility

In the majority of companies I studied, employees did identify with and were committed to their companies, and as a result a strong sense of collective and personal, or what I shall term 'joint and several', responsibility for the decisions and actions of their company seemed to be engendered. In most companies, the importance of *collective* involvement in and responsibility for decisions seemed to be entirely taken for granted. For example, in one of the longest-established companies I studied, an employee told me:

Not one single person can make a decision at companies like [company name]. I've been to several overseas companies with our management, sometimes not the top management but part of the management, and we'd go like, ten people from [our company] would go and two people would receive us, and they'd make the decision there and we'd say, 'oh we'll have to go back and make the decision when we get back'. That kind of difference still persists, so whenever I want to make a major decision I have to go first to make a round to all the related companies and organizations and convince them first.

This tendency towards collective actions and responsibilities did not seem to result in the *dissipation* of responsibility among employees for their consequences, as some might expect, for two main reasons. First, as discussed earlier, individual responsibilities were usually systematized in the carefully crafted hierarchies, systems, and procedures that most companies had. But second, the strong sense of identification with one's colleagues and the corporate community, and the understanding that one's whole life (not just work) was inextricably bound up now and in the future with one's colleagues, seemed to create the conditions for a 'joint and several' responsibility for the actions of the company as a whole. For example, in one company, which was facing grave financial problems, the comments of a senior director suggested that the responsibility for solving the problem was at the same time a collective and a personal matter:

[Our industry] is facing very serious problems, so the time required to discuss matters is very long, as we need to assess all the possible situations, and we need to think through all of the risks. The time for consideration is long. I do my *nemawashi* at my level, and my staff do their *nemawashi* at their level; *nemawashi* has too broad a meaning, but for me it really means collecting information and opinions from everyone, so that I can analyse issues well, before suggesting decisions.

Moreover, personal responsibility for the collective actions of the company seemed to be taken for granted in most of the companies I studied. For example, an employee at one company, who had overseen the construction of the company's two overseas plants, did not seem to be able to comprehend why neither the foreign contractor company nor their staff would assume any responsibility for the problems which had been encountered:

Things are different here—I actually think the [nationality] and the [nationality] are the same, neither say sorry, it's always excuse excuse excuse, and they say no problem, no problem, but after that when you find a problem, they say it is not my responsibility. In [country] we used one company to construct the plant, and it was the same thing there, we had to have so many arguments with the engineers. [. . .] Why don't they feel any responsibility for what they do?

In sum, in the majority of companies I studied, the long-term commitment of core employees to their colleagues and the company seemed to create the conditions where employees feel a strong joint and several responsibility for their own actions, as well as those of their colleagues and the company as a whole. One employee summed up succinctly what this meant for him:

We employees think that we are the owners. When I am doing a job I sometimes think what is best for our company, not just for myself—I tend not to work just for our official responsibility, but acting as if I am the president of chairman. This is the strong point of Japanese company.

7

Japanese Directors—Elders of the Corporate Community

7.1. INTRODUCTION

Economists, policy-makers, and the media tend to attribute especial significance to the governance role of the board of directors, which is posited as a bridge between company management and shareholders. As discussed in Chapter 2, the Japanese board is commonly believed to be representative of employee rather than shareholder interests, which for many suggests that directors tend to be entrenched and Japanese corporate governance arrangements as a whole are fundamentally flawed. Recently, there have been some studies which suggest that Japanese senior managers may not be as entrenched as has widely been assumed, but in the absence of empirical research it is difficult to explain why this is so.

In this chapter I present my analysis of the role of senior management (I use this term to include directors, senior directors, and corporate auditors) in the governance of the companies I studied. At one level, the arguments I present here tend to support the analysis put forward by mainstream critics of Japanese senior management. The board of directors appears to be little more than a ceremonial body, decision-making power is concentrated in the hands of a small executive management committee, the board of auditors does not monitor management, external directors are not independent, and the Annual General Meeting (AGM) does not give shareholders any real opportunity to communicate with managers. However, I argue that putting these forward as evidence that Japanese senior management must therefore be 'entrenched', misconstrues the role of senior management in the governance of their companies. Rather than acting as a bridge between shareholders and management, senior managers appear to be the linchpin of the corporate community, and in this respect are at the heart of a robust system of governance: they act to cohere a system of responsibilities, reciprocal obligation, and trust, which operates through interpersonal relationships within and between companies.

7.2. AN ENTRENCHED MANAGEMENT ELITE?

The 'Ceremonial' Board of Directors

Outside of the companies I studied, there seemed to be a widespread feeling among interviewees that the way the Japanese board of directors functioned was out of step with best practice in the rest of the world, and as such the board needed to be reformed. Invariably interviewees referred to the high-profile restructuring of the board at Sony, using this as anecdotal evidence of apparently 'dramatic' or 'fundamental' board changes under way in Japan generally. For example, the director of a securities company claimed:

Sony has decided to reduce the number of directors to 8, 9, or 10, and it is very necessary to get good outsiders to manage well. . . . Before '94 Japanese companies used very traditional ways of decision-making, but now we have found that it does not work well, and to catch-up with rivals from abroad it is very necessary to reduce the size of the board and accept outside directors. For example, Nissan is trying another way; they have 40 members and hold the meeting every week, but I don't think it works well—in the future the company will be forced to change.

However, the pictures of change suggested by interviewees outside of the companies I studied, rarely matched the descriptions of the actual changes that were discussed by interviewees inside. One of the companies in the sample did modify its board during the course of the research, reducing the number of directors from more than thirty to just ten. At the time this happened, it was reported in the media as evidence of the trend among Japanese companies to adopt 'global best practice'. However, inside the company, I was told that what the company had done was simply re-label the *jomu-kai* (senior management committee: this is discussed in the following subsection) as the board, and re-name the board 'executive officers'. One senior director acknowledged to me:

What [we] have done is actually what every Japanese company already really does, but it allows the Americans to understand us more easily. This has to be understood, as theoretically the board meeting is really a formality, it is just a festivity, and in the US the board of directors is the key for corporate governance.

In this case, there was no evidence of operational decision-making being decentralized, or the powers of the board being revised in any significant way. Indeed, in all of the other companies I studied, there was also no evidence of any substantive changes taking place in the way the board functioned or was constituted.

In many companies, it seemed that the board meeting was appreciated principally as a means of ensuring that decisions ratified by directors were disseminated and carried out throughout the company. For example, one (junior) board director claimed that his main role as a director was to communicate company policy to the department he was responsible for, and to ensure that his department operated in line with company policies. Furthermore, in most companies directors acknowledged that board meetings principally comprised operational reporting, as this director told me:

Yes, we usually have the [board] meeting around the tenth, and we report what we've done on the last cycle and what we're expecting on the next cycle. We pretty much report on what we did and what we think is going to happen in the month that we're in.

In view of this communication role, it appeared to be considered important that the board of directors was representative of the company as a whole. As such, in most of the companies I studied all departments were usually represented on the board of

Table 7.1. *Sizes of boards in sample (averages are given in bold)*

# Employees	7500	4000	875	20,500	22,000	150	11,500	1450	2250	11,500	12,125	1075	50	80	
Board size	27	26	16	38	10	10	30	20	20	26	34	14	7	11	**20.64**
President	1	1	1	1	1	1	1	1	1	1	1	1	1	1	**1.00**
Chairman	1	0	1	1	0	1	1	1	1	1	0	1	1	1	**0.79**

directors, and, consequently, the larger the number of employees, the larger the board tended to be (Table 7.1 shows the boards sizes for all the companies in the sample correlated against the number of employees).

Beyond this communication role, the board of directors (*torishimariyaku-kai*) *as a group* was described as little more than a ceremonial body, with no real authority of its own. For example one company president told me:

The board is considered a formality, as certain matters have to be approved by the board, and then by the shareholders meeting.

In another company, where members of the founding family held the most senior management position, I was told by the company president that she[1] and her husband (the chairman) made the strategy and policy decisions in conjunction with the directors at executive management meetings, which were then just rubber-stamped at the board meeting afterwards:

For us the board meeting is much more of a ceremony, well, I mean, a signing [hesitates for a while] well whatever is needed in the law, but the place where we make our real decision or where the directors actually get to do the decision-making is the management meeting which we hold every month and at that meeting all the staff report what they have done that month and what they think they should do next month. My husband and I talk about the strategy and policies we are thinking about in the long- and mid-term, and the board will decide whether they should say something or agree or whatever, I mean we ask them whether they agree with our strategy.

In sum, it was widely held that the board meeting was mainly a legal formality, and usually entailed the ratification of decisions taken elsewhere: as a group, the board did not have any input into the generation or revision of these decisions. As one director put it, 'when the proposals are on the [board-room] table they are already really agreed. . . . Board meetings are really very ceremonial'.

The Authority of the jomu-kai

Although the boards of directors I observed seemed to be in most cases singularly different from the widely held (Anglo-American) idea of what constitutes a 'proper'

---

[1] There are very few women directors in Japan, but in this (family-dominated) company the wife of the founder was the President. A survey by Corporate Women Directors International in 1998 identified 198 women among the 53,759 Japanese directors of Japanese listed and Over The Counter (OTC) traded companies. Three per cent of listed companies have a woman on the board, and 0.2% of the total number of directors are women. For OTC companies, the number of companies with women directors rises to 11.2%, and 1.1% of the total number of directors are women.

Table 7.2. *Jomu-kai membership (averages are given in bold)*

President	1	1	1	1	1	1	1	1	1	1	**1.0**
Vice chairman				1		1				1	**0.2**
Executive vice-president	1	3		4	4	2			2	2	**1.3**
Senior managing director	1	2	4	6		3	2	2	2		**1.6**
Managing director	4	5		7		8	5	7	6		**3.0**
Total committee #	7	11	5	19	5	15	8	10	11	4	**8.1**

board, most companies had another 'inner' grouping of senior directors which seems far closer to the conventional idea of what a board is and does. In ten of the fourteen companies I studied, a separate *jomu-kai* (senior management committee) was distinguished from the board of directors, and was consistently described as the locus of corporate decision-making. Members of the *jomu-kai* were also members of the board of directors, and were usually designated managing director, senior managing director, vice-president, or vice-chairman. It was usually members of the *jomu-kai* who were selected to be 'representative directors'[2] of their companies. The four companies that did not have a separate board and *jomu-kai*, were the smallest companies in the sample with the smallest boards (7–10 members each); in these companies it appeared that the roles of *jomu-kai* and board of directors were combined. The company chairman generally was not a member of the *jomu-kai*. A breakdown of the membership of the *jomu-kai* in the ten companies which had such a body appears in Table 7.2.

In all of the companies I studied, I was told that most of the important policy decisions were taken by the *jomu-kai*. For example, one senior director told me:

Well most, well important strategies or important matters are discussed in the managing directors' committee. As for the board of directors' meeting well, er, not, the purpose is not to discuss, we simply inform the meeting of important things and simply say we agree. It's kind of a decision ceremony.

According to the president of another company, the 'real' decisions were not taken at the board meeting, but at the *jomu-kai*. In another company a director told me:

The *jomu-kai* is the place where the real discussion takes place, and the board meeting just has the decisions presented to them—it is just a ceremony.

Interviewees frequently emphasized the seniority and authority of the *jomu-kai* vis-à-vis the board of directors. For example, one senior director indicated that the board of directors would rarely reject a decision taken by the *jomu-kai*. This is not to say that the board was forbidden to discuss such matters, simply that the relevant discussion would have taken place earlier, before it was presented to the board for ratification. Moreover, it was clearly understood that the board's role was not to take

---

[2] According to the Japanese Commercial Code (Article 261. I) one or more representative directors are required to be elected *by the board* to sign official documents on behalf of the company.

any decisions, but simply to authorize decisions taken by the *jomu-kai*. For example, a senior director in one company was eager to emphasize that the *jomu-kai* had the ultimate decision-making authority, over and above the board, with regard to important company issues:

The *jomu-kai* consists of nine board members, and this is where substantial decisions are made. Do you understand? Many of the issues are decided in the departments, but the more important matters go further up, the final decision being made here in the *jomu-kai*.

In sum, interviewees seemed keen to stress that the *jomu-kai*, not the board of directors, was the more important corporate decision-making body. A directorship was a junior position, or as this company president described it, was an 'entrance exam' for the more senior role in the *jomu-kai*:

The criteria to select a board member is that he has the potential to become a top executive of the future. First, you are elected as a board member. Then you might be chosen as managing director in charge of some function when you join the *jomu-kai*, then executive VP which covers a slightly wider responsibility rather than one particular field, then from these three or four executive VPs the president will be chosen. . . . In this country to become a board member is the first step of an entrance exam; I think in general this system has worked well.

Dependent External Directors

At the time of the research fieldwork, there was increasing pressure from the Japanese and international media for companies to introduce 'independent' external directors onto their boards. Most interviewees were very aware of the debate about whether Japanese companies should appoint more external directors, but only in the largest, most international company I studied was I told that any 'independent' (in this case two non-Japanese) directors had actually been appointed. These particular appointments were widely reported in the media at the time as a 'revolution' for Japanese corporate governance. However, one of the (internal) directors explained to me that although the new directors did appear to come from unrelated companies, the appointments had in fact been made on the basis of close, existing relationships:

There was a strong relationship with [foreign bank name], so we said we would welcome some outside directors, but they must have some knowledge and understanding of our business so they can make the right decisions. That is why those directors have a strong relationship with [us]. [Our] businesses are so globalized and so diverse that they must understand the current situation and [our] future.

A further two companies I studied claimed to have seriously considered appointing independent directors. In one of these companies, which seemed to be attempting to present itself as a 'non-traditional' Japanese company, I was told that they had tried to appoint an independent external director to their board, but as there was no other relationship between the companies the appointment had been vetoed by the other company. Instead, a family member (who, moreover, was believed to be able to exercise far more independent judgement than any non-related director could have done) had been appointed instead:

Well at the moment we have to be realistic, we won't be able to find anybody, well the fourth person we were trying to have is working for a huge, well a large company as a chairman, well he's a chairman but he doesn't have any control of . . . there's a parent company of that company, and that company doesn't want him to be going out doing directorships of other companies, and I think that's the reality in Japan, you can't really have any good outside director, really outside, so at the moment the only people that we really have is the people that are our directors who are not actually employees. One is my father, he's pretty, well I mean, by what we say by being outside is that they don't depend on our salary, and he's pretty much the only person that could speak upfront to my uncle [the chairman], so he's the most outspoken, so in a way he's the most independent director, I mean from a standpoint of American standards a brother would be an insider director, but looking at it from the substance he's pretty much an outside director.

In another of the more recently established companies in the sample, I was told that, at the time of their flotation, they had tried to recruit an 'independent' director (albeit a personal acquaintance of the company chairman), but his company too had not allowed the appointment, because of concerns about financial liabilities when there was no other relationship between the companies:

. . . we tried to have a new outside director, but his company would not allow him to join our board—the business environment in Japan does not allow one of their board members to become the director of another company which is not directly related to their company. They are really afraid. [. . .] In the US you can limit individual director's liabilities, but in Japan there is no law allowing that, so there is no limit—that company may be liable for any of our problems.

The point that this interviewee raised was an important one. The Japanese Commercial Code has always offered recourse for shareholders against the personal assets of company directors in certain instances of malfeasance and corporate bankruptcy. For many companies, this alone seems to militate against the appointment of external directors in Japan.[3]

   Many other interviewees also told me that it was impossible for a company to contemplate sending an employee to be a director on another company's board unless there was a strong relationship between the companies, as the transfer of staff would be bound up with a raft of other responsibilities and obligations between the companies. For example, the director of a recruitment consultancy told me that he had approached one company president to ask whether his company might recommend some names to the board of one of the companies in the sample for consideration

---

[3] The problem was underscored in a September 2000 court ruling against eleven Daiwa Bank executives who were held accountable for the losses generated by an employee's fraudulent bond trading over eleven years in its New York office. The bank suffered losses of over $2 billion, and the court ordered the eleven men to personally repay shareholders $1.5 billion. Although some have seen this as a victory for greater accountability in Japan, it has generally been recognized as overkill in terms of vicarious liability for the fraudulent acts of an employee. To this end, the Japanese Government has decided to limit external company directors' liabilities to a maximum of two years' salary. It is possible that this may pave the way for more company directors to consider non-executive positions on other company's boards.

as independent directors, as it was considered a forward-looking organization which already had appointed a number of apparently 'independent' directors. However, the reply he received had convinced him that it was unlikely that many Japanese firms would appoint external directors who were not already linked to a company in some way or another:

[Name] will soon retire and at the same time the three outside directors that are currently on the board will also retire. I asked him whether he would use our services to recruit new outside directors but he said that this was impossible. It is very important he said that he knows the other directors personally, so probably when he retires there will again be no outside directors. We have never introduced any director-level appointment or policy-making people and frankly we cannot see this changing.

In sum, in the companies I studied it seemed that the appointment of truly 'independent' directors to the board was considered difficult, if not impossible. It was not that companies were unwilling to invite external directors to serve on their boards, but that given the responsibilities, obligations, and liabilities that accompanied the appointment of an external director, many companies were unwilling to allow their directors to join another board. As discussed in Chapter 6, the appointment of external directors tends to be bound up with relationships between partner companies, and according to the majority of interviewees seemed likely to continue that way.

Encumbered but Diligent Auditors

Corporate Auditors (*kansayaku*) are probably unfamiliar to most non-Japanese, but are integral to the Japanese corporate governance system and were widely discussed by most interviewees. All Japanese companies are required to have one corporate auditor, and companies with paid-up capital in excess of ¥500 million or with total liabilities in excess of ¥20 billion must have at least three, one of whom must be full-time and one of whom must be independent of the company (in this case, independence is defined as not being employed by, or serving as director of the company during the preceding five years). Legally, the role of the auditor is limited to reviewing the execution of directors' duties as laid down in a company's articles of incorporation, forestalling their dereliction of duty, and verifying and reporting on company documents (including financial statements) before they are submitted to the Annual General Meeting. In practice, as company statutes always include an obligation of due diligence on the part of directors, the auditor is also expected to report on any breaches of this due diligence. In this last respect in particular, the corporate auditor is believed to play a key role in the system by which Japanese companies are governed.

Every company I studied had a board of four auditors (rather than the statutory three), comprising two 'internal' auditors, and two 'external' auditors (the latter were also often referred to in many of the companies as 'part-time' auditors). Most interviewees, especially junior employees and those outside of companies, were nonetheless highly sceptical about whether the board of auditors (*kansayaku-kai*) did actually fulfil any useful governance role. The following comment was fairly typical:

Let me tell you about the statutory auditors, which as you know here is really just a retirement post—the statutory auditor has no real power, and is just a way of phasing out the board directors before they retire so they have the prestige of a position but really do not actually do anything.

In some cases, auditors themselves voiced concerns about how effective they could be as 'management monitors', given how they were appointed, their authority *vis-à-vis* the board and the *jomu-kai*, and so on. For example, the internal auditor of one company told me:

It's stipulated that the auditors role is to check the situation of the executives and board, but because of the Japanese system where it is customary for the president to choose the auditors, in practice this is very difficult. Because of this structure if we need to say things to do with operations it is relatively easy to point out, but if they are issues to do with the adequacies of management it is difficult to say. As for skills themselves, in concrete terms there are management issues like suggestions as to cost-reduction and effectiveness where our views are not taken into account, so we produce the report and it is just disregarded. So we are in a weak position, so it is important to have a structure where these reports are followed up and considered seriously.

Although the Commercial Code demands that at least one auditor should be an external appointee, in the companies I studied the external auditors were all either former employees (invariably referred to as 'Old Boys' (OBs)) who had been retired for the minimum five-year period, had come from affiliated companies or banks, or had been otherwise closely involved with the company for a long time (e.g. having acted as the company lawyer).[4] Moreover, in every company I studied, the external auditors were part-time, and most of the information these external auditors received was second-hand, usually from reports made by the internal 'full-time' auditors (nine of the companies had two full-time auditors, even though the law requires just one), as described to me by an internal auditor in one of the larger companies:

The other full-time auditor I meet every day because he works next door. With the other two [external auditors] we have a rule to meet as auditors at least once every three months, but during the previous fiscal year we met six times. There we exchange opinions and information. Apart from this there is a board meeting every month, and an important part of that is the two full-time auditors will go and meet the part-time auditors to explain the agenda, and at the meeting the auditors will consult and exchange views on the particular issues raised. On top of this if there are particularly important issues we will telephone each other.

Another of the larger companies in my sample had appointed the president of its main bank and the president of its largest shareholder, an insurance company, as its

---

[4] A survey by Toyo Keizai (1995) showed that for large companies with capital in excess of ¥500 million or liabilities of ¥20 billion, 30.3% of external auditors came from group companies, 12.5% from banks or insurance companies, 16.1% from other large shareholders or business partners, 11.7% were former employees, 15.7% were professionals (e.g. lawyers or accountants), and the remaining 13.7% were from the public sector or 'others'.

external auditors, but as the internal auditor explained to me, they were not expected to contribute much:

. . . we do not expect our outside auditors to visit [our] job sites or plants. As presidents of their own companies they do not have the time. Nor do we expect them to go into much detail as far as technical matters are concerned. We are the ones to gather information and supply necessary information and detail to them.

In another case, one external auditor claimed that he had initially been unwilling to become an external auditor precisely because he feared that the company would restrict his access to relevant information:

The outside auditor position is usually occupied by someone with lots of idle time. They are not really expected to participate—it's more a puppet-like thing. And the rights and responsibilities of the outside auditor to look into the papers, and the actual treatment given to auditors is not up to the level of the heavy legal responsibility. I personally did not like the idea of being an auditor. I do not have enough time or energy to participate or perform, but as a final thing I accepted with the proviso that my health remains good. I am now trying to get enough information, and also making sure that I put everything down in writing so as to avoid any problems if there are any legal problems later on.

As all of the preceding quotations indicate, it was widely acknowledged that auditors were not really felt to be independent of company management, and as such were not able to 'monitor' or hold company managers accountable in the agency sense of these words. However, this is not to say that the actions and decisions of the company were not scrutinized by auditors at all. In the previous chapter I discussed the formal systems and procedures which were commonly used in many of the companies I studied to ensure the checking and cross-checking of corporate decisions. As part of these carefully constructed systems and procedures, *internal* auditors did play an important role, and moreover seemed to carry out their duties assiduously and conscientiously. In one company, for example, an internal auditor described his general routine in some detail, and suggested that although he was more proactive, the external auditor did perform a crucial moderating role:

We receive most of the important documents, for example the *shacho kessai* [president's decisions], and we will then check all of these documents on a daily basis, and on top of that the full-time auditors will go out and regularly visit at least two or three places each month, including headquarters, branches and subsidiaries, and there we will ask about the current activities and check that nothing illegal is going on, and whether there are any problems in terms of collecting (*saiken*) credits, and then we will report back to the part-time auditors, and then we will write up a report which will be circulated to all of the board members.

In sum, conceiving the auditor as a non-partisan representative of outside interests may be fallacious. The idea of checking up on, or directly 'monitoring' (in the economic sense) other executives seemed to be incompatible with the trusting interpersonal relationships that I have discussed in previous chapters. Nonetheless, in the majority of companies I studied, the (internal) auditor did appear to be considered an important company resource, who played an important role ensuring the legal compliance of corporate activities.

The Annual General Meeting and Sokaiya

All of the foreign investors and analysts I interviewed criticized company AGMs for being little more than rituals, and not the opportunity for shareholders to meet and question the board of directors as laid down in the Commercial Code. For example the director of a non-Japanese securities company described the AGM of one of the companies being studied thus:

At the shareholders meeting, which lasts 20 or 30 minutes, there is no real content, and the executives just pay attention to the extortionists rather than the real shareholders.

Most foreign investors and analysts especially criticized companies for holding their AGMs on the same day. This was often discussed as evidence of the disrespect companies had for the rights of shareholders, as it made attendance at more than a couple of meetings impossible for those with a portfolio of shareholdings. Of the companies in my sample, ten held their AGMs on the same days as each other (along with most other Japanese companies) in 1998, 1999, 2000, and 2001.

A Japanese business journalist I interviewed suggested that increasing media scrutiny might ultimately force companies to change the way AGMs were held:

. . . year by year Japanese media are becoming interested in the annual shareholder meetings, especially the ugly side, and last year there was a very big scandal, a bribery case where they [the board of the company being discussed] gave money to *sokaiya*, so perhaps this year more media will watch. . . . companies will eventually have to change their ways, there is now so much attention on them.

Yet in spite of the criticisms from outsiders and the predictions of imminent change, the majority of interviewees responsible for or involved with dealing with shareholders, claimed that the AGM was simply an opportunity for corporate extortionists (*sokaiya*) and special interest groups to attack and embarrass management, and therefore timings and formats were unlikely to change significantly in the foreseeable future. In many of the larger companies I studied, interviewees recounted to me their experiences with *sokaiya*. A typical attack was described to me by an investor relations manager responsible for organizing the AGM of his company:

Sometimes there are special stockholders who we call *sokaiya*, so in order to protect the directors from *sokaiya*, companies traditionally put their own employees on the first, second and third rows—three years ago [at out company AGM] there was so much violence, throwing whisky bottles at the chairman, some *sokaiya* went up to the podium and hit the chairman [laughs nervously]. Sometimes I feel that Japan is a low-level, underdeveloped country. They were all arrested though, that was '94, a remarkable year. They were arrested, and released at the end of '97 so we might have some fun in '98. And the length of the meeting is usually 30 minutes—people usually say the shorter the better. When the chairman announces the agenda, the employees clap and shout out 'we agree', so the chairman usually says that the agenda is carried—I think probably 70 per cent of Japanese companies are still like this. . . . Of course we invite [employees] and we invite *sokaiya*, but actually they didn't attack us last year because we had 1300 stockholders, which is very big. So we reserved an even bigger place for this year.

In another company, I was told how *sokaiya* tried to extort money from the companies they targeted:

They do a lot of things, these right-wing *sokaiya* hold a lot of demonstrations [outside our offices], and they are waiting for us to contact them—they want us to say please stop this, if you stop this we will buy your group magazines or pay you some money. But we haven't done this, we have just sued them. But this group is quite violent; *sokaiya* and *yakuza* [Japanese Mafia] are very close, there is no difference.

In this company, and all of the other larger companies, there was a person or small team of people, usually in the General Affairs Department or President's Office who would be responsible for dealing with *sokaiya*. Interviewees in these departments, as well as other employees involved with AGMs and investor relations, seemed to be clear that dealing with *sokaiya* was illegal, especially as the law regarding corporate extortion had been clarified and toughened in 1997 (tightening up ambiguities about which kinds of relationships were illegal, and imposing a maximum fine of ¥3 million and a jail sentence of up to three years for contraventions). Nonetheless, employees charged with overseeing company dealings with *sokaiya* often reported that their job was not as clear-cut as the media suggested it ought to be. Many expressed feeling a significant dilemma, as although they knew *sokaiya* activities were illegal, on the one hand they were intimidated by them and on the other they were legally required to respond to them as shareholders. All of the companies in the study maintained that their policy was to sue *sokaiya* if there was unequivocal evidence of attempted extortion or demonstrations outside their offices, but wanted to convey how tricky and invidious their task was in practice, as the gangster's tactics were becoming more sophisticated:

They are quite smart you know. They have specialists in traditional Japanese companies, and they know how to build home pages. And their questions at the stockholders meetings are usually very reasonable, but they repeat the same thing over and over. They don't just come individually either, they come as a group. And one person starts a question, and at the end another guy will ask, and then the third, and then the first guy again. They sit separately, and the chairman has the right to control the meeting, but as soon as this person finishes the other guy will say 'My question is quite closely related to this question' so it is hard for the chairman to stop. They are well-organized, and their intention is to make the meeting long, and the directors feel uncomfortable.

It may seem strange to non-Japanese readers that company employees could apparently feel so intimidated by extortionists, but it is important to remember that Japanese *sokaiya* are closely linked to organized crime syndicates, and have been known to resort to violence and even murder if a company does not comply with their demands (e.g. *sokaiya* are suspected of murdering a director of Fuji Photo Film and a branch manager of Sumitomo Bank in 1994).

Not only was the AGM felt to be open to abuse by *sokaiya,* many interviewees also felt that it served little useful purpose anyway. As in most other countries, voting on company policy is principally carried out in Japan by proxy in advance of the AGM, and the show of hands at the meeting is meaningless: it is only the proxy votes that are of real consequence. Furthermore, many company directors argued that the AGM was not an appropriate forum for meaningful discussion with shareholders. For example one company president claimed:

No—as you know it is just a 30-minute meeting, and most of the attendees are insiders, employees who own the company shares. I don't think the AGM is the right opportunity to discuss with the investors—I think one-to-one meetings are the best opportunity. In every country the AGM is really a ceremony.

In sum, although many company interviewees appeared to understand the criticisms levelled against them concerning the AGM, given the potential for intimidation by *sokaiya* it was generally perceived that the AGM was not terribly relevant for the way that their companies were governed.

7.3. ALLEGIANCE TO THE COMPANY AND ALL ITS CONSTITUENTS

The issues I have discussed in the previous section seem to indicate a general concern, inside and outside of the companies I studied, about how the governance roles of Japanese senior managers seemed to be out of step with 'global best practice'. However, the changes that have been effected as a result of these concerns are, in many respects, limited. In this section I will argue that the principal reason for the lack of substantive change is that most senior managers I interviewed seemed to find it difficult to reconcile the notion of 'accountability to shareholders', which was widely recognized as underpinning the idea of international corporate governance best practice, with their deeper sense of responsibility to the company itself and *all* of its constituents.

Knowing the Company

In spite of all the discussion about reforming the Japanese board and appointing more external directors, in every company I studied profound knowledge of a company was consistently declared to be the most important requirement for any senior management position. For example, one senior director told me:

[For me to be effective as a senior director] one of the most important things is experience of the company's operations. Our senior management think that knowing every job site information is important to decide everything, so for example our president reads more than 1000 reports every month. . . . And if we do not know every detail then we would not [be able to] decide correctly, that is our present philosophy,

In another company, the president described how surprised he had been at first when he was appointed, as he had a sales and marketing background rather than an engineering background. As a technology-centred manufacturing company, he claimed to have truly expected one of his colleagues who had worked as an engineer to be selected as president. On his appointment though, he had been told that the single reason that he had been preferred was that by virtue of his particular career path, he was believed to have the best all-round knowledge of the company's operations. In another company, the president also told me that he would not be able to work effectively with his colleagues in the *jomu-kai* unless he had an intimate understanding of the whole business:

. . . I know all our strengths and negatives, and how our competitors are doing and so forth, and I have access to all the relevant information and so when we have a discussion [in the *jomu-kai*] touching upon strategy or tactics and certain kinds of business positions, the views expressed by those in charge of a certain part of that division may appear to me to be a little bit partial, not taking into account the total picture, or maybe showing their lack of knowledge or experience in some respect and so forth. It is important that a president is able to judge this.

The importance attributed to knowing a company intimately has been discussed at length in the previous chapter. To reiterate, in the majority of cases I studied, intimate knowledge and close identification with a company seemed to be bound up with the notion that a company was not just a production mechanism, but also a social organization. As such, the purpose of a company was not simply to maximize profits, but to maximize the value of the company as a whole. One company president made this point very clearly:

We don't only want a profitable business. Our company philosophy is to take care and educate people from babies to retirement. Our aim is to create a business which serves this corporate philosophy. It is a very difficult task. . . . In this way we are good for society, we are good for our employees, we are good for our shareholders, but if we do not follow our corporate philosophy we cannot be successful at all.

In this context, having a thorough, experience-based knowledge of all aspects of the company was considered indispensable for a senior management position, as only through this was it possible to really understand all the intricacies of the company as a whole. By knowing the company intimately, senior managers, and the president in particular, would be able to make sagacious judgements about how the corporate community was best run taking account of the long-term interests of every participant. The president of one company made this point explicitly in discussing his reticence to invite external directors to serve on the board. He claimed that whatever managerial skills an external director might have, these were largely irrelevant unless they were accompanied also by a deep understanding of the company as a whole. Without such knowledge, he doubted whether the company could be directed effectively:

[External Directors] may have very good managerial skills, but they may not know a particular business well enough and may not have a good enough knowledge about the culture and the way of thinking of the members of a company. If an outside director tries to steer the company without knowing the inside of the company well enough, they are likely to make mistakes. . . . Employees who have worked within the company for many years may have a lower risk of making such mistakes.

Balancing the Interests of all Corporate Participants

As discussed at length in this and in previous chapters, the notion that senior managers *ought to* be more accountable to shareholders was an important topic of debate during the period that I carried out the research. However, the difficulty many senior managers had in reconciling this idea with their felt commitment to employees, was frequently made apparent during many interviews. This was exemplified by the prevarication of one corporate auditor, who struggled to answer a question about who he was legally responsible to:

. . . as an auditor I should be saying [I represent] 100 per cent the shareholder but this is a sort of formal or legalistic answer. But this does not really reflect my sentiment—more frankly with my background I should say employees are a very important part because having been in charge of human resources management throughout so many years, so with a small voice I would say employees are always in my mind, but probably I could not say this outright in front of the shareholders. Therefore, the formal good student answer should be 100 per cent to the shareholders but again in terms of my sentiment and my background I should say employees are very important and always in my mind because through employees' efforts and contributions this company could be sustained and this company's management could continue and I would never like to see a situation where employees are put in a difficult position. I don't know if worrying about the employees should be the job of the auditor or the president but I would have to sort out my thinking before I come up with a clear answer to that. [Long pause]. You invited me to speak honestly so I disclosed some aspect of my sentiment but I have to correct myself and this is my formal correction as an auditor I was elected by the shareholders meeting and not by the employees and besides among our shareholders many of them are in fact employees through the employees' shareholding union. I think now almost 15 per cent or more of our shares are held by our employees. In that sense my formal and candid answer is shareholders, 100 per cent, that is the actual and precise answer.

I have elucidated at length what seemed to be a genuine desire among most company directors to meet the expectations of all their shareholders, in so far as they were considered valued constituents of the company. Yet in spite of the many different measures being implemented, in each of the companies I studied senior managers implicitly or explicitly acknowledged that the interests of shareholders did not for them have priority over the equally important interests of employees, customers, business partners, and banks. For example, one company president claimed:

Well, basically we're responsible to the shareholders [laughs]. No, it's the employees. We are really responsible to our employees . . . and consumers. If we cannot make and sell our product we do not survive.

As this quotation exemplifies, many senior managers seemed to rank the interests of employees above those of shareholders, but only because they were considered to be more fundamental to the survivability of the company as a unit. In another company, the president also seemed to perceive customers and employees to be more fundamental to the existence of the company than shareholders were:

[Our purpose is] to develop new products which give people joy, to give our employees excellent working conditions so they can achieve their own potentials, and to improve society by providing excellent technology. And then the fourth thing is returns for shareholders, we have to provide a good return for shareholders.

Comments such as these, which were common to most of the companies I studied, did not indicate that shareholders' interests were ignored, but simply that fulfilling responsibilities to the whole range of corporate participants was considered essential in order to promote the long-term interests of the company as a whole. In sum, those who acceded to the highest executive positions in Japanese companies, did not appear to conceive themselves as 'agents' of any one particular group, but instead seemed to constitute above all a body of employees who were committed to promoting the long-term interests of the company as a whole, which involved making judgements about the relative importance of *all* of its various constituents:

[. . .] the Japanese respect shareholders but also employees, and certainly consumers are important. We have to maintain our relationship with society, with suppliers and all of these various groups who are important.

7.4. LINCHPINS OF THE CORPORATE COMMUNITY

The board of directors may be conceived of as a bridge between shareholders and managers by agency theorists, but in this section I want to argue that in the companies I studied, senior management as a group appear to act more as a linchpin around which all constituents of the company cohere. Not only are senior managers recognized as elders of the corporate communities I discussed in the previous chapter, they also act as a central focus and point of contact for the external business relationships discussed in Chapters 4 and 5. As such, I suggest that they facilitate and guarantee the form of governance I have discussed in previous chapters, which seems to be based on interpersonal responsibilities, reciprocal obligations and trust, and which depends on the close involvement of both employees and committed outside parties in the affairs of the company as a whole.

Elders of the Corporate Community

The close and frequent interaction of senior managers with other employees at all levels of the organization was often commented upon in the companies I studied. For example, a senior director in one of the largest companies I studied told me:

There are board meetings once a month, and a *jomu-kai* meeting twice a month. Apart from that, there are heads-of-department meetings, such as the sales director meeting the director of accounting, and we also talk individually with other directors, and the people beneath them such as heads of branches and business offices, heads of factories. We are doing such meetings rather energetically.

In another company a senior director claimed:

We have so many meetings—board meetings and management meetings, which are often very intensive one or two days, and headquarters meetings and also we have business leader meetings twice or three times a year, where their business plans and budgets are presented—our president likes such presentations. So each month there are ten meetings, and then there are morning meetings with all the employees where the president talks to the employees. For me it is very easy to see how the company is going, at these high-level, middle-level, and junior-level meetings.

The relevance of this close and frequent interaction of directors with other members of the company is understandable in the context of my discussion in the previous chapter. Not only does it seem to make it difficult for employees (or directors in this case) to act exclusively in their own personal interests, but more importantly perhaps it serves to reinforce the sense of interdependence that employees feel with their colleagues in the company. This seems to engender the strong sense of responsibilities and obligations to colleagues which I suggested were common in most of the companies I studied, which in turn seems to encourage employees to act in the long-term interests of the company as a whole.

Moreover, as well as having regular interaction with junior colleagues, senior management appeared to interact very closely with their peers. This was particularly commented upon at the *jomu-kai* level, where it appeared that any opportunity for the most senior members of the company to act autonomously was strongly circumscribed. Discussion between the members of this group was claimed to be relatively frequent (every week or fortnight, as opposed to once a month for the board), and unlike the board of directors, far from ceremonial:

The executive vice-presidents make up the inner board. The board meets once a month, but the *jomu-kai* meets once a week. This comprises managing directors, around ten people. This inner board discusses quite severely and consults what to do.

Even company presidents, whose powers are commonly believed to be fairly unrestrained, appeared to be strongly moderated by the *jomu-kai*. For example, a senior managing director told me:

One thing I must point out is that looking from outside the president looks like a dictator, but on the contrary, this *jomu-kai* is the real decision-making body, and the president really just chairs this group and does not really have the power to overcome their decision. In other words the unanimous decision of this group really is the decision of the company. As a formality then the board approves the decisions which are presented to it.

In another company, where the president was a member of the founding family, he told me that members of the *jomu-kai* could, and would if necessary, veto any decision that they felt was inappropriate, including the choice of his successor. Statements such as these were quite common, and seemed to indicate that even where the president's authority appeared to be fairly strong (e.g. in the family firms in the sample), they felt their authority to be bound up with and dependent on others in the company.

As well as being closely integrated with current employees and their immediate peers, senior directors also appeared to feel a strong sense of responsibility to former employees ('OBs') for the well-being of the company. In all of the larger, well-established companies, 'OBs' would meet fairly frequently together as a group, and regularly with the incumbent management. If the company was facing a particularly important issue they would invariably offer their help, advice, or opinions. This direct link with former employees, buttressed by stories about the company's past, seemed to play an important role in reinforcing to senior employees their sense of responsibility for the *long-term* future health of the company. The potential influence of former employees was demonstrated most clearly in the case of one of the companies which was involved in a scandal during the period of the research. Here a senior director claimed:

The pressure on us after the scandal has come from inside the company, from employees and OBs [Old Boys] and also the [name] group companies. . . . They exert pressure, explicit, and implicit. For example the OBs come to my room, and sometimes when I drink with employees or influential people from [name] Group companies they confer with us quite seriously.

As implied in this quotation, the pressure brought to bear by OBs was considered as strong as that from any external party, even though they did not have any easily identifiable 'power' to exert over senior management. This suggests that the felt pressure emanated from a sense of responsibility to the OBs, rather than from any fear of possible sanctions they could bring to bear.

In sum, although the role and responsibilities of the company board were discussed as being primarily 'ceremonial', the internal governance role of senior managers as a body needs to be understood in the context of the discussion in the previous chapter. Close and frequent interaction with employees, peers, and retired former colleagues, seemed to mitigate the potential for senior managers to act against the interests of the corporate community as a whole. But more importantly, as discussed in the previous chapter, the resultant strong identification that senior managers felt with their colleagues past and present and the company as a whole, seemed to engender an obligation to promote the long-term interests of the company as a whole, and to shoulder responsibility quickly for any failures.

External Links

As well as being important to the internal governance processes, it is senior managers who tended to have the closest relationships with colleagues in partner companies, which I suggested in Chapters 4 and 5 are also important for the way that the majority of companies were governed. Senior managers I interviewed frequently emphasized the importance of communication they had with colleagues in partner companies, as in this example from one of the company presidents:

The relationship doesn't depend on the shareholding, but more on trust and the personal relationship. . . . Without the personal connection with someone in a high position in the company I think it is impossible to do business with them. I have very good contacts with key people in these companies, for example in [company name] one of the people I have known well since I was a manager, but from next June he will be the president.

As discussed in Chapters 4 and 5, it seemed that close and frequent dialogue with colleagues from business partners (including investors, customers, and suppliers), was important in producing and reproducing the strong sense of responsibility and reciprocal obligations felt between partner companies. The stability and long-term nature of these interpersonal relationships seemed to engender not just a punctilious approach to business relationships, but in many cases a sense of kinship and trust. This was discussed in some detail in Chapter 6, and was often explicitly expressed by interviewees as in the quotation above.

Most senior managers I interviewed expressly recognized the dangers of a company becoming too introverted. For example one internal auditor expressed some concerns about whether he might become too complacent given his intimate knowledge of the company: not only did he know the company's operations intimately, he also had close relationships with many of the company's directors, which he accepted could potentially make him overly 'lenient' or not inquisitive enough about the company's operations or his colleagues' actions. In this context, advice and opinions from colleagues unconnected with the company were extremely valuable, and moreover, tended to be warmly appreciated. For example, one senior company director told me:

Most important is that the top management really wants to have outside advice or checking—this is most important, but it is important that they have someone they trust.

As discussed in previous chapters, the relationships between colleagues at different companies and main banks usually seemed to be informal, and to characterize them as entailing the 'monitoring' of one party by another would in most cases be misleading. Sometimes this was made explicit, for example one director at a main bank told me:

We cannot say anything to [company name] directly about their performance, but our directors can *discuss* the issue with them.

Often consultation between colleagues at different companies was described, as in the preceding example, as 'dialogue' or 'discussion'. In another company, a senior managing director spoke of the 'good dialogue' that his company enjoyed with its main bank, which he attributed in part to having developed a strong relationship with colleagues at the bank throughout his career with his company:

The special factor advantage I could point to is that [the current president and chairman] were in a good position to have a good working relationship with me personally when I was in charge of finance, as managing director and senior managing director and when I was in charge of general affairs and they were some twenty some years ago in charge of [name] department so they know [our] management very very well and we have a very good working relationship, still having very free discussion and good dialogue, not the discussion amongst strangers but we all know the situation very well.

Even if such inter-company relationships appeared to be informal, they nonetheless seemed to be important for the way that most of the companies I studied were governed. As discussed in previous chapters, high levels of dialogue between companies, their banks, their suppliers, their customers, and their affiliates, regardless of whether they are part of an established business group, are institutionalized in Japan and seem to entail a strong sense of mutual responsibility and mutual scrutinization. This took place at many different levels, but appeared to be particularly formalized at the most senior echelons of a company. For example, in the following quotation, the general manager of a major city bank discussed how different staff would continually be discussing different issues with a particular client company, but when it came to important issues it was always the most senior directors who were involved:

Yes, if it comes to very critical or difficult issues, I myself, or my boss, [name] who is the managing director, will negotiate with the more senior people. That often happens, say once a week or at least a few times a month, because sometimes management decisions are necessary to agree on some issues. And also our deputy president and our president and our chairman have personal and official contacts with [company president's name]. Just yesterday our deputy president met with Mr. [company president's name].

In sum, as well as being the apogee of the internal corporate system, it seemed that the well-developed networks of personal contacts that most senior managers were bound up with, were important in ensuring that a corporate community did not itself become introverted or entrenched. However, as discussed in Chapters 5 and 6, this did not seem to be an issue of colleagues 'monitoring' each other in the economic sense. Instead it seems that it is the reciprocal responsibilities and obligations between colleagues at different companies, which were important for their governance role. A senior director of one company which belonged to a *keiretsu* described the regular meetings between him and colleagues from partner companies thus:

[Our group companies meet together] twice a year for four or five days, at a hotel where we discuss general matters, and during the night we drink and chat, so we have very close relationships between the class. The new president of [company name] is my good friend, so for example we talk easily, informally, and individually, what do you think [name] of our company's results, or our reputation. It is very informal, but it's also tough. It is like university colleagues.

8

What can be Learned?

8.1. INTRODUCTION

When each individual perceives the same sense of interest in all his fellows, he immediately performs his part of any contract, as being assur'd that they will not be wanting in theirs. All of them, by concert enter into a scheme of actions, calculated for the common benefit, and agree to be true to their words; nor is there anything requisite to form this concert or connection, but that everyone have a sense of interest in the faithful fulfilling of engagements, and express that sense to other members of society.

(David Hume, A *Treatise of Human Nature*, 1740)

I should begin by re-emphasizing that the research I have carried out and reported in this volume is based on empirical studies of corporate governance in fourteen Japanese companies. The particular research design I employed aimed to elucidate information about actual governance practices, rather than attitudes towards them or inferences about them. Because of the number of cases I examined, the study to a certain extent falls between two stools: in some respects it lacks company-specific contextual detail, but at the same time it is not a controlled sample that enables generalities about Japanese corporate governance to be drawn. Notwithstanding, I trust that in the previous four chapters I have gone some way towards achieving one of the aims of the book. Namely, given the scarcity of previous empirical research of Japanese governance processes and practices in context, I have provided a useful contribution to our knowledge about Japanese corporate governance, by giving some voice to the sense that participants make of their own experiences of the system in practice. In some instances over the course of the previous four chapters, I have been able to draw on macro-level data in order to generalize from the company-specific findings to Japanese business in general. Notwithstanding, further research employing different methodologies, for example structured interviews, questionnaire surveys, and statistical analyses, would be required to allow more extensive extrapolation from the themes and trends that I have identified as important.

In this concluding chapter I want to focus on addressing the principal aim I set out at the beginning of the book, that is to draw out some of the general implications of this empirical study for the way that 'corporate governance' is currently conceived. I begin by recapping the main issues discussed in the previous four chapters. I go on to sketch a tentative model of how a system of responsibilities and reciprocal obligations, within and between companies, which was highlighted in these four chapters, seems to operate as a form of corporate governance. I then relate this conceptualization to existing theoretical approaches to corporate governance. Finally, I consider some of the critical implications of the study as a whole for corporate governance policy and research generally.

8.2. RECIPROCAL RESPONSIBILITIES, OBLIGATIONS, AND TRUST

Shareholding

In Chapter 4 I began by discussing some important changes associated with share-holders and shareholding practices, which were affecting most of the companies I studied. These included the selling of cross-shareholdings, financial innovations such as new share issuing procedures, the establishment of investor relations teams and departments, the greater influence of non-Japanese shareholders, and so on. However, in spite of these apparently important changes, it seemed that the concepts and practices associated with share ownership *per se* were not being radically transformed. For example, for most of the companies I studied, managers continued to control the allocation of equities, tending to select their majority shareholders on the basis of on-going business relationships. Also, most companies carefully monitored who their ultimate shareholders were, and did not appear to be particularly concerned with their company's share price. In sum, I argued that there was little evidence that managers felt, or in any practical sense were becoming, more *accountable to* shareholders, even though they claimed to be far more conscious of shareholders than had been the case in the past.

In spite of the fact that managers did not appear to behave in a way consistent with feeling *accountable to* shareholders, they did appear to feel a strong *responsibility* to all shareholders. However, in the case of shareholders who were also long-term business partners, the sense of responsibility and obligation appeared in many cases to be especially strong, although I argued that this did not appear to be a product of the shareholding *per se*, but was an attribute of the business relationships itself. The exchange of equities between business partners is simply a symbol of the relationship.

In highlighting the importance of business relationships, my empirical findings accord with a long tradition of work on the Japanese corporate system which has focused on the importance of business networks (Caves and Uekusa 1976; Futatsugi 1986; Fruin 1992), especially many recent studies which have explicitly attempted to understand the implications of these networks for the way that Japanese companies are governed (Gerlach 1992; Gilson and Roe 1993; Fukao 1995). Within this line of research, some studies have questioned the appropriateness of the mainstream, economics-derived models of corporate governance, which tend to focus attention solely on how principals are able to protect their financial investments in the context of these business relationships (Gerlach 1992; Gilson and Roe 1993; Ito 1995). For example Gilson and Roe claim:

> . . . complex multi-level monitoring is part of the production process, but this monitoring is motivated not just by financial institutions seeking a return on capital, but also by product market competition. (1993: 874)

Such analyses resonate with my findings in one respect, that the relationships between the companies I studied and their business partners cannot always be adequately explained solely on the basis of financial, especially equities exchanges. However, my empirical findings also differ in one very important respect. This is that in many of the relationships with cross-shareholders which I examined, especially where the relationship had existed for a long time, there appeared to be no direct 'monitoring' (in the economic sense discussed in Chapter 1) taking place at all. Indeed it seemed that in many cases, to 'monitor' a business partner was perceived to risk destroying the relationship.

The idea that it is the responsibilities and reciprocal obligations between business partners which are important for the way that companies are governed, accords with Dore's (1983) notion of 'relational contracting' between companies, which he puts forward as a key distinguishing feature of the Japanese corporate system. Relational contracting depends on the establishment and maintenance of 'goodwill' between business partners in the corporate system. Dore suggests that the stability of relationships is central to the establishment of goodwill, enabling personal relationships to develop which allow both sides to recognize and maintain mutual obligations. Dore does not develop these ideas explicitly to explore their implications for the corporate governance system in Japan, but in his recent work he does posit them as an alternative to (Anglo-American) organizational systems based around self-interest (Dore 1998, 2000).

In sum, shareholding *per se* appears to be largely irrelevant for understanding the way that most of the companies I studied are governed. (Cross-) shareholding appears to be an important embodiment (or 'expression' in Clark's (1979) terms) of the relationship between business partners, but it seems that it is the relationships themselves which are more important for understanding how the companies I studied are governed.

Main Bank

In Chapter 5 I examined the relationships between companies and their main banks. I found that the financing arrangements of many of the companies I studied were undergoing dramatic changes during the period of research. Interviewees claimed that there were greater opportunities for companies to source finance directly from the capital markets, and that as banks were experiencing severe financial problems, their capacity to provide debt finance to client companies had been reducing; in many of the cases I studied there was no debt relationship between a company and its main bank at all. The changes taking place in the financial environment appeared to be generally regarded as permanent, and as a result, all of the Japanese banks where

I carried out interviews were restructuring their operations, reducing their focus on the provision of debt, and repositioning themselves as financial services companies. Employment practices were being revised, and most banks were considering, or were in the process of, merging or allying themselves with domestic or foreign institutions. During the course of researching and writing up this book, all of the banks where I originally carried out interviews have merged, and now there are only four major banking groups in Japan (see Table 5.2).

Yet, in spite of many interviewees claiming that the 'balance of power' was being transformed as a result of these changes, the relationships between banks and the majority of companies I studied appeared to be as strong, if not stronger than ever. There was evidence of continuing extensive communication between companies and their main banks, and exchanges of staff at all levels of the organizations. Where companies were making use of capital market finance, this was often channelled through their main bank, and where companies were experiencing financial distress, the main banks continued to provide support and advice.

Again, within these relationships there was not always evidence of the main bank 'monitoring' or 'disciplining' its client companies, especially where a relationship was well established. This strongly contradicts conventional notions of the main bank's role within the Japanese corporate governance system, which posits the main bank as a 'corporate monitor' in place of shareholders. Some other researchers have recently challenged this traditional conceptualization of the main bank, based on the observation that, given changes in patterns of corporate finance away from debt financing, the relationship between companies and banks has remained durable (Gerlach 1992; Gilson and Roe 1993; Aoki *et al.* 1994). For example, Gilson and Roe (1993) suggest that banks may be motivated to perform a monitoring function to protect their position as factors of production and providers of credit as well as enjoying a return on their equity investments. My findings concur with such analyses, in suggesting that the main bank relationship is based on more than just the debt relationship. However, my findings go further, in suggesting that the *protection* of investments, however broadly defined, is not elemental to the company–main bank relationship; the relationship seems to be often based on shared goals and a sense of cooperation, which creates a system of reciprocal obligation, responsibilities, and trust between employees at companies and their main banks. This system appears to be significant for the way that the majority of companies I studied are governed.

Employees

Although there has been fairly extensive research on Japanese employees and the employment system, especially in the context of the relative success of Japanese companies during the 1980s, there are contradictory interpretations of their importance for corporate governance. Mainstream economic interpretations suggest that the interests of employees have been prioritized in Japanese companies at the expense of shareholders, which is now commonly argued to be an indication of poor corporate governance. An opposing view is that the Japanese company is more accurately described as a community rather than a production mechanism; although the governance implications of this have not been fully developed, research in areas such as industrial relations suggest that it engenders a participatory, communitarian system of employee–management relations and consultation processes, which is significant for the way that companies are governed.

The analysis I presented in Chapter 6 is broadly congruent with this latter perspective. In the majority of companies I studied, core employees appeared to identify strongly with their companies, to the extent that they do not seem to be so much *contracted* to the company, but are perceived and perceive themselves as intrinsically *constituting* the company. This close identification with the company did not seem to be an inherently dispositional phenomenon. Indeed, many younger employees appeared cautious about committing themselves to such intricate, cohesive corporate communities. However, it appears that given lifetime employment and its associated practices, over time core employees come to identify strongly with, and become progressively more committed to, their companies. This coincides with a number of studies which have argued that the relatively high proportion of 'mobile' younger workers in Japan is not just a recent phenomenon, nor is it symptomatic of a disillusionment with the lifetime employment *per se*; it can be explained by the desire among young workers to find and commit themselves only to a company that can offer them an attractive lifetime career (Nitta 1995; Ornatowski 1998).

Identification with and commitment to a company among core employees seems to engender a strong sense of participation and involvement in the company, which in turn results in a keenly felt sense of 'joint and several' responsibility for the actions and decisions of the company as a whole. Although in most companies there tended to be systems and procedures to ensure the proper checking of decisions and actions, it seems that these are to some extent just safeguards, as the strong sense of corporate community goes a long way towards producing a system where employees can be trusted to act in the long-term interests of the company as a whole, and not exclusively in their own personal interests.

In many of the companies I studied, it seems that the strong commitment of core employees to their colleagues and the company serves to engender a form of participatory governance, where the best interests of the company as a whole are promoted. Moreover, the close and intimate corporate community means employees are less inclined or able to act exclusively in their own self-interest. This may well diminish, or in some cases even eliminate, the need for shareholders to 'monitor' or 'discipline' companies, which in turn helps perpetuate the company as a community.

Many aspects of the 'traditional' Japanese employment system were clearly being modified to fit the needs of the changing commercial and economic environment. Recruitment, training, and promotion practices were all being adapted; wage structures were being modified; fewer employees were being recruited as 'core employees'; and it seemed that many companies were adding a new category of 'specialist employee' to the two traditional categories of long-term, generalist core employees and non-regular employees. However, this did not mean that underlying principles of the employment system, such as the commitment to core employees was diminishing.

For example, even when companies were forced to reduce the number of employees in order to reduce salary costs or to scale-back production, efforts were made to ensure that this was done through voluntary rather than compulsory redundancies. As such, I would argue that predictions about the imminent demise of lifetime employment, seniority promotion and wages, and so on will prove to be misguided, in the same way that they have been following each of the previous downturns in the Japanese economy (Rohlen 1974; Abegglen 1985; Tsuru 1994). The lifetime employment system and associated practices as a whole were not being abandoned, and accordingly it did not seem that the participatory form of governance I have described was under any immediate risk of reducing in importance.

Senior Management

As discussed in Chapter 1, economists and policy-makers tend to attribute especial significance to the governance role of the board of directors, which is posited as a bridge between company management and shareholders. In the case of Japanese companies, the board is often believed to be representative of employee rather than shareholder interests, which for many commentators suggests that Japanese corporate governance arrangements are flawed. Recently some researchers have shown that Japanese senior managers are not as entrenched as has sometimes been assumed, but in the absence of empirical research it has been difficult to elucidate why this is so.

In Chapter 7 I presented the findings of my analysis relating to senior management. Many interviewees claimed to be concerned about the issue of corporate governance, in particular whether the governance role of Japanese senior managers was out of step with global best practice. Nonetheless, most senior managers appeared to find it difficult to reconcile the notion of 'accountability to shareholders' with their sense of responsibility and obligation to a broader range of corporate constituents, including colleagues, current and past employees, business partners (especially the main bank), shareholders, and customers. As such, although there were some limited 'reforms' being undertaken to accommodate the perceived expectations of (foreign) shareholders (e.g. reducing the size of the board of directors and improving investor relations), these changes often did not appear to be substantive.

According to the mainstream economic characterization of 'good' corporate governance, my analysis of the board of directors, the *jomu-kai*, external directors, corporate auditors, and the AGM might be interpreted as confirmation that senior management are entrenched: there appear to be no clear lines of accountability, no explicit monitoring mechanisms, no obvious sanctions that can be brought to bear in the case of managers acting irresponsibly, and so on. However, I argued that it is more likely to be mainstream ideas of what constitutes 'good corporate governance' that are inadequate, as they appear to misconstrue the relevance of senior management for the governance of their companies. One of the principal roles of senior management in the companies I studied appears to be to facilitate and guarantee the participatory system of governance by employees (past and present), discussed in Chapter 6. Furthermore, it is senior managers who tend to have the closest relationships with colleagues in partner companies, which I suggested in Chapters 4 and 5 are important for the way that their companies are governed. As such, rather than acting as a bridge between shareholders and management, I argued that senior managers in many of the companies I studied are recognized as the linchpin of the corporate community: they are at the centre of a system of reciprocal responsibilities, obligations, and trust, which is associated with strong interpersonal relationships within and between companies.

8.3. 'SOCIALLY ENDOGENOUS' CORPORATE GOVERNANCE

The idea that reciprocal responsibilities, obligations, and trust are important attributes of Japanese companies and corporate relationships is not a novel finding (Ouchi 1981; Dore 1983, 1987; Gerlach 1992; Sako 1992; Powell 1996; Das and Teng 1998; Hagan and Choe 1998; Dyer and Chu 2000). There is, however, no firm consensus about their origins and nature. For example, some researchers assume them to be essentially dispositional phenomena and characterize Japan as a society comprising high-trust individuals (Hofstede 1980; Triandis 1994), while others discuss them as primarily institutional phenomena (Powell 1996; Hagan and Choe 1998). In this section I add to this discourse, by *tentatively* outlining how certain social and psychological processes may help to explain how the reciprocal responsibilities, obligations, and trust identified in my analysis are produced and sustained, which also helps to clarify how they may serve as a means of corporate governance.[1] The discussion elucidates the possibility of a form of 'socially endogenous' corporate governance, which draws on the voluntary reciprocal obligations and responsibilities enacted in everyday individual-level and organizational-level socio-economic interactions, rather than the exercise of hierarchical controls of individual behaviour.

Intra-Group Physical, Psychological, and Emotional Proximity

Evolutionary psychologists, social exchange theorists, and cultural researchers among others have put forward various ideas to explain the origins of other-oriented (generally termed prosocial) behaviour, many of which highlight the importance of face-to-face interaction and high levels of communication. For example, Axelrod (1984) suggests that reciprocity between individuals in a relationship or group is encouraged by making 'interactions more durable, and making them more frequent' (p. 129). This is because this type of interaction means that a person's behaviour is under constant scrutiny, making it much more difficult to behave in a way that goes against the interests of the relationship or group as a whole: not only are transgressions likely to be identified more easily, they can also be sanctioned very quickly. Furthermore, Axelrod suggests that frequent and repeated interaction has the effect of 'enlarging the shadow of the future'. In other words, an individual is more likely to recognize and take into account the long-term consequences of her behaviour within that particular relationship or group. Social dilemma research has shown that even in

---

[1] To recap, I define corporate governance as 'the system by which business corporations are directed and controlled' (Cadbury 1992; OECD 1999).

relationships where no future interaction is expected, high levels of communication tend to promote cooperation as members are more easily able to discover whether others plan to act in a cooperative or trustworthy manner, and can also persuade partners to act in the best interests of the group as a whole (Bouas and Komorita 1996). Also, repeated interaction and communication has been argued to facilitate feedback that is likely to make a person aware of the effect of their behaviour on known others: social conformity research suggests that a full and immediate awareness of the effect of one's own behaviour on others is important in preventing the fragmentation of personal responsibility for one's actions, which promotes responsible, other-oriented behaviour (Milgram 1976). Finally, relationship research has shown that the more we communicate and interact with others, the more likely it is that friendships will grow (so-called 'propinquity effect', Segal, 1974; Berscheid and Reis, 1998),[2] and in friendly relationships, behaviour tends to be guided by a concern for the needs and welfare of the other (Mills and Clark 1994).

As well as high levels of communication and face-to-face interaction being important for the development of reciprocal responsibilities, obligations, and trust, many empirical studies indicate that committed membership of an identifiable group is also relevant. For example, committed membership of a clearly identified organization makes it clear to members that they are likely to interact in the future with other members, which is likely to encourage them to act in the best interests of the group as a whole, whether or not there is any history of interaction (Pruit and Kimmel 1977). Even in a large group, colleagues are not anonymous others; they may not have met or know personally all other members, but they are identifiable and knowable others, who are part of an immediate social network. Also, social psychologists have shown that in a group, again even if the group is a temporary one, members are likely to conform to the needs and expectations of the group as a whole as a result of normative social influence (Asch 1951, 1956; Allison 1992). With commitment to a clearly identified and proximate group, the effect of normative social influences is likely to be stronger than in a temporary or more ambiguously defined group: Latané (1981) has demonstrated that the extent to which a given group member will respond to the social influence of a group is dependent on how close the group is to the member in space and time, how big the group is, and how important the group is to the member. Many of the companies I studied would rate highly on each of these dimensions in the eyes of their employees.

In the cases I studied, core employees were not just committed to their companies, but also closely identified with their company and colleagues; in other words, membership of the organization was often inextricably intertwined with core employees' self-image. Social psychologists suggest that one of most powerful determinants of human behaviour stems from need to maintain a stable and positive self-image (Festinger 1957; Aronson 1969, 1998), and in the cases I explored, the company is intrinsic to this self-image. In this context, acting against the interests of the company

---

[2] That is, however, in the absence of negative qualities; the more exposure one has to an unpleasant person, the greater dislike is likely to ensure (Swap 1977).

or one's colleagues as a whole, is likely to be deeply upsetting and strongly resisted, as it would constitute an affront to one's own self-image. This resonates with descriptions in my study of profound emotions varying between social discomfort, shame, and humiliation (Crozier 1990; Retzinger 1995) experienced by directors and employees if they felt they had let their company (in other words their colleagues) down in any way. In such cases, these emotions acted as powerful levers of conduct, prompting either urgent effort to put things right (not always successful) or painful public apologies and resignations where a situation could not be saved.

To sum up, it seems that various social and psychological processes may be useful in helping to clarify how responsible, other-oriented behaviour is generated and sustained *within* a close-knit group, such as in many of the companies I studied. In particular, high levels of face-to-face interaction between core employees and an unambiguous commitment to the company seem to be important in creating the conditions where employees are induced into acting in the interests of their colleagues and the company as a whole, rather than exclusively in their own self-interest.

Inter-Company Obligated Interpersonal Relationships

In this subsection I want to consider some of the factors that might enable the processes discussed thus far to help produce a system of reciprocal responsibilities, obligations, and trust between employees *in different companies*.

Frequent visits, telephone calls, and socializing together were important constituents of most of the established business relationships I studied, and were intrinsic to all of the well-established company–main bank relationships. This regular and intensive interaction provides the opportunity for the processes discussed in the previous subsection to engender some interpersonal responsibility and trust between employees who regularly work together as part of an inter-organizational relationship (generally known as 'boundary-spanners'). However, these boundary-spanners are relatively few in number, may only be in the role for a few years, and primarily interact at certain boundaries of the relationship, for example in the finance department or at board level. Also, the processes I discussed earlier are facilitated by a stable, clearly identified group environment; here we are talking about separate organizations. The relevant question therefore is how is it possible to talk of inter-organizational responsibility and trust, when communication and interaction is limited to a few boundary-spanners who do not share a common group identity? On the basis of this current study, I would suggest that at least three factors are important: clear organizational structures and procedures, highly socialized boundary-spanners, and a clear commitment to the relationship on the part of both companies.

Zaheer *et al.* (1998) argue even if individual boundary-spanners come and go, the establishment of stable role definitions, organizational structures, and institutional processes can serve to codify informal commitments which over time become established routines and practices. Interpersonal responsibilities and trust in this way become institutionalized and re-institutionalized, in turn influencing the orientation of other members of the organization. The clear hierarchical structures and formal operating system and procedures discussed in Chapter 6 that were common to most of the companies I studied are important in this respect, enabling the interpersonal reciprocal responsibilities, obligations, and trust generated between boundary-spanners, to be translated up to the inter-organizational level.

The fact that the boundary-spanners in the companies (and banks) I studied are invariably core employees who are highly socialized within their companies, also seems to be important in facilitating the extension of interpersonal responsibility and trust up to a more generalized inter-organizational level. First, because of the processes discussed in the previous subsection, boundary-spanners who are highly socialized core employees are likely to act in a responsible and trustworthy way within the relationship. Second, as it is generally known within the relationship that boundary-spanners are highly socialized core employees, it is likely that all employees within a relationship will recognize the behaviour of the boundary-spanners to be a reliable proxy for the behaviour of the non-interacting members at the partner organization, which (as the boundary-spanners act responsibly) produces a general understanding among employees at each organization that the partner organization as a whole is responsible and trustworthy.

A third factor which seems to be important in enabling inter-organizational responsibility and trust to develop, is the strong commitment to inter-organizational relationships, which seems to serve a similar purpose as the clear group identity discussed in the previous section. In this current study, such commitment was most commonly seen between members of company groups (such as *keiretsu*) or among genealogically related firms (e.g. between parent companies, subsidiaries, and spin-offs), but it was also evident between initially unrelated organizations (for example between some companies and their main banks). In all cases, mutual commitment was evidenced and reproduced by numerous symbols and rituals, which appeared to embody and reinforce the ongoing, interdependent relationship between partner organizations, and make unambiguous the understanding among all employees that their actions and behaviour were likely to have long-term repercussions for and within the relationship. In the cases I studied, these symbols included *otsukiai*, exchanges of equities, exchanges of staff, invitation of external directors to the board, group meetings, and so forth (see Chapter 5). Also, the recounting of shared histories seemed to be relevant. For example, in the cases I studied many of the company–main bank relationships were associated with stories about the past relationship, in particular about incidents where one partner helped the other in times of need, which were shared and retold by employees in both partner companies. Such retelling of stories is significant in reinforcing and personalizing the mutual commitment of the two organizations in the minds of employees, and may supplement and substitute for the lack of more frequent personal direct face-to-face contact, as shared memory contributes to the creation and maintenance of a sense of shared group identity (Halbwachs 1950; Douglas 1980).

It is beyond the scope of this current book to go much further in trying to elucidate and further refine the operational and theoretical details of how reciprocal responsibilities, obligations, and trust are developed within and between companies, and to draw out all of their implications for the way that the companies I studied are governed. The research design I have used does not allow it. My aim in this section has simply been to draw attention to some empirical research in a number of different fields that can account for a 'socially endogenous' form of corporate governance. The empirical studies that I have cited begin to clarify how an exacting system of close interpersonal scrutiny and sanctioning on the one hand, and processes that encourage and reward prosocial behaviour on the other, come to form the basis of a system by which companies can be governed. Such a system does not seem to constitute a straightforward alternative for a system of corporate governance based on hierarchical control, as it is contingent on the socio-economic context. However, given this context, it does appear to represent a highly effective means of directing and controlling a company, as the system not only inheres close social monitoring and sanctioning of exclusively self-serving behaviour, it also rewards behaviour that supports and enhances the collective goals and values of the whole social network of which the company is a part (which includes shareholders, creditors, suppliers, customers, as well as employees). Overall, I would suggest that the notion of 'socially endogenous' corporate governance warrants far greater empirical and theoretical enquiry, and existing research in disciplines that deal with human motivation and behaviour may prove especially fruitful in this respect.

8.4. RELATION TO EXISTING THEORIES OF CORPORATE GOVERNANCE

In this section I want to discuss the 'socially endogenous' form of corporate governance I have sketched out thus far in relation to the existing approaches to corporate governance outlined in Chapter 1. By exploring various similarities and differences, I want to draw attention to some of the limitations of current approaches to corporate governance, and develop further some specific details of a socially endogenous corporate governance.

Although some economists have recognized that trust or 'social controls' (Ouchi 1979, 1980) may be relevant for the way that companies are governed (Bromiley and Cummings 1995), most economic analyses tend to assume these are possible only in very small groups where there is repeated interaction, and seek to explain them mainly in terms of calculation and hierarchical controls such as fiat, incentives, and monitoring mechanisms (Williamson 1993) that proscribe individual self-interested behaviour (Varian 1990; Stiglitz 1993). The reciprocal responsibilities, obligations, and trust that I have described were not exclusive to the smaller companies I studied, nor did they depend solely on repeated interactions between individuals, direct calculation, or hierarchical controls (although these may play a role where relationships are not well established). For example, in several of the well-established company–main bank relationships, there were high levels of trust but no evidence of overt monitoring or other explicit controls. Indeed, many interviewees claimed that for a bank to actively monitor a client company, or to attempt to take advantage of a position of relative power, would have the effect of destroying trust in the relationship. This is consistent with psychological research which has shown that external rewards, pressures, constraints, or sanctions are more likely to reduce or destroy intrinsic motivation (say, to act in a trustworthy or responsible manner) than encourage it (e.g. Harackiewicz 1979; Deci and Ryan 1985; Kohn 1993; Tang and Hall 1995; Ryan and Deci 1996). Williamson (1993) also recognizes that this may be the case in particular types of relationship, such as exist between family members and close friends:

There are some transactions for which the optimal level of conscious metering is zero... Conscious monitoring, even of a low-grade kind, introduces unwanted calculativeness that is contrary to the spirit of certain very special relations and poses intertemporal threats to their viability (p. 481).

This present empirical study suggests, however, that the 'very special relations' that Williamson refers to might also be feasible between employees within a company, or even between employees at different organizations. This indicates that transaction cost economic approaches might usefully revise at least some of its assumptions, to explore further the possibility that direct calculation may not account for all types of trust within and between companies.

Many of the 'organizational approaches' to corporate governance that I discussed in Chapter 1 resonate with various aspects of this present study. For example stewardship theory (Davis *et al.* 1997) emphasizes trust and pro-organizational motivation and behaviour in explaining the actions of managers. There are also some affinities with the stakeholder approaches to the company, which see managers as being accountable not just to a single principal, the shareholder, but to multiple stakeholders. However, the socially endogenous governance I have described differs from both stewardship and stakeholder approaches, in appearing to entail no sense of managers being *accountable to* a conspicuous other or others. Instead, the sense of responsibility and obligation towards others, embedded in a complex system of inter-individual relationships within and between companies, appear to do the work of being explicitly called to account by others.

In this respect, there are similarities to Kay and Silberston's (1995) concept of trusteeship, which although not fully elaborated theoretically, does not depend on a notion of accountability to a specific other. The departure point of their version of trusteeship is that in spite of some theoretical claims to the contrary, company assets are not legally, or in any practical sense, 'owned' by anyone. As such, it is difficult to state clearly to whom managers are accountable; it is this difficulty that Kay and Silberston suggest creates many of the controversies around the issue of corporate governance. They argue that the idea of trusteeship circumvents such problems, by suggesting that in a company, managers control broadly defined company assets in trust (trust here is a legal concept which gives notional control of assets to a party, but with a legal obligation to administer the assets in a certain way). Kay and Silberston see this conceptualization as being closer to the social reality of organizations than the neoclassical economist's notion that the company is essentially an artificially constructed bundle of contracts. Nonetheless, the idea of trusteeship is argued still to require a system of monitoring and surveillance, to ensure that company assets are administered in the best interests of the company. Kay and Silberston suggest that these principally should take the form of legal mechanisms, rather than accountability to a specified other. The system of governance based around reciprocal responsibilities, obligations and trust that I have enunciated differs from Kay and Silberston's conceptualization of trusteeship on this point.

Of the various strands of theory I discussed in Chapter 1, the findings of this study seem to be most closely in line with notions of 'trust-based' governance. However, this is still an underdeveloped area of research. Although the potential for trust as a governance mechanism is frequently touched upon in the organizational literature (Kramer and Tyler 1996; Powell 1996; Lane and Bachmann 1998), it has not yet received significant attention in the evolving corporate governance literature. One notable exception is Roberts (2001*b*), who discusses the different effects of trusting behaviour and controlling behaviour on processes of accountability in Anglo-American systems of corporate governance. In particular, he claims that the 'individualizing' form of accountability that is produced by agency theory promotes a preoccupation with self rather than an awareness of reciprocal dependence. 'Socializing' forms of accountability by contrast allow the testing of assumptions through dialogue, which is a vital form of learning that can 'produce complex relationships of respect, trust and felt reciprocal obligation' (p. 1567), which, he argues, are essential for the effective operation of companies. He is careful to argue that neither form of accountability is necessarily better than the other, but valuably delineates their associated (intended and unintended) effects. The potential for 'socializing' forms of accountability inherent in trusting relationships which Roberts outlines, strongly corroborates the findings of this present study. Moreover, this study supports his 'more complex' conceptualization of the corporate governance problem: it is not just about monitoring and controlling self-interested agents, but concerns the need for effective processes of corporate accountability.

8.5. IMPLICATIONS FOR CORPORATE GOVERNANCE POLICY AND RESEARCH

I want to re-emphasize that I am not proposing 'socially endogenous corporate governance' to be the definitive description of the Japanese system of corporate governance. What I would contend though is that a form of corporate governance which draws on the voluntary reciprocal responsibilities, obligations, and trust enacted in everyday socio-economic interactions may prove significant in reassessing many of the existing studies on Japanese corporate governance referred to in Chapter 2, which have produced results consistent with an effective system of corporate governance in Japan, but which have been unable to reconcile these results with the apparent lack of accountability of managers to an identifiable other. It may also prove, with further theoretical elaboration, valuable for research into corporate governance in a variety of other contexts outside of Japan. For example, the possibility of a system of corporate governance that draws on reciprocal responsibilities, obligations, and trust may be useful in considering the direction and control of companies where extant economics-derived approaches are largely silent, such as family companies, other closely held companies, start-up companies, and public-sector companies. It may also prove equally useful in understanding more fully the direction and control of large public companies, as mainstream economic approaches tend to assume away any meaningful internal governance processes (despite many corporate governance codes of practice implicitly recognizing their importance, for example emphasizing the need to balance the relative power of company chairman and chief executive (Cadbury 1992)). In addition, it offers one way of exploring the link between a company's system of governance and its production/innovation system, which mainstream economics-informed approaches fail to do (Lazonick and O'Sullivan 1996; O'Sullivan 2000). Trust, for example, has not only been recognized as a coordination mechanism but has also been explored in terms of impact on production, and has even been proposed as a precondition for superior competitive performance (Sako 1998).

A related implication of this study is to urge a more refined view of how *change* in systems of corporate governance occurs. For example, in the case of Japan there is a tendency to view changes that are taking place simply as the replacement of anachronistic 'culturally determined' practices by more modern 'rational economic' practices (Kikuchi 1999; Wakasugi and Yanai 2000). However, this study suggests that change is more complex; it rarely involved the straightforward adoption or transplantation of new initiatives (such as investor relations departments, stock options plans, ROE measurement), but instead entailed a process of adaptation and often significant modification as new practices were assimilated. The more simplistic view of change is informed to a certain extent by a commonly held idea that (Anglo-American) 'rational-economic' practices are more advanced in evolutionary terms than 'traditional, culturally bound' ones. But also, the primitive approach to culture and cultural change in economics and organizational studies does not help to encourage debate about the nature of change. Most empirical work in these disciplines seems to centre around a fairly static view of culture as an enduring, autonomous phenomenon, and as such seeks out to discover the most relevant combination of artifacts, values, beliefs, and assumptions that can best describe a particular culture. The work of Hofstede (1980, 1991) is typical in this respect. In other disciplines, such as anthropology, cultural psychology, and evolutionary psychology, far more sophisticated conceptualizations of culture as an active, selective, and constructive process are extant and have been long explored (Cole 1996; Tomasello 1999; Douglas 2000; Saito 2000, 2001). Such ideas would seem invaluable in attempting to explore how an existing culture and institutional framework serves to inform and mediate new ideas as they are assimilated, and would be especially useful in understanding the way that new corporate governance practices are being incorporated in Japan and elsewhere around the world. I suggest that this is an important area for future research, and will provide productive insights for policy-makers concerned with global corporate governance standards.

Arguably the most important implication of this study, however, relates to the understanding and definition of the 'corporate governance problem'. As discussed in Chapter 1, capital-centred economic models of the firm, in particular agency theory, dominate thinking about corporate governance, and see it primarily in terms of a 'problem' resulting from the 'separation of management and control'. Blair (1995) describes the resultant current stream of research on corporate governance as 'a long and somewhat arcane scholarly effort to explain large enterprises in a way consistent with neoclassical economic theory' (p. 228). Arcane though it may be, it has undeniably come to eclipse broader thinking about how companies are or should be governed, not only among researchers (Shleifer and Vishny 1997), but also among practitioners (Monks 2001) and policy-makers (OECD 1998*b*, 1999).

The possibility of a 'socially endogenous' corporate governance does not necessarily impugn the value of economic approaches to corporate governance, nor does it undermine the relevance of their 'solutions' for improving corporate governance. But, as it provides a feasible alternative means of understanding the direction and control of companies, it does call into question the all-pervasive *normative* application of economic theories to corporate governance across the world.

One particular problem with the normative application of economic theories to corporate governance policy, is that where actual governance processes are not adequately explained by these theories, any 'reforms' that are proposed may well be seen as impractical or irrelevant by practitioners, and as a result their implementation is likely to be either resisted or (at least initially) presentational rather than substantive (for details on the transformation of knowledge, practice, and other artefacts transferred to a new milieu, see e.g. Bloor 1997, 2000; Cole and Cole 2000; Saito 2000, 2001). This may partly explain why in this present study, even though many new corporate governance related reforms were being introduced at the company level, their relevance and practicality was sometimes questioned by company interviewees, and actual modification of underlying company practices was often negligible. This in turn risks generating suspicion and criticism from those whose views on corporate governance are guided by economic theories. Again, this was evident in this present study, where foreign analysts, bankers, and the media frequently lambasted many of the changes being undertaken by Japanese companies, as variously 'superficial', 'immature', 'amateurish', or 'spurious'. In this respect, the pre-eminence of economic approaches to corporate governance appears to have the potential to *perpetuate* mistrust between economies which operate differently, as much as facilitate the introduction of globally accepted standards. Consequently, this current study urges more careful consideration of corporate governance policy proposals, better questioning of the assumptions that underlie such proposals, and above all far more empirical research on national systems of corporate governance which does not define *a priori* the 'governance problem'.

Calling into question the hegemony of economics-informed approaches will enable more sophisticated analyses of different systems of corporate governance in their own terms, allowing in particular the 'failings' of systems to be addressed more adequately. For example, one possible drawback of a socially endogenous system of corporate governance, which I raised in Chapter 6, is that without adequate links across its boundaries a close-knit group may be deprived of valuable forms of diversity, and in extreme cases may become a closed system, entrenched and introverted, and convinced of its own invulnerability (Janis 1982). This is not to say that employees in close-knit companies which are not part of an extensive business network will necessarily act irresponsibly to those outside their company, as it is likely that the social and psychological processes I have described will produce a generalized other-oriented behaviour. However, without regular interaction beyond the boundaries of the firm, it does seem more likely that the group will become inward-looking.

Another potential shortcoming, which is particularly relevant in the context of globalization, is that if a company performs badly or acts perfidiously, responsibility for the problem may appear from the outside to be dispersed among the company as a whole, rather than being assumed by any identifiable individual or individuals. Although this is not a weakness in itself (indeed as discussed earlier breaking trust is likely to entail powerful social recriminations among the group), it is inconsistent with the current, more widespread notion of 'accountability' which requires an identifiable individual, typically the company's chief executive, to bear responsibility or blame for the problem. In the case of Japan, usually one or more senior members of a company will assume some public responsibility for a company misdemeanour, by apologizing publicly or resigning from their position. However, those outside the system may misinterpret this as the senior members having assumed individual responsibility for the problem. Hence, there is likely to be an outcry when it is discovered that these individuals continue to be supported by the company after their resignation (which is usually the case).

Possibly the most important drawback of a socially endogenous system of corporate governance, is that it is likely to be inefficacious where (intra- and inter-) company interactions are infrequent or distant, or where partner companies are not committed to one another. If, as part of the globalization process, this type of atomized business relationship becomes more common in Japan, the system as it stands is likely to founder. Whether this is actually happening in Japan is arguable, but, given the hegemony of economic approaches to corporate governance, there is only one possible solution: move towards the Anglo-American system of corporate governance based around clear hierarchical controls. By questioning the pre-eminence of economic approaches to corporate governance though, and attempting to understand the existing system of governance in its own terms, it is possible that more reasoned and diverse strategies to cope with the pressures of globalization can be sought out, and also the way that change is actually happening in practice can be better understood.

Given the scope of this current study, it is not possible to recommend a list of strategies to 'improve' corporate governance in Japan, but it does seem that further empirical and theoretical study that seeks to recognize and better appreciate the processes by which the governance of companies in Japan operates in practice, would be invaluable. This would allow the drawbacks of the Japanese system, especially in the context of globalization, to be addressed in far more skilful ways than is currently the case, and the advantages and disadvantages of different reform proposals to be more completely understood. By way of example, this study suggests that measures to encourage the appointment of independent directors would be both difficult to implement and unlikely to bring about workable or effective change, at least in the short-term. By contrast, encouraging (international) institutional investors to interact more frequently with companies they have invested in, could be relatively easy to realize and highly advantageous to both parties.

In conclusion, this study has suggested that social monitoring and sanctioning on the one hand and the promotion of prosocial behaviour on the other, can together produce a diffuse *and therefore* powerful social accountability, to oneself, one's colleagues, one's company, and partner companies. Like any other system of corporate governance, the resulting 'socially endogenous' system cannot *entirely* prevent exclusively self-serving behaviour (although as discussed particular social and psychological processes may make it more unlikely), but it does appear to be able to identify and sanction such behaviour at least as effectively as any system constructed around hierarchical controls.

The form of corporate governance I have delineated requires a particular context where there are high levels of face-to-face interaction and communication, and commitment to ongoing relationships. Where this context is possible, it may have some advantages over a 'selfish' system (Axelrod 1984), including, for example, the relatively low cost of maintaining it (Williamson 1993). However, I would like to make clear that I am not proposing that a socially endogenous system of corporate governance can necessarily substitute for a system based around hierarchical controls. In the case of more infrequent 'transactions' between 'individuals' at a distance, the other is likely to be perceived as anonymous and separate, and actors probably feel little personal significance or relevance or emotive closeness to the 'transaction'. In these circumstances, the hierarchical controls such as those described by agency theorists and transaction costs economists could well be more appropriate mechanisms to attenuate the potential opportunism of self-interested actors.

However, what is perhaps not well understood by those who ascribe to approaches to corporate governance based on economic theories of the firm, is that the 'self-interested actor' is possibly the product of these theories' own self-fulfilling assumptions (Ghoshal and Moran 1996; Roberts 2001a). Economics-derived models of governance are built on the assumption that without external control, human beings are prone to act self-interestedly. This empirical study suggests that the assumption of self-interested human behaviour is one-sided at best. Human beings are at least equally capable of taking into consideration the interests of others alongside their own in making decisions and taking action, and are not only motivated by incentives, monitoring, and fiat. There is a substantial amount of empirical work which discredits this limited view of human motivation and behaviour, some of which I have cited in this chapter, and yet the work of corporate governance researchers and policy-makers, wittingly or unwittingly, continues to be strongly informed by it.

The ideas I have presented in this book require a great deal more empirical and theoretical elaboration. However, I hope that even in their relatively underdeveloped state, they commend greater recognition that alongside the currently dominant concern with the elaboration of mechanisms to 'control' the behaviour of company managers, the governance of companies might equally be considered in terms of the complex system of reciprocal responsibilities, obligations, and trust inherent in the everyday socio-economic interactions within and between companies.

Bibliography

Abe, Y. (1997). 'Chief executive turnover and firm performance in Japan', *Journal of the Japanese and International Economies*, 11(1): 2–26.

Abegglen, J. (1958). *The Japanese Factory*. Glencoe, IL: Free Press.

—— and Stalk, G. (1985). *Kaisha: The Japanese Corporation*. New York: Basic Books.

Albert, M. (1991). *Capitalisme contre Capitalisme*. Paris: Editions du Seuil.

Alchian, A. A. and Demsetz, H. (1972). 'Production, information costs and economic organisation', *American Economic Review*, 62(5): 777–95.

Allison, P. D. (1992). 'The cultural evolution of beneficent norms', *Social Forces*, 71: 279–301.

Andrews, F. M. (1984). 'Construct validity and error components of survey measures: a structural modelling approach', *Public Opinion Quarterly*, 48: 409–42.

Aoi, J. (1997). 'To whom does the company belong? A new management mission for the Information Age', in D. H. Chew (ed.), *Studies in International Corporate Finance and Governance Systems*. Oxford: Oxford University Press.

Aoki, M. (1984). *The Economic Analysis of the Japanese Firm*. Boston: North Holland.

—— (1988). *Information, Incentives and Bargaining in the Japanese Economy*. Cambridge: Cambridge University Press.

—— (1994). 'The Japanese firm as a system of attributes: a survey and research agenda', in M. Aoki and R. Dore (eds), *The Japanese Firm: Sources of Competitive Strength*. Oxford: Oxford University Press.

—— and Dore, R. (1994). *The Japanese Firm: Sources of Competitive Strength*. Oxford: Oxford University Press.

—— Patrick, H., and Sheard, P. (1994). 'The Japanese Main Bank System: an introductory overview', in M. Aoki and H. Patrick (eds), *The Japanese Main Bank System: its Relevance for Developing and Transforming Economies*. New York: Oxford University Press.

Aronson, E. (1969). 'The Theory of Cognitive Dissonance: a current perspective', in I. L. Berkowitz (ed.), *Advances in Experimental Social Psychology*, Vol. 4. New York: Academic Press.

—— (1998). 'Dissonance, hypocrisy and the self-concept', in E. Harmon-Jones and J. S. Mills (eds), *Cognitive Dissonance Theory: Revival with Revisions and Controversies*. Washington, DC: American Psychological Association.

Asch, S. (1951). 'Effects of group pressure upon the modification and distortion of judgment', in H. Guetzkow (ed.), *Groups, Leadership and Men*. Pittsburgh, PA: Carnegie Press.

—— (1956). 'Studies of independence and conformity: a minority of one against a unanimous majority', *Psychological Monographs*, 70 (9, Whole No. 416).

Axelrod, R. (1984). *The Evolution of Co-operation*. New York: Basic Books.

Bartlett, F. C. (1932). *Remembering: a Study in Experimental and Social Psychology*. Cambridge: Cambridge University Press.

Batson, C. D. (1998). 'Altruism and prosocial behavior', in D. Gilbert, S. Fiske, and G. Lindzey (eds), *The Handbook of Social Psychology*, Vol. 2, 4th edn. New York: McGraw-Hill.

Bauman, Z. (1993). *Postmodern Ethics*. Oxford: Blackwell.

Bell, D. (1973). *The Coming of Post-Industrial Society*. New York: Basic Books.

Belson, W. (1986). *Validity in Social Research*. Aldershot: Gower.

Berger, S. and Dore, R. (eds) (1996). *National Diversity and Global Capitalism*. Ithaca: Cornell University Press.

Berle, A. (1932). 'For whom corporate managers are trustees: a note', *Harvard Law Review*, 45: 1365–72.

Berle, A. A. and Means, G. C. (1932). *The Modern Corporation and Private Property*. New York: Macmillan.

Berscheid, E. and Reis, H. T. (1998). 'Attraction and close relationships', in D. Gilbert, S. Fiske, and G. Lindzey (eds), *The Handbook of Social Psychology*, Vol. 2, 4th edn. New York: McGraw-Hill.

Black, B. (1992). 'The value of institutional investor monitoring: the empirical evidence', *UCLA Law Review*, 39(4): 895–939.

Blair, M. (1995). *Ownership and Control: Rethinking Corporate Governance for the Twenty-first Century*. Washington, DC: Brookings Institute.

Blois, K. J. (1999). 'Trust in business to business relationships: an evaluation of its status', *Journal of Management Studies*, 36(2): 197–215.

Bloor, D. (1997). 'Remember the strong programme?', *Science, Technology and Human Values*, 22: 373–85.

—— (2000). 'Whatever happened to "social constructiveness"?', in A. Saito (ed.), *Bartlett, Culture and Cognition*. Hove: Psychology Press.

Boon, S. D. and Holmes, J. G. (1991). 'The dynamics of interpersonal trust: resolving uncertainty in the face of risk', in R. A. Hinde and J. Groebel (eds), *Cooperation and Prosocial Behaviour*. Cambridge: Cambridge University Press.

Borio (1990). *Patterns of Corporate Finance, BIS Economic Papers 27*. Basel: Bank for International Settlements.

Bouas, K. S. and Komorita, S. S. (1996). 'Group discussion and cooperation in social dilemmas', *Personality and Social Psychology Bulletin*, 22: 1144–50.

Boyd, B. K., Carroll, W. O. *et al.* (1996). 'International governance research: a review and an agenda for future research', *International Comparative Management*, 11: 191–215.

Bratton, W. W. (1989). 'The new economic theory of the firm: critical perspectives from history', *Stanford Law Review*, 1: 1471–527.

Brewer, M. B. and Kramer, R. M. (1986). 'Choice behavior in social dilemmas: effects of social identity, group size and decision framing', *Journal of Personality and Social Psychology*, 50: 543–49.

Briggs, C. L. (1986). *Learning How to Ask: a Sociological Appraisal of the Interview in Social Science Research*. Cambridge: Cambridge University Press.

Bromiley, P. and Cummings, L. L. (1995). 'Transactions costs in organizations with trust', in R. Bies, B. Sheppard, and R. Lewicki (eds), *Research on Negotiation in Organizations*. Greenwich, CT: JAI Press.

Butler, D. and Kitzinger, U. (1976). *The 1975 Referendum*. London: Macmillan.

Cadbury, A. (1992). *Report of the Committee on the Financial Aspects of Corporate Governance*. London: Gee.

—— (2000). 'Introduction', in World Bank, *Global Corporate Governance Forum*. Washington: World Bank.

CalPERS (1998). *CalPERS Corporate Governance Principles for Japan*. http://www.calpers-governance.org/principles/international/japan/.

Cassell, C. and Symon, G. (eds) (1994). *Qualitative Methods in Organizational Research*. London: Sage.

Caves, R. and Uekusa, M. (1976). *Industrial Organization in Japan*. Washington: Brookings Institution.

Chandler, A. (1962). *Strategy and Structure: Chapters in the History of American Industrial Enterprise*. Cambridge, MA: MIT Press.

Chang, H.-J., Palma, G., and Whittaker, D. H. (1998). 'The Asian Crisis: introduction', *Cambridge Journal of Economics*, 22: 649–52.

Charkham, J. (1992). 'Corporate Governance: lessons from abroad', *European Business Journal*, 4(2): 8–16.

—— (1994). *Keeping Good Company: a Study of Corporate Governance in Five Countries*. Oxford: Clarendon Press.

Chell, E. (1998). 'Critical incident technique', in G. Symon and C. Cassell (eds), *Qualitative Methods and Analysis in Organizational Research*. London: Sage.

Chen, R., López-Gelormino, C. S., and Shaw, S. M. (2001). 'Asia's performance challenge', *The McKinsey Quarterly*, 3: 6–9.

Cicourel, A. V. (1982). 'Interviews, surveys and the problem of ecological validity', *American Sociologist*, 17: 11–20.

Clark, J. M. (1916). 'The changing basis of economic responsibility', *The Journal of Political Economy*, 24(3): 209–29.

Clark, R. (1979). *The Japanese Company*. New Haven: Yale University Press.

Coase, R. H. (1937). 'The Nature of the Firm', *Economica*, 4: 386–405.

Coffee, J. C. (1991). 'Liquidity vs. Control: institutional investors as corporate monitors', *Columbia Law Review*, 91: 1277–368.

Coffey, A., Holbrook, B. *et al.* (1996). 'Qualitative data analysis: technologies and representations', *Sociological Research Online*, 1(1): 1–16.

Cole, M. (1996). *Cultural Psychology*. Cambridge, MA: Belknap Press.

Cole, J. and Cole, M. (2000). 'Re-fusing anthropology and psychology', in A. Saito (ed.), *Bartlett, Culture and Cognition*. Hove: Psychology Press.

Converse, J. M. (1984). 'Strong arguments and weak evidence: the open/closed questioning controversy of the 1940s', *Public Opinion Quarterly*, 48: 267–82.

Corbett, J. (1987). 'International perspectives on financing: evidence from Japan', *Oxford Review of Economic Policy*, 3(4): 30–55.

—— (1994). 'An overview of the Japanese financial system', in N. Dimsdale and M. Prevezer (eds), *Capital Markets and Corporate Governance*. Oxford: Clarendon Press.

Crabtree, B. F. and Miller, W. L. (eds) (1992). *Doing Qualitative Research*. Newbury Park, CA: Sage.

Crouch, C. and Streeck, W. (eds) (1997). *Political Economy and Modern Capitalism: Mapping Convergence and Diversity*. London: Sage.

Crozier, W. R. (ed.) (1990). *Shyness and Embarrassment: Perspectives from Social Psychology*. Cambridge: Cambridge University Press.

Das, T. K. and Teng, B.-S. (1998). 'Between trust and control: developing confidence in partner cooperation in alliances', *Academy of Management Review*, 23(3): 491–513.

Davies, P. L. (1997). 'Institutional investors as corporate monitors in the UK', in K. J. Hopt (ed.), *Comparative Corporate Governance*. Berlin: Walter de Gruyter.

Davis, G. F. and Thompson, T. A. (1994). 'A social movement perspective on corporate control', *Administrative Science Quarterly*, 39(1): 141–73.

Davis, J. H., Schoorman, F. D., and Donaldson, L. (1997). 'Toward a stewardship theory of management', *Academy of Management Review*, 22(1): 20–47.

Dawes, R., van de Kragt, A., and Orbell, J. (1990). 'Cooperation for the benefit of us—no me, or my conscience', in J. Mansbridge (ed.), *Beyond Self-Interest*. Chicago: University of Chicago Press.

Deci, E. L. and Ryan, R. M. (1985). *Intrinsic Motivation and Self-Determination in Human Behavior*. New York: Plenum.

Dodd, E. M. (1932). 'For whom are corporate managers trustees?' *Harvard Law Review*, 45: 1145–63.

Donaldson, L. and Davis, J. H. (1991). 'Stewardship theory or agency theory: CEO governance and shareholder returns', *Australian Journal of Management*, 16(1): 49–64.

Donaldson, T. and Preston, L. E. (1995). 'The stakeholder theory of the corporation: concepts, evidence and implications', *Academy of Management Review*, 20(1): 65–91.

Dore, R. (1973). *British Factory–Japanese Factory: the Origins of National Diversity in Industrial Relations*. Berkeley: University of California Press.

—— (1983). 'Goodwill and the spirit of market capitalism', *British Journal of Sociology*, 34: 459–82.

—— (1987). *Taking Japan Seriously: a Confucian Perspective on Leading Economic Issues*. Stanford, CA: Stanford University Press.

—— (1996). 'Convergence in whose interest?', in S. Berger and R. Dore (eds), *National Diversity and Global Capitalism*. Ithaca: Cornell University Press.

—— (1998). 'Asian Crisis and the Future of the Japanese Model', *Cambridge Journal of Economics*, 22: 773–87.

—— (2000). *Stock Market Capitalism: Welfare Capitalism*. Oxford: Oxford University Press.

Douglas, M (1980). *Evans-Pritchard*. London: Fontana.

—— (2000). 'Memory and selective attention; Bartlett and Evans-Pritchard', in A. Saito (ed.), *Bartlett, Culture and Cognition*. Hove: Psychology Press.

Durkheim, E. (1893). *De la Division du Travail Social*. Paris: Felix Alcan.

Dyer, J. H. and Chu, W. (2000). 'The determinants of trust in supplier–automaker relationships in the US, Japan, and Korea', *Journal of International Business Studies*, 31(2): 259–85.

Dyer, W. G. and Wilkins, A. (1991). 'Better stories, not better constructs, to generate better theory: a rejoinder to Eisenhardt', *Academy of Management Review*, 16(3): 613–19.

The Economist (1994). 'A survey of corporate governance', *The Economist*, 330(7848), 29 January: 3–18.

—— (1995). 'Japan Inc frays at the edges', *The Economist*, 335(7917), 3 June: 67–68.

—— (1999). 'No more tears', *The Economist*, 353(8147), 25 November: 3–4.

Eisenhardt, K. M. (1989). 'Agency theory: an assessment and review', *Academy of Management Review*, 14(1): 57–74.

Eli, M. (1990). *Japan Inc: Global Strategies of Japanese Trading Companies*. Maidenhead: McGraw-Hill.

Etzioni, A. (1975). *A Comparative Analysis of Complex Organizations: on Power, Involvement and their Correlates*. New York: Free Press.

Fama, E. (1980). 'Agency problems and the theory of the firm', *Journal of Political Economy*, 88(2): 288–307.

Festinger, L. (1957). *A Theory of Cognitive Dissonance*. Stanford, CA: Stanford University Press.

Financial Times (1997). 'The impact of governance', 14 February.

—— (1998). 'Anglo-Solutions: Japan's ray of hope', 6 May.

—— (2000). 'Equities: from slow start to relentless build-up', 11 January.

Fingleton, E. (1995). 'Jobs for life: why Japan won't give them up', *Fortune*, 131(5), 20 March: 119–24.

Freeman, R. E. (1984). *Strategic Management; a Stakeholder Approach.* Boston: Pitman/Ballinger.

Friedman, M. (1953). 'The methodology of positive economics', in M. Friedman (ed.), *Essays in Positive Economics.* Chicago: University of Chicago Press.

Friedman, M. (1970). 'The social responsibility of business is to increase its profit', *New York Times Magazine,* 13 September.

Fruin, W. M. (1992). *The Japanese Enterprise System.* Oxford: Clarendon Press.

Fukao, M. (1995). *Financial Integration, Corporate Governance, and the Performance of Multinational Companies.* Washington, DC: Brookings.

Futatsugi, Y. (1986). *Japanese Enterprise Groups.* Kobe: Kobe University Press.

G7 (1999). *Strengthening the International Financial Architecture: Report of the G7 Finance Ministers to the Köln Economic Summit,* Cologne, 18–20 June 1999.

Garvey, G. T. and Swan, P. L. (1992). 'The interaction between financial and employment contracts: a formal model of Japanese corporate governance', *Journal of the Japanese and International Economies,* 6(2): 247–74.

Gerlach (1992). *Alliance Capitalism.* Berkeley: University of California Press.

Ghoshal, S. and Moran, P. (1996). 'Bad for practice: a critique of the transaction cost theory', *Academy of Management Review,* 21(1): 13–47.

Gilson, R. J. (1994). 'Corporate governance and economic efficiency', in M. Isaksson and R. Skog (eds), *Aspects of Corporate Governance.* Stockholm: Juristforlaget.

—— and Roe, M. J. (1993). 'Understanding the Japanese keiretsu: overlaps between corporate governance and industrial organization', *The Yale Law Journal,* 102(4): 871–906.

Glaser, B. and Strauss, A. (1967). *The Discovery of Grounded Theory.* Chicago: Aldine.

Granovetter, M. (1985). 'Economic action and social embeddedness', *American Journal of Sociology,* 91(3): 481–510.

Gritching, W. (1986). 'Public opinion versus policy advice', *Australian Psychologist,* 21: 45–58.

Gronning, T. (1997). 'Accessing large corporations: research ethics and gatekeeper-relations in the case of researching a Japanese-invested factory', *Sociological Research Online,* 2(4): 1–12.

Hagan, J. M. and Choe S. (1998). 'Trust in Japanese interfirm relations: institutional sanctions matter', *Academy of Management Review,* 23: 589–600.

Halbwachs, M. (1950). *La Mémoire Collective.* Paris: Presses Universitaires de France.

Hammersley, M. and Atkinson, P. (1995). *Ethnography: Principles in Practice* (2nd edition). London: Routledge.

Hammersley, M. and Gomm, R. (1997). 'Bias in social research', *Sociological Research Online,* 2(1): 1–13.

Harackiewicz, J. M. (1979). 'The effects of reward contingency and performance feedback on intrinsic motivation', *Journal of Personality and Social Psychology,* 37: 1352–63.

Hart, O. and Moore, J. (1990). 'Property rights and the nature of the firm', *The Journal of Political Economy,* 98: 1119–58.

Hawley, J. P. and Williams, A. T. (1996). *Corporate Governance in the United States: the Rise of Fiduciary Capitalism.* Working paper, St. Mary's College of California.

Hazama, H. (1964). *The History of Labour Management in Japan.* Basingstoke: Macmillan.

Hill, I. and Duffield, S. (2001). *Share Ownership—A Report on the Ownership of Shares at 31 December 2000.* London: Office for National Statistics.

Hill, S. (1995). 'The social organization of boards and directors', *British Journal of Sociology,* 46(2): 245–78.

Hinde, R. (1997). *Relationships: a Dialectical Perspective.* Hove: Psychology Press.

Hirschman, A. O. (1972). *Exit, Voice and Loyalty: Responses to Decline in Firms, Organizations and States.* Cambridge, MA: Harvard University Press.

Hirschmeier, J. and Yui, T. (1981). *The Development of Japanese Business.* London: George Allen & Unwin.

Hofstede, G. (1980). *Culture's Consequences.* Beverly Hills, CA: Sage.

—— (1991). *Cultures and Organizations.* New York: McGraw-Hill.

Holmes, J. and Murray, S. (1996). 'Conflict in close relationships', in E. T. Higgins and A. Kruglanski (eds), *Social Psychology: Handbook of Basic Principles.* New York: Guilford Press.

Hopt K. J. (ed.) (1997). *Comparative Corporate Governance: the State of the Art and Emerging Research.* Berlin: Walter de Gruyter.

Horiuchi, A., Packer, F. *et al.* (1988). 'What role has the "main bank" played in Japan?', *Journal of the Japanese and International Economies,* 2: 159–80.

Hoshi, T., Kashyap, A., and Scharfstein, D. (1990*a*). 'The role of banks in reducing the costs of financial distress in Japan', *Journal of Financial Economics,* 27: 67–88.

—— —— and —— (1990*b*). 'Corporate structure, liquidity and investment: evidence from Japanese industrial groups', *Quarterly Journal of Economics,* 106: 33–60.

Hume, D. (1740). *A Treatise on Human Nature.* London: Thomas Longman.

Ide, M. (1998). *Japanese Corporate Finance and International Competition: Japanese capitalism versus American capitalism.* Basingstoke: Macmillan.

Imai, K. and Komiya, R. (eds) (1994). (translated by R. Dore and H. Whittaker). *Business Enterprise in Japan: Views of Leading Japanese Economists.* Cambridge, MA: MIT Press.

—— and —— (1994). 'Characteristics of Japanese firms', in K. Imai and R. Komiya (eds) (translated by R. Dore and H. Whittaker), *Business Enterprise in Japan: Views of Leading Japanese Economists.* Cambridge, MA: MIT Press.

Itami, H. (1994). 'The "Human-Capital-ism" of the Japanese firm as an integrated system', in K. Imai and R. Komiya (eds) (translated by R. Dore and H. Whittaker), *Business Enterprise in Japan: Views of Leading Japanese Economists.* Cambridge, MA: MIT Press.

Ito, K. (1995). 'Japanese spinoffs: unexplored survival strategies', *Strategic Management Journal,* 16: 431–46.

Itoh, H. and Teruyama, H. (1998). 'Do positions and tenure of top executives affect their attitude?', in T. Tachibanaki (ed.), *Who Runs Japanese Business?* Cheltenham: Edward Elgar.

Jackson, N. and Carter, P. (1995). 'Organizational Chiaroscuro: throwing light on the concept of corporate governance', *Human Relations,* 48(8): 875–99.

Jaikumar, R. (1986). 'Postindustrial manufacturing', *Harvard Business Review,* Nov.–Dec.

Janis I. L. (1982). *Groupthink.* Boston, MA: Houghton Mifflin.

Japan Institute of Labour (1997). *Labour-Management Relations in Japan.*

Japan Securities Research Institute (1998). *Securities Market in Japan 1998.* Tokyo: Tokyo Shoken Kaikan.

Jensen, M. C. (1983). 'Organization theory and methodology', *Accounting Review,* 58: 319–39.

—— (1994). 'Self-interest, altruism, incentives and agency theory', *Journal of Applied Corporate Finance,* Summer: 40–5.

—— and Meckling, W. H. (1976). 'Theory of the firm: managerial behavior, agency costs and ownership structure', *Journal of Financial Economics,* 3: 305–60.

JETRO (1991). *Business Facts and Figures.* Tokyo: JETRO.

Johnson, R. A. and Ouchi, W. G. (1974). 'Made in America (under Japanese management)', *Harvard Business Review,* Sept.–Oct.

Jones, R. S. and Tsuru, K. (1997). 'Japan's corporate governance: a system in evolution', *OECD Observer,* 204, Feb.–Mar.: 40–1.

Jones, T. M. (1995). 'Instrumental stakeholder theory: a synthesis of ethics and economics', *Academy of Management Review,* 20(2): 404–38.

Kang, J. -K. and Stulz, R. M. (1997). 'Why is there a home bias? An analysis of foreign portfolio equity ownership in Japan', *Journal of Financial Economics*, **46**(1): 3–28.

Kaplan, S. N. (1994). 'Top executive rewards and firm performance: a comparison of Japan and the United States', *Journal of Political Economy*, **102**(3): 510–45.

—— and Minton, B. A. (1994). 'Appointments of outsiders to Japanese boards: determinants and implications for managers', *Journal of Financial Economics*, **36**(2): 225–58.

Kay, J. and Silberston, A. (1995). 'Corporate governance', *National Institute Economic Review*, **153**, August: 84–98.

Keidenran (Japan Federation of Economic Organisations) (1997). *Urgent Recommendations Concerning Corporate Governance*. Tokyo: Keidanren.

—— (2000). *Points of Discussion Relating to Corporate Governance in Japanese Public Companies (Interim Report)*. Tokyo: Keidanren.

Kelle, U. (1997). 'Theory building in qualitative research and computer programs for the management of textual data', *Sociological Research Online*, **2**(3): 1–18.

Kester, W. C. (1991). *Japanese Takeovers: the Global Contest for Corporate Control*. Boston, MA: Harvard Business School Press.

—— (1996). 'American and Japanese corporate governance: convergence to best practice?', in S. Berger and R. Dore (eds), *National Diversity and Global Capitalism*. Ithaca: Cornell University Press.

Keynes, J.-M. (1936). *The General Theory of Employment Interest and Money*. London: Macmillan and Co.

Kikuchi, M. (1999). *Kigyokachi Hyoka Kakumei* [The Revolution in Corporate Valuation]. Tokyo: Toyo Keizai.

King, N. (1994). 'The Qualitative Research Interview', in C. Cassell and G. Symon (eds), *Qualitative Methods in Organizational Research*, pp. 14–36. London: Sage.

—— (1998). 'Template analysis', in C. Cassell and G. Symon (eds), *Qualitative Methods and Analysis in Organizational Research*. London: Sage.

Kohn, A. (1993). *Punished by Rewards*. Boston: Houghton Mifflin.

Kono, T. (1984). *Strategy and Structure of Japanese Enterprises*. London: Macmillan.

Kramer, R. M., Brewer, M. B., and Hanna, B. A. (1996). 'Collective trust and collective action: the decision to trust as a social decision', in R. M. Kramer and T. R. Tyler (eds), *Trust and Organizations: Frontiers of Theory and Research*. Sage: Thousand Oaks.

—— and Tyler, T. R. (eds) (1996). *Trust in Organizations: Frontiers of Theory and Research*. London: Sage.

Kuwahara, Y. (1989). *Industrial Relations System in Japan: a New Interpretation*. Tokyo: The Japan Institute of Labour.

Lane, C. and Bachman, R. (eds) (1998). *Trust within and between Organizations*. Oxford: Oxford University Press.

LaPiere, R. T. (1934/35). 'Attitudes vs. Actions', *Social Forces*, **13**: 230–37.

Latané, B. (1981). 'The psychology of social impact', *American Psychologist*, **36**: 343–56.

Lawson, T. (1997). *Economics and Reality*. London: Routledge.

Lazonick, W. and O'Sullivan, M. (1996). 'Organization, finance and international competition', *Industrial and Corporate Change*, **5**(1): 1–49.

Learmount, S. (2001). 'International institutional investors and UK corporate governance', in T. Seki and S. Learmount (eds), *Corporate Governance in the UK*. Tokyo: Shoji Homu.

Lewicki and Bunker (1996). 'Developing and maintaining trust in work relationships', in R. M. Kramer and T. R. Tyler (eds), *Trust in Organizations: Frontiers of Theory and Research*. London: Sage.

Manne, H. G. (1965). 'Mergers and the market for corporate control', *Journal of Political Economy*, 73: 110–20.

Martin, R. (1993). 'The new behaviorism: a critique of economics and organization', *Human Relations*, 46(9): 1085–101.

Masaki, H (1979). 'The financial characteristics of the zaibatsu in Japan: the old zaibatsu and their closed finance', in K. Nakagawa (ed.), *Marketing and Finance in the Course of Industrialization*. Tokyo: Tokyo University Press.

Masuyama, S. (1994). 'Role of Japanese capital markets: the effect of cross-shareholdings on corporate accountability', in N. Dimsdale and M. Prevezer (eds), *Capital Markets and Corporate Governance*. Oxford: Clarendon Press.

Matsumoto, K. (1991). *The Rise of the Japanese Corporate System: the Inside View of a MITI Official*. London: Kegan Paul.

Maug, E. (1998). 'Large shareholders as monitors: is there a trade-off between liquidity and control?', *Journal of Finance*, 53(1): 65–98.

Maurice, M., Sellier, F. *et al*. (1986). *The Social Foundations of Industrial Power*. Cambridge, MA: MIT Press.

McNulty, T. and Pettigrew, A. (1999). 'Strategists on the Board', *Organization Studies*, 20(1): 47–74.

Milgram, S. (1976). 'Obedience to criminal orders: the compulsion to do evil', in T. Blass (ed.), *Contemporary Social Psychology*. Itasca, IL: F. E. Peacock.

Mills, J. and Clark, M. S. (1994). 'Communal and exchange relationships: controversies and research', in R. Erber and R. Gilmour (eds), *Theoretical Frameworks for Personal Relationships*, Hillsdale, NJ: Erlbaum.

Ministry of Labour (1993). *Survey on Retirement Allowance System and Payments*. Tokyo: Ministry of Labour.

—— (1997). *Basic Survey on Wage Structure*. Tokyo: Ministry of Labour.

Mitchell, R. K., Agle, B. R., and Wood, D. J. (1997). 'Toward a theory of stakeholder identification and salience: defining the principle of who and what really counts', *Academy of Management Review*, 22(4): 853–86.

Monks, R. and Minow, N. (1995). *Corporate Governance*. Oxford: Blackwell.

—— (2001). *The New Global Investors*. Oxford: Capstone.

Moran, P. and Ghoshal, S. (1996). 'Theories of economic organization: the case for realism and balance', *Academy of Management Review*, 21(1): 58–72.

Muth, M. and Donaldson, L. (1998). 'Stewardship theory and board structure: a contingency approach', *Corporate Governance*, 6(1): 5–29.

Myners, P. (2001). *The Myners Review of Institutional Investment: Final Report*. London: HMSO.

Nada, T. (1998). 'Determinants of top executives promotion and remuneration', in T. Tachibanaki (ed.), *Who Runs Japanese Business?* Cheltenham: Edward Elgar.

Nakamura, J. I. (1981). 'Human capital appreciation in pre-modern rural Japan', *Journal of Economic History*, 41(2): 263–81.

Nakane, C. (1972). *Japanese Society*. Berkeley: University of California Press.

Nakatani, I. (1984). 'The economic role of financial corporate grouping', in M. Aoki (ed.), *The Economic Analysis of the Japanese Firm*. Amsterdam: North Holland.

Nikkei Weekly (1998). 'The end of cross shareholding?', 15 June.

—— (1997). 'LDP, Keidanren target shareholder lawsuits', 8 September.

—— (1998). 'Scandals offer opportunity to push change', 12 July.

Nippon Life Insurance Research Institute (2000). *The Present Status of Unwinding of Cross-Shareholding—The Fiscal 1999 Survey of Cross-Shareholding*. Tokyo: NLI Research Institute.

—— (2001). *The Present Status of Unwinding of Cross-Shareholding—The Fiscal 2000 Survey of Cross-Shareholding*. Tokyo: NLI Research Institute.

Nitta, M. (1995). 'The employment practices and employment of young workers in Japan: past experience and present situation', *Japan Labor Bulletin*, **34**(10): 1–10.

—— (2001). 'Corporate governance, Japanese style: roles of employees and unions', *Social Science Japan*, **20**: 6–11.

Nomura Research Institute (2001). 'Rebirth of Japanese companies through governance reforms', *NRI Report 25*. Tokyo: NRI.

Odagiri, H. (1992). *Growth through Competition, Competition through Growth*. Oxford: Clarendon Press.

OECD (1977). *The Development of Industrial Relations Systems; some Implications of the Japanese Experience*. Paris: OECD Publications.

—— (1995). 'Financial markets and corporate governance', *Financial Market Trends*, **62**: 13–22.

—— (1996). 'Corporate governance: a system in evolution', *OECD Economic Surveys—Japan 1996*. Paris: OECD.

—— (1997). 'The impact of institutional investors on OECD financial markets', *Financial Market Trends*, **68**: 15–54.

—— (1998*a*). *Corporate Governance: Improving Competitiveness and Access to Capital in Global Markets*. Paris: OECD.

—— (1998*b*). 'Shareholder value and the market in corporate control in OECD countries', *Financial Market Trends*, **69**: 15–37.

—— (1999). *OECD Principles of Corporate Governance*. Paris: OECD.

Okazaki, T. (1994). The Japanese firm under the wartime planned economy', in M. Aoki and R. Dore (eds), *The Japanese Firm: the Sources of Competitive Strength*. Oxford: Oxford University Press.

Okumura, H. (1975). *Houjin shihonshugi no kouzou: nihon no kabushiki shoyuu [The Structure of Corporate Capitalism: Share Ownership in Japan]*. Tokyo: Nihon Hyouronsha.

Ornatowski, G. (1998). 'The end of Japanese-style human resource management?', *Sloan Management Review*, **39**(3): 73–84.

O'Sullivan, M. (2000). *Contests for Corporate Control*. Oxford: Oxford University Press.

Ouchi, W. G. (1979). 'A conceptual framework for the design of organizational control mechanisms', *Management Science*, **25**: 833–48.

—— (1980). 'Markets, bureacracies and clans', *Administrative Science Quarterly*, **23**: 293–317.

—— (1981). *Theory Z*. New York: Avon.

Pascale, R. and Rohlen, T. (1983). 'The Mazda turnaround', *Journal of Japanese Studies*, **9**(2): 219–63.

Pencavel, J. and Craig, B. (1994). 'The empirical performance of orthodox models of the firm: conventional firms and worker cooperatives', *Journal of Political Economy*, August: 718–44.

Perrow, C. (1986). 'Economic theories of organization', in C. Perrow (ed.), *Complex Organizations*. New York: Random House.

Pettigrew, A. M. (1992). 'On studying managerial elites', *Strategic Management Journal*, **13**: 163–82.

Powell, W. (1996). 'Trust-based forms of governance', in R. Kramer and T. Tyler (eds), *Trust in Organizations: Frontiers of Theory and Research*. Thousand Oaks, CA: Sage.

Prowse, S. (1992). 'The structure of corporate ownership in Japan', *Journal of Finance*, **47**(3): 1121–40.

Pruitt, D. and Kimmel, M. L. J. (1977). 'Twenty years of experimental gaming: critique, synthesis, and suggestions for the future', *Annual Review of Psychology*, 28: 363–92.

Rajan, R. G. and Zingales, L. (1998). *Power in a Theory of the Firm*. NBER Working Paper Series, National Bureau of Economic Research.

Retzinger, S. M. (1995). 'Shame and anger in personal relationships', in S. Duck and J. T. Wood (eds), *Confronting Relationship Challenges*. Thousand Oaks, CA: Sage.

Roberts, J. (2001*a*). 'Corporate governance and the ethics of Narcissus', *Business Ethics Quarterly*, 11(1): 109–28.

—— (2001*b*). 'Trust and control in Anglo-American systems of corporate governance: the individualizing and socializing effects of processes of accountability', *Human Relations*, 54(2): 1547–72.

Rock, E. B. and Wachter, M. L. (2001). 'Islands of conscious power: norms and the self-governing corporation', *University of Pennsylvania Law Review*, 149(6): 1607–18.

Roe, M. J. (1997). 'Path dependence, political options and governance systems', in K. J. Hopt (ed.), *Comparative Corporate Governance*. Berlin: Walter de Gruyter.

—— (1997). 'Norms and corporate law: introduction', *Journal of Applied Corporate Finance*, 9(4): 8–22.

Rohlen, T. (1974). *For Harmony and Strength: Japanese White-Collar Organization in Anthropological Perspective*. Berkeley: University of California Press.

Romano, R. (2001). 'Less is more: making institutional investor activism a valuable mechanism of corporate governance', *Yale Journal on Regulation*, 18: 1–78.

Rousseau, D. M., Sitkin, S. B., Burt, R. S., and Camerer, C. (1998). 'Not so different after all: a cross-discipline view of trust', *Academy of Management Review*, 23(3): 393–404.

Ryan, R. M. and Deci, E. L. (1996). 'When paradigms clash: comments on Cameron and Pierce's claim that rewards do not undermine intrinsic motivation', *Review of Educational Research*, 66: 33–8.

Saito, A. (1996). 'Social origins of cognition: Bartlett, evolutionary perspective and embodied mind approach', *Journal for the Theory of Social Behaviour*, 26(4): 399–422.

—— (1998). 'Lifespan development and phylogeny of interactive minds', *Culture and Psychology*, 4(2): 245–58.

—— (2000). 'Multilevel analyses of social basis of cognition', in A. Saito (ed.), *Bartlett, Culture and Cognition*. Hove: Psychology Press.

—— (2001). 'Phylogeny, history, and ontogeny of human cognition', *American Journal of Psychology*, 114(4): 628–34.

Sako, M. (1992). *Prices, Quality and Trust: Inter-Firm Relations in Britain and Japan*. Cambridge: Cambridge University Press.

—— (1998). 'Does trust improve business relations?', in C. Lane and R. Bachmann (eds), *Trust Within and Between Organizations*. Oxford: Oxford University Press.

Sampson, E. E. (1993). *Celebrating the Other: a Dialogical Account of Human Nature*. Hemel Hempstead: Harvester Wheatsheaf.

Segal, M. W. (1974). 'Alphabet and attraction: an unobtrusive measure of the effect of propinquity in a field setting', *Journal of Personality and Social Psychology*, 30: 654–7.

Seki, T. and Learmount, S. (eds) (2001). *Corporate Governance in the UK* [in Japanese]. Tokyo: Shoji Homu.

Sen, A. (1987). *On Ethics and Economics*. Oxford: Blackwell.

Shapiro, D., Sheppard, B. H., and Cheraskin, L. (1992). 'Business on a handshake', *Negotiation Journal*, 8(4): 365–77.

Sheard, P. (1987). 'Intercorporate shareholdings and structural adjustments in Japan', *Pacific Economic Papers* no. 151.

—— (ed.) (1992). *International Adjustment and the Japanese Firm.* Sydney: Allen & Unwin.

—— (1994). 'Reciprocal delegated monitoring in the Japanese main bank system', *Journal of the Japanese and International Economies*, 8(1): 1–21.

Sherman, H. D. and Babcock, B. A. (1997). 'Redressing structural imbalances in Japanese corporate governance', in D. H. Chew (ed.), *Studies in International Corporate Finance and Governance Systems.* Oxford: Oxford University Press.

Shleifer, A. and Vishny, R. W. (1997). 'A survey of corporate governance', *Journal of Finance*, 52(2): 737–83.

Shoji Homu Kenkyu Kai (1990). *Antei Kabunushi ni Taisuru Jittai Chosa.* Shoji Homu: Tokyo.

Someya, K. (1996). *Japanese Accounting: a Historical Approach.* Oxford: Clarendon Press.

Starkey, K. (1995). 'Opening up corporate governance', *Human Relations*, 48(8): 837–44.

Stiglitz, J. E. (1993). 'Peer monitoring and credit markets', in K. Hoff, A. Braverman, and J. E. Stiglitz (eds), *The Economics of Rural Organization: Theory, Practice and Policy.* Oxford: Oxford University Press.

Suzuki, S. (1980). 'Kyuusai yuushi ni okeru "meinu banku" chikara', [The strength of relief capital from main banks]. *Keiou Keiei Ronshuu*, December: 18–39.

Swap, W. C. (1977). 'Interpersonal attraction and repeated exposure to rewarders and punishers', *Personality and Social Psychology Bulletin*, 3: 248–51.

Symon, G. and Cassell, C. (1998). *Qualitative Methods and Analysis in Organizational Research,* London: Sage.

Tachibanaki, T. (ed.) (1998). *Who Runs Japanese Business? Management and Motivation in the Firm.* Cheltenham: Edward Elgar.

Tang, S and Hall, V. C. (1995). 'The overjustification effect: a meta-analysis', *Applied Cognitive Psychology*, 9: 365–404.

Tokyo Stock Exchange (2001). *Survey on Listed Companies' Corporate Governance.* Tokyo: Tokyo Stock Exchange.

Tomasello, M. (1999). *The Cultural Origins of Human Cognition.* Cambridge, MA: Harvard University Press.

Triandis, H. C. (1994). *Culture and Social Behavior.* New York: McGraw-Hill.

Tricker, R. I. (1984). *Corporate Governance.* Vermont: Gower.

—— (1994). 'Editorial—on theories of corporate governance', *Corporate Governance*, 2(2), April: 55–7.

—— (1996). 'Corporate Governance—on papers and paradigms', *Corporate Governance*, 4(4), October: 199–201.

Tsuru, K. (1994). *The Japanese Market System: its Strengths and Weaknesses.* Tokyo: LTCB.

Tsutsui, W. M. (1997). 'Rethinking the paternalist paradigm in Japanese industrial management', *Business and Economic History*, 26(2): 561–72.

Turnbull, S. (1997). 'Corporate governance; its scope, concerns and theories', *Corporate Governance*, 5(4), October: 180–205.

Tyler, T. R. (1993). 'The social psychology of authority', in J. K. Munighan (ed.), *Social Psychology in Organizations: Advances in Theory and Practice*, 141–60. Englewood Cliffs, NJ: Prentice Hall.

Useem, M. (1984). *The Inner Circle.* Oxford: Oxford University Press.

Varian, H. R. (1990). 'Monitoring agents with other agents', *Journal of Institutional and Theoretical Economics*, 46(1): 153–74.

Viner, A. (1993). 'The coming revolution in Japan's board rooms', *Corporate Governance*, 1(3): 112–19.

Wakasugi, H. and Yanai, H. (2000). *Good Governance, Good Company.* Tokyo: Chuo Keizaisha.

Wakasugi, T (1997). 'EVA and the Japanese corporate governance problem', *Journal of Applied Corporate Finance*, **9**(4): 144–67.

Watanabe, S. and Yamamoto, I. (1993). 'Corporate governance in Japan: ways to improve low profitability', *Corporate Governance*, 1(4), October: 208–25.

Weber, R. P. (1985). *Basic Content Analysis*. Beverley Hills, CA: Sage.

Weinstein, D. E. and Yafeh, Y. (1998). 'On the costs of a bank centered financial system: evidence from the changing main bank relations in Japan', *Journal of Finance*, **53**(2): 635–72.

Westphal, J. D. and Zajac, E. J. (1998). 'The symbolic management of stockholders: corporate governance reforms and shareholder reactions', *Administrative Science Quarterly*, **43**(1): 127–53.

Whittaker, D. H. (1990). *Managing Innovation: a Study of British and Japanese Factories*. Cambridge: Cambridge University Press.

—— (1990). 'The end of Japanese-style employment?', *Work, Employment and Society*, **4**(3): 321–47.

—— (1998). 'Labour unions and industrial relations in Japan: crumbling pillar or forging a "third way"?', *Industrial Relations Journal*, 29(4): 280–94.

Whittaker, H. and Kurosawa, Y. (1998). 'Japan's crisis: evolution and implications', *Cambridge Journal of Economics*, 22: 761–71.

Williamson, O. E. (1975). *Markets and Hierarchies: Analysis and Antitrust Implications*. New York: Free Press.

—— (1979). 'Transaction-cost economics: the governance of contractual relations', *Journal of Law and Economics*, 22: 233–61.

—— (1984). 'Corporate governance', *The Yale Law Journal*, 93: 1197–230.

—— (1985). *The Economic Institution of Capitalism*. New York: Free Press.

—— (1991). 'Comparative economic organization: the analysis of discrete structural alternatives', *Administrative Science Quarterly*, 36: 269–96.

—— (1993). 'Calculativeness, trust and economic organization', *Journal of Law and Economics*, **34**: 453–500.

—— (1996). *The Mechanisms of Governance*. Oxford: Oxford University Press.

—— (1996). 'Economic organization: the case for candor', *Academy of Management Review*, 21(1): 48–57.

Womack, J. P., Jones, D. T., and Roos, D. (1990). *The Machine that Changed the World: the Story of Lean Production*. New York: Macmillan.

Wood, D. J. and Jones, R. E. (1995). 'Stakeholder mismatching: a theoretical problem in empirical research on corporate social performance', *The International Journal of Organizational Analysis*, 3(3): 229–67.

World Bank (1999). *Corporate Governance: a Framework for Implementation*. Washington: World Bank.

Yamamura, K. (1997). *The Economic Emergence of Modern Japan*. Cambridge: Cambridge University Press.

Yin, R. K. (1984). *Case Study Research: Design and Methods*. Beverly Hills, CA: Sage.

—— (1993). *Applications of Case Study Research*. Thousand Oaks, CA: Sage.

Yonekawa, S. and Yoshihara, H. (1987). *Business History of General Trading Companies*. Tokyo: Tokyo University Press.

Yoshimori, M. (1995). 'Whose company is it? The concept of the corporation in Japan and the West', *Long Range Planning*, 28(4): 33–44.

Yui, T. (1984). 'The development of the organisational structure of top management in Meiji Japan', *Japanese Yearbook on Business History*, 1: 1–23.

Zaheer, A., McEvily, B., and Perrone, V. (1998). 'Does trust matter? Exploring the effects of interorganizational and interpersonal trust on performance', *Organization Science*, 9(2): 141–59.

—— and Venkatraman. (1995). 'Relational governance as an interorganizational strategy: an empirical test of the role of trust in economic exchange', *Strategic Management Journal*, 16: 373–92.

Zingales, L. (1997). *Corporate Governance*. NBER Working Paper Series, National Bureau of Economic Research.

Index